CW01455266

Virgil's *Aeneid*: A Study Guide

Athena Critical Guides

Table of contents

Virgil's *Aeneid*: A Study Guide

This study guide will assist you in your studies of Virgil's *Aeneid*.

At the time of writing several UK examination boards offer A Level examinations in Classical Civilisation. One popular and key part of these examinations is the study of Greek and Roman epic poetry, including Virgil's *Aeneid,* as well as Homer's *Iliad* and *Odyssey.*

Virgil's *Aeneid* is a Latin epic poem that, although inspired by the epic poetry of Homer, was a poem written very much for his own time and in order to celebrate the greatness of Rome.

Studying GCE Classical Civilisation

This study guide has been written to provide a rewarding experience for those who are, or are interested in, studying Classical Civilisation. In particular, this study guide will assist you in understanding and examining the subject matter of epic poetry; Virgil's *Aeneid.*

Who is this study guide for?

This study guide is intended to offer a satisfying experience for those learners who undertake an AS or A level qualification in Classical Civilisation. This qualification pathway is offered by OCR and CIE examination boards. This resource is primarily designed to assist those who are studying this topic for a Classical Civilisation qualification.

This study guide will help to lay a sound foundation for those who go on to study the Ancient World at a higher (degree) level as well as appeal to those who are interested in learning more about the ancient world generally and in particular, the epic poetry of Virgil.

The aims and objectives of A Level GCE in Classical Civilisation include;

- Develop an interest in and enthusiasm for Classical Civilisation and develop an understanding of the intrinsic value and significance of Epic Poetry.

- Acquire an understanding of different identities within society and an appreciation of aspects such as social, cultural, religious and ethnic diversity, as appropriate.

- Build on your understanding of the past through experiencing a broad and balanced course of study.

- Improve as an effective and independent learner.

- Develop the ability to ask relevant and significant questions about the past and to research these questions.

- Acquire an understanding of the nature of ancient literature and poetry.

- Develop your use and understanding of literary terms, concepts and skills.

- Make links and draw comparisons within and/or across different kinds of literature and thematic aspects.

- Organise and communicate your knowledge of Epic poetry and understanding in different ways, arguing a case and reaching substantiated judgements.

Examination Boards offering study in Classical Civilisation

This product is designed to be used as a study aid in order for learners to attain a qualification in the following examination units;

OCR Examination Board

- Advanced Level GCE in Classical Civilisation

(H408/11) The World of the Hero

CIE Examination Board

- Advanced Level GCE in Classical Civilisation

(9274) Component 4: Gods and Heroes: the importance of epic

AQA Examination Board

- *Advanced Level GCE in Classical Civilisation (2020): Component 2: CIV2B*

Please note that the AQA A level is an outgoing specification that is not being replaced

A study of Virgil's *Aeneid* at A level requires the following points to be covered;

Key topics	Content
Literary techniques and composition	• composition of the epic • structure and plot of the epic • language of the epic including the use of speeches, themes, flashback, similes and other narrative and descriptive techniques and their effects • Homeric influence
The heroic world: characterisation and themes	• concepts, values and behaviour of a Greek and Roman hero • characterisation of major and minor characters • role of Aeneas in Rome's Imperial destiny • portrayal of war • the portrayal of different peoples; Trojans, Greeks, Carthaginians, Italians
The social, cultural and religious context	• moral values implicit in the *Aeneid* including *pietas* (duty to gods, state and family) and its contrast with *furor* • importance of fate and destiny • role of the immortals and the relationship between mortals and immortals • family and friendship • relationships between men and women, parents and children • part played by women in the epic and their position in society
Historical and political background	• Augustan context in which the *Aeneid* was produced including: • the political and historical background of the civil war • Augustus' rise to power and consolidation of his rule • Virgil's relationship to Augustus and his regime and the extent to which they are promoted within the epic • promotion of the Roman Empire

How to use this guide

This A Level study guide has been organised in such a way so as to help an A Level student of Classical Civilisation more easily understand the *Aeneid* and also to correspond to the major topic areas identified by the major examination boards.

To this end this Athena Critical Guide is divided into multiple *Parts* each containing four or five sections that relate to the overall theme of the relevant Part. Each sub-section discusses a specific aspect or series of related aspects relevant to the A level student, so for example Part Two covers the background to Virgil and introduces his techniques and each section deals with a specific aspect as identified below;

PART TWO

2.1: Book One: Aeneas arrives at Carthage

2.2: Book Two: The Fall of Troy

2.3: Book Three

2.4: Presentation of character: Aeneas and Anchises

2.5: Homeric Influences in Books I-III

2.6: The Supernatural in Books I-III

Each section is introduced with a number of bullet points that will help the reader to identify the focus of the section and also to help correlate the section to their relevant examination specification.

Within each section are a number of tasks and activities as well as glossary terms and additional points of information that are considered useful or thought provoking to an A Level student.

The tasks and activities are based on the structure and duration of questions posed by the examination boards therefore it is envisaged that they will be especially valuable in aiding the reader to prepare for their respective examinations.

Please note that this study guide is not endorsed by the examination boards and as such is not an officially recognised product by AQA, OCR or CIE examination boards.

Which translation of the *Aeneid* should I use?

This study guide does not recommend a specific translation of the *Aeneid*. No specific edition or translation of a text is set because of copyright availability issues in different parts of the world.

> *According to the OCR and CIE examination boards, A level and AS level learners sitting the A Level examination in Classical Civilisation may use any translation of the text.*

However where a translation is printed on an OCR examination question paper two versions will be provided, these will be taken from:

- *Virgil, 'Aeneid' translated by D. West, (Penguin)*

- *'Virgil, 'The Aeneid', translated by A.S. Kline, online at http://www.poetryintranslation.com*

These are excellent translations and readily available to learners.

Free translations of the *Aeneid* can be obtained from;

The Perseus digital Library; *www.perseus.tufts.net*

MIT; *http://classics.mit.edu/Virgil/Aeneid.html*

Kindle and iBook versions

Both Kindle and iBook versions may also offer free or purchasable versions of the *Aeneid* which are translated by different academics which may be used accompany this critical study guide

Exams related to this study guide

OCR PAPER ONE: The world of the hero (H408/11)

This compulsory component is an externally assessed, written examination testing AO1 and AO2.

The examination is worth 100 marks and lasts 2 hours and 20 minutes. This represents 40% of the total marks for the A Level.

The examination will consist of three sections.

Section A focuses solely on Homer and will contain two sets of questions; one on the *Iliad* and one on the *Odyssey*. Learners should answer the questions on the text they have studied.

Section B contains questions focusing solely on Virgil's *Aeneid,* and all questions in this section are compulsory.

Section C contains a stimulus question in which students draw on both a passage from Homer (either the *Odyssey* or the *Iliad*) and one from Virgil; and a choice of essays. In these essays learners will be expected to make use of secondary sources and academic views to support their argument.

There are three question types in this exam, they are:

- 10 mark stimulus question

- 20 mark essay

- 30 mark essay

CIE: PAPER TWO: Roman Civilisation, option 2: Virgil: A critical examination of Virgil's *Aeneid* in context

Students taking this examination should focus on the following aspects;

•*the structure and design of the poem and its plot*

•*literary techniques*

•*characterisation of Aeneas and other secondary figures*

•*the portrayal of women*

•*the fall of Troy*

•*the function of the gods*

•*the theme of Rome's mission*

Candidates will be expected to have a working knowledge of the socio-political circumstances of the period so that the *Aeneid* may be understood in context. Detailed historical knowledge is not expected.

Set text: Virgil *Aeneid* Books 1, 2, 4, 6

Exam structure

No particular edition is set. A Penguin Classics edition is available and this will be used for the setting of questions.

The exam paper is worth 50 marks and is timed (90 minutes).

Exam candidates answer two questions one each from a different option each worth 25 marks.

PART ONE: Introduction to the *Aeneid*

PART ONE

1.1 Introduction

In this section we will;

- *Introduce the Aeneid of Virgil*

- *Begin to explore the nature and structure of the Aeneid*

- *Begin to introduce some of the characters*

A Brief overview of the *Aeneid*

The *Aeneid* is an account in twelve books of the travels and toils of the Trojan hero, Aeneas. The *Aeneid* covers Aeneas' escape from Troy at the end of the Trojan War, his wanderings and efforts to find a new home for his people and his battles in Italy in order to found a new home for the survivors of the Trojan War.

Written in the epic style, it was (and still is) inevitably compared to Homer's *Iliad* and *Odyssey*. As we explore the *Aeneid* further we will identify numerous examples of references to the epic poems of Homer.

The basic framework of the *Aeneid* mirrors the *Odyssey* and to a lesser extent the *Iliad*. The first half of the story describes the wanderings of the Hero, and is sometimes referred to as the *'Odyssey of Aeneas'*. The second half of the *Aeneid* describes the fight for victory in order to establish a home and is sometimes referred to as the *'Iliad of Aeneas'*.

The Books of the *Aeneid*

Book One	Aeneas' fleet is blown to Africa by Juno
Book Two	Aeneas meets Dido and tells of the fall of Troy
Book Three	Aeneas tells of his adventures to this point
Book Four	Aeneas and Dido
Book Five	Aeneas arrives in Sicily
Book Six	The Underworld
Book Seven	Aeneas arrives in Italy; the Latins prepare for war
Book Eight	Aeneas and Evander, the shield of Aeneas
Book Nine	Nisus and Eurylaus
Book Ten	The deaths of Pallas and Mezentius
Book Eleven	Camilla fights and dies
Book Twelve	The confrontation of Turnus and Aeneas

Dramatis Personae in the *Aeneid*

There are a lot of characters in the *Aeneid* and if this is the first time that you have studied the *Aeneid* it can get a little confusing remembering who is who. Below is a selection of characters;

❖ **Olympian Gods**

Juno – The Queen of the Gods who hates Aeneas and the Trojans (In Greek *Hera*)

Jupiter – The king of the Gods (in Greek *Zeus*)

Venus – The Goddess of Love and Mother of Aeneas (in Greek *Aphrodite*)

Vulcan – The husband of Venus and God of crafting (in Greek *Hephaestus)*

Neptune – The Sea God (in Greek *Poseidon*)

Diana – Goddess of the Hunt (in Greek *Artemis*)

Cybele – Goddess of prophecy and fertility

Apollo – God of prophecy, healing amongst others and favourite God of the emperor Augustus

❖ **Minor Gods**

Aeolus – God of Winds

Tiber – River God

Allecto – A Fury

Juturna – Nymph – sister of Turnus

Opis – nymph and attendant of Diana

❖ **Trojans**

Aeneas – the 'Hero' of the *Aeneid*

Creusa – the wife of Aeneas

Ascanius – Aeneas' son (also called Iulus)

Anchises– Aeneas' father

Achates – Aeneas' comrade and attendant

Ilioneus – A Trojan Elder

Nisus – A Trojan warrior

Eurylaus – A young Trojan

Palinurus – A Trojan sailor

❖ **Those encountered during the wanderings of Aeneas**

Dido – Queen of Carthage

Polydorus – A Trojan ghost

Calaeno – A Harpy

Helenus – A Trojan and son of King Priam

Andromache – Wife of the Trojan Hector

Acestes – A Trojan settled in Sicily

Sibyl – Priestess and prophetess of Cumae

❖ **The Dead Heroes and inhabitants of the Underworld**

Hector – a Trojan, Son of King Priam, killed in the Trojan War

Deiphobus - a Trojan, Son of King Priam, killed in the Trojan War

Anchises – Trojan and father of Aeneas (also seen alive)

❖ **Latins**

King Latinus – King of the Latins

Queen Amata – Queen of the Latins

Lavinia – only daughter of Latinus and Amata

Drances – a councillor and hostile to Turnus

Turnus – prince of Ardea and enemy of Aeneas

❖ **The army of Turnus**

Mezentius – Etruscan King in exile

Lausus – Son of Mezentius

Messapus – Son of Neptune

Camilla – a fearsome warrior woman

Note: There are many more characters in the *Aeneid*. It may be useful to create a reference guide of these characters.

1.2 Virgil, Aeneas and the Aeneid

This section will help you to;

- *Understand who Virgil was*

- *Understand what we know of his life and works*

- *Explore some of the reasons why the Aeneid was composed*

- *Begin to understand the role and importance of Aeneas*

Who was Virgil?

Publius Virgilius Maro was born around 70BC and died in 19BC. Virgil's work was extensive and included the *Georgics,* and *Eclogues,* as well as poetry. Virgil is most remembered however for his epic poem; the *Aeneid.*

Sometimes in academic writing you will see Virgil spelt as 'Vergil' – this is also correct as an anglicized spelling and closer to the pronunciation of his name, but we shall continue throughout with the Latinised 'Virgil'.

Unlike some other writers and historical personages, no near contemporary biographer of Virgil exists; therefore what is written about his life below is best guess fit derived from Virgil's own writings and other incidentals.

Virgil was an Italian from Mantua who was educated at Mediolanum (Milan) before moving to Rome in the late 50s-early 40s BC, where he wrote poetry. Virgil may have also been a member of an Epicurean philosophy school near Neapolis prior to his arrival in Rome.

During the period of the First Triumvirate (43-37BC) Virgil's father may have had his some of his property seized as a result of the proscriptions of those suspected of supporting the assassins of Caesar Brutus and Cassius.

In addition to the *Aeneid*, Virgil wrote several poems which are still extant;

- *Eclogues* 39/38BC - 10 short poems on farming

- *Georgics* 29BC – a poem spanning 4 books on farming, current affairs and hinting at an epic yet to be written – the *Aeneid*.

At some point after the Eclogues were published, Virgil became a member of the loose literary society that emerged under the guidance and patronage of Maecenas – a close friend and supporter of Augustus. Virgil is thought to have performed his *Georgics* to

Augustus in person and also parts of the *Aeneid* (Books II, IV and VI) at some point after 23BC.

Having drafted the *Aeneid* in the 20s BC, Virgil travelled to Greece and the Aegean Sea around 22/21BC with the intention of completing his epic poem away from Rome. In 20BC Virgil encountered Augustus on his tour of the Eastern provinces and accompanied him on his journey back to Italy. Unfortunately, Virgil contracted a fever near Athens and this illness remained with him on the journey back to Italy. When he landed at Brundisium in Italy, Virgil was dying and passed away soon after, in 19BC.

Virgil was buried at Neapolis and is thought to have written his own epitaph on his deathbed;

'Manuta bore me, Calabria carried me off, now

Neapolis holds me; I sang of pastures, fields and kings'.

The *Aeneid*

The *Aeneid* is an epic poem comprised of twelve books which depicts the mythical account of the journey of the Trojan prince Aeneas. Fleeing the fall of Troy at the end of the Trojan War, Aeneas journeys across the seas with the surviving Trojans and after many adventures establishes a new home in Italy. His arrival in Italy initiates a series of battles against the Latins. The hero Turnus leads the Latin forces that oppose Aeneas. From Aeneas and the Trojan survivors in time will emerge the city and people of Rome.

Despite the Roman conquest of Greece, Virgil was well aware of his own cultural heritage and the legacy of the greatest of Greek poets, Homer. Therefore Virgil sets out self-consciously to *write* (rather than compose in the oral tradition of Homer) using both the *Iliad* and the *Odyssey* as core texts. In fact, Virgil mirrors both the *Iliad* and the *Odyssey* in the *Aeneid*.

Books One through Six typically being thought of as his *"Odyssey"*, in so far as they are the story of Aeneas' journey to Latium. Books Seven through Twelve being his *"Iliad"*, in so far as they are the story of the Trojan War but set in a different land, motivated by a marriage dispute and the anger of the gods. The echoes of the original myth of the Trojan War are plain.

As mentioned earlier, Virgil seems to have recited books II, IV and VI personally to Augustus and his friends and family. Throughout the *Aeneid* there are many allusions to Augustus and it is form these books that passages that are of most relevance for the study of Augustus and the Principate are to be identified.

According to some traditions it seems that Virgil was disappointed with the *Aeneid* and he went so far as to order the *Aeneid* burned –

this was countermanded by Augustus himself and the *Aeneid* was published after the death of Virgil.

The *Aeneid* became an instant hit and for centuries thereafter it became a standard school text for young Romans of all social classes across the Empire. That it was well known among the wider Roman populace is attested to the identification of lines of poetry drawn from the *Aeneid* found as graffiti on the walls of the streets of Pompeii. The *Aeneid* was also used by the superstitious as a form of an oracle, with random readings being used to answer questions – obviously with varying degrees of success!

Even if the *Aeneid* had been published in the lifetime of Virgil, it would have made a wealthy many even wealthier – when he died Virgil was estimated to have the wealth and property matching the minimum requirements of ten Senators.

Who was Aeneas?

Aeneas was the son of the Trojan mortal Anchises and the Goddess of Love Venus (Aphrodite in Greek). He is a leading Trojan character in Homer's *Iliad*. A brave warrior, he is good at fighting in the *Iliad*, but he is not the very best. In the *Iliad* Aeneas has duels with Diomedes and Achilles – in both he needs to be rescued by his mother from certain death.

Where he exceeds all however is through his piety towards the Gods and even in the *Iliad* he has an important destiny to fulfil; he will lead the Trojans after their city is destroyed and find them a new home.

The myths and legends of Aeneas reached Italy certainly by the 6th century BC. Etruscan produced pottery has been unearthed with painted images of Aeneas.

The earliest known theory that Rome was founded by both Odysseus and Aeneas together came from the 5th century writer Hellanicus of Lesbos. By the late 4th century BC the Roman senatorial families were willing to associate the idea that the Trojans were linked to the foundation of Rome. They saw that this allowed the Roman elite to associate themselves with the Hellenistic cultural tradition that dominated the Mediterranean, whilst preserving their own distinct Italian identity.

Aeneas in writings between Homer and Virgil

In the lost epic poem called *'The Sack of Troy'* Aeneas leaves Troy before the city falls to the Greeks during the Trojan Horse episode. Quite clearly, Virgil elects to have Aeneas present during the sack of Troy in order to make his escape more exciting and also to head off accusations that Aeneas was either a coward or a deserter.

In Gnaeus Naevius' *Punic War* (a late 3rd C BC writing) Aeneas is reported as travelling to Carthage and his desertion of Dido is seen as one of the major reasons for enmity between Rome and Carthage. Whilst in Quintus Ennius' *Annals* (an early 2nd C BC narrative historical poem) Aeneas leaves Troy during the sack of the city and settles in Italy.

Why Aeneas?

Aeneas already had an established role in mythology as a character in Greek mythical traditions. In the *Iliad* Homer mentions him in several parts of his epic and especially in Book Twenty, where it was prophesised that it was Aeneas' destiny as a member of the Trojan royal family to take the sacred things of Troy to a safe place with the surviving Trojans, and to continue their race.

But this is Greek myth – not Italian.

Italy had its own myths and legends peculiar to itself about Rome's own cultural traditions and the founding of the city, the most famous being the story of Romulus and Remus, the twin brothers who were suckled by a female wolf on the banks of the River Tiber. These twins would found Rome and one, Romulus, would kill the other in an argument over boundaries.

Virgil *could* have concentrated on some of these other myths associated with the early history of Rome, as did a famous Roman historian Livy (who was a contemporary of Virgil) but instead Virgil chose Aeneas for his clear link to Homer, and so to the respected culture and literary heritage of the Greeks and Greek epic poetry.

Using the hero Aeneas also allowed Virgil to write an '*Iliad* II' or a sequel to the *Iliad,* though one with a particularly Roman slant.

The *Aeneid* is also in the tradition of the *Odyssey,* which is also a sequel to the *Iliad*, since it concerns the journey home of one of its most famous heroes. Unlike the *Odyssey*, Virgil's central character comes from Troy, not Greece and is the very man that Homer predicted was destined to establish the Trojans in a new home.

This makes the Homer/Virgil parallel even clearer: both the *Aeneid* and the *Odyssey* can therefore be seen in parallel, and there are clear links to be made between both Aeneas and Odysseus (the heroes' names in both cases give rise to the title of their respective poem) the journeys, one to Ithaca, the other to establish a new home, take place in the same mythical time as each other.

An early representation of Aeneas: Aeneas carrying Anchises

1.3 The legacy of Homer

In this section we will;

- *Understand who Homer is and why he is important*

- *Begin to explore the nature of epic poetry*

- *Consider other later writers that influenced Virgil*

Homer the poet

Homer is a shadowy semi-historical figure about which even the Ancient Greeks could not agree. His birthplace, date of birth and even (in more recent times) gender have all been disputed along with whether or not Homer was blind or not, or able to write or not.

A very approximate timeline for Homer

1600-1100 BC: approximate dates between which Mycenaean civilisation flourished.

850 BC: approximate date of the life of Homer given by Herodotus.

850-750 BC: many modern estimates place the creation of the oral versions of the *Iliad* and *Odyssey*

750 BC: earliest probable date of the *'pithekoussai cup'* – which is inscribed with lines from Homer.

750-650 BC: Likely date for the first written versions of the *Iliad* and the *Odyssey*.

Very, very, little can be said with any degree of certainty about Homer, beyond stating that the Ancient Greeks believed that there was a poet called Homer who is credited with creating the epic poems of the *Iliad* and the *Odyssey*.

Conventional dating places Homer as having lived *circa* 750-700 BC, and identifies him as either being born, or living in, one of several possible Greek cities along the coast of Asia Minor, the western seaboard of Turkey. This date is very arbitrary though.

Homer was clearly removed in time from the legendary events about which he describes. It is safe to say that Homer was not a historian and was not concerned with recording actual, historical events. Tradition and attempts by some archaeologists have attempted to associate Homer's poems and the towns and societies of which he speaks with sites and finds dating back to the Mycenaean period of Greece.

However, it must be said that despite this Homer and the Bronze Age sites discovered by archaeologists such as Schliemann and Arthur Evans at 'Troy', Mycenae and Knossos are inextricably linked in the popular mind. In fact Homer comes from a period much later than these sites. Homer's world should be more accurately associated with the Greece of the 7-8th centuries BC. This is because many 'non-Mycenaean' elements can be identified in Homer's poems, which are clearly an intrusion from Homer's contemporary world (that of the Greek Dark Age) and stand at odds with many of the things we know about the earlier Mycenaean period.

The works of Homer were considered by the Ancient Greeks to be the cornerstone of their culture and Homer's poetry remains an important foundation for modern literature. Homer's epic poems possess a unique composition, and the exciting tales of gods and heroes that they contain form an excellent starting point for the exploration of the ancient world and classical civilisation.

Who wrote the *Odyssey* and the *Iliad*?

So far we have assumed that the author of both the *Iliad* and *Odyssey* was an individual poet called 'Homer'.

It has been assumed that;

- One individual created both works.

- This individual went by the name 'Homer'.

- The *Iliad* and the *Odyssey* were created in that order.

- The *Iliad* and the *Odyssey* were first performed between the 8th and 6th century BC.

- That these works were called *'Iliad'* and the *'Odyssey'*.

- That 'Homer' was a man.

In fact, all of these are just that; *assumptions*. However, none of these assumptions can be argued to be definitely accurate due to the great age of the works we are dealing with.

The Ancient Greeks certainly believed that there was one, sole author of both works, and the tradition has also painted this man as being called 'Homer', a blind bard whose birth has been claimed by at least seven cities states.

Modern academics have pointed out inconsistencies in both the *Iliad* and the *Odyssey* which suggest that different parts of both works come from different times and from different poets. For example, in the *Iliad,* Book Ten; the Greek heroes Diomedes and Odysseus steal and ride horses away from the Thracians they have just raided. Everywhere else in both works horses are used exclusively to pull chariots. They are never ridden. Another example often used by academics seeking to identify different poets writing at different times is the rather odd ending of the *Odyssey*; Book Twenty Four of the *Odyssey* seems an addition, an appendix to the whole, and a rather disappointing one at that.

However, though there remain enough links and similarities between the two works that it is certainly still a possibility. It seems likely enough that even if the author of the *Odyssey* did not himself compose the *Iliad*, he certainly knew about it in enough detail to reproduce much of its flavour and linguistic style in his own work.

It has often been argued that both the *Iliad* and the *Odyssey* could have been composed not by a single individual; instead, the argument runs that these are the work of a group of loosely associated poets who collaborated and updated these works to produce many variants which were in turn written down and codified into 'one' definitive version which survived down to 1488 when a manuscript of Homer was first printed in Italy.

Despite the strength and plausibility of these kinds of arguments, many academics prefer the theory that both the *Iliad* and the *Odyssey* were created by one individual called Homer. The simple truth is that given our lack of firm evidence one way or another; *we simply do not know*. The argument continues, and will probably continue for some time to come without a definitive answer.

The Oral nature of Epic poetry

> **Remember!**
>
> *When reading epic poetry, it is important to remember that epic poetry was meant to be <u>heard</u>, not read.*

The poet or poets who constructed the *Odyssey* and the *Iliad* utilised many different stylistic and linguistic techniques. Many of these techniques and styles were subsequently adapted by Virgil to a greater or lesser extent. Virgil also introduced other styles as we shall see.

These techniques not only add depth and complexity to the narrative of epic poetry, but also were used to help the poet be able to time his performances and also to be able to remember the events and order of them. Remember after all that epic poetry were long poems that would have been performed over a period of several days. As such, techniques such as repetition and regression of the story would help the audience to also keep track.

When reading Homer or Virgil, it is important to remember that this epic poem was meant to be **heard**, not read. Oral poetry is designed to be listened to. It is almost certain that Homer's poetry comes from a pre-literate period. With one bare exception, there is no mention of writing in either the *Iliad* of or the *Odyssey* and the techniques used in both poems strongly suggest that the poet (or poets) that created these stories was illiterate.

Virgil however is different. He comes from a time period when writing was widespread (amongst the elite in any event) and he, unlike Homer wrote his poetry prior to performance to an audience. Virgil's target audience is also the very highest of the Roman elite in the city of Rome; whereas Homer's audience varied depending upon who, when and where he was.

In the ancient world the idea of silent reading was somewhat unusual; typically someone reading a book would read out aloud as they read. When considering the epic poetry of Homer or Virgil, it is important to bear in mind that the poet would recite and the audience would listen.

Why is Homer important to Virgil?

Virgil's *Aeneid* is an epic poem in the form, composition and tradition of Homer's *Iliad* and *Odyssey*. Since Epic poetry is the sustained narrative of so called 'Great Events' of the past as told by a much more modern author, for Virgil or any other aspiring epic poet to attempt to add to this narrative of 'Great Events' inevitably led the audience to compare future epics to Homer which were (and arguably are) the greatest poems of the ancient world.

Instead of trying to write something different to Homer, Virgil deliberately embraces Homer, his techniques and his world narrative.

If you have read Homer previously, as you read the *Aeneid* you will no doubt identify similarities in the poems. Virgil draws deliberately on Homer's poems; the plot, character, stylistic techniques and deployment of language is all deliberately similar.

But it is important to understand Virgil is not re-writing or attempting to ape Homer. Instead he is inspired by the works of Homer to write in the same tradition; a story that has some of its own roots in Homer, yet at the same time Virgil is creating something unique; an epic poem in the Homeric tradition that explains in part the rise and greatness of Rome.

3rd and 2nd Century BC Influences on Virgil

Homer was not the only poet or writer that inspired Virgil.

There are several intertextual references in the *Aeneid* from the following poets;

- Apollonius of Rhodius' *Argonautica*

- Quintus Ennius' *Annals*

Apollonius of Rhodius' *Argonautica*

Apollonius of Rhodius was a 3rd century BC writer and poet.

Apollonius spent much of his life in the city of Alexandria and served as a royal tutor to some of the children of the Ptolemies. He wrote an epic poem called the *Argonautica*.

Heavily influenced by the *Odyssey,* The *Argonautica* was written like Homer's epics in Hexameter verse and comprised of four books. It told the story of Jason and the Argonauts and their search for the Golden Fleece of Colchis. The *Argonautica* was a major influence on the *Aeneid* and, like the *Odyssey* and the *Aeneid*, the *Argonautica* has episodes that involve epic sea voyages, meetings of the gods and a catalogue of the assembled heroes. In the *Argonautica* the hero Jason bears strong resemblance to Odysseus and Medea more resembles Nausicaa than she does the Medea of Euripides' play by the same name.

Quintus Ennius' *Annals*

Quintus Ennius lived from 239-169BC and like Virgil, was a Roman poet of Italian origin; Ennius was granted Roman citizenship in 184BC. Ennius served as a Soldier in the Roman armies in Sardinia and also worked in Rome as a tutor. He wrote many plays and poems and seems to have been over fond of alcohol.

The Annals were a narrative poem of Roman History. Spanning some fifteen books, the Annals recorded the history of Rome from the fall of Troy to the Roman capture of Ambracia (a region in Western Greece) which occurred only a few years before his death.

Ennius' *Annals* begins like Homer and Virgil with an invocation to the Muses which was particularly apt as a temple to the Muses had just been constructed in Rome by Ennius' patron Fulvius Nobilior. Like Virgil too, the *Annals* details the link between the fall of Troy and the establishment of the Trojans in Italy by Aeneas, in their efforts the Trojans were aided and abetted by the Olympian Gods.

An early presentation of Aeneas

1.4 Linguistic and stylistic techniques in Virgil's Aeneid

In this section we will;

- *Identify the distinctive features of the style and language of the Aeneid*

- *Explore and understand some key linguistic and stylistic techniques used in Virgil's Aeneid*

- *Consider the main descriptive features of Virgil*

- *Examine the main narrative techniques of Virgil*

- *Explore and understand some key linguistic and stylistic techniques used in Virgil's Aeneid*

- *Understand the narrative techniques, including flashback, retardation and episodes in the Aeneid*

- *Practise finding and analysing some of these linguistic features present in the Aeneid*

- *Understand some of the techniques Virgil adopted from Greek Tragedy*

Introduction

In this topic we will introduce some of the linguistic and stylistic techniques of Virgil's *Aeneid*. By introducing some linguistic and stylistic features of the *Aeneid* at this early stage in the guide we will establish a sound basis of understanding of oral composition.

Introducing features of Epic poetry

Epic poetry differs from regular modern written poetry in several ways. The main difference we can identify is length. An epic poem is well, epic!

If you have already explored Homer's Odyssey or Iliad you will recognize several of the techniques that Virgil uses in the *Aeneid*.

Below are some of the key features of epic poetry used by Virgil

- *Epithets - Adjective phrases*

- *Recycling of descriptive language*

- *Digression or Retardation of the plot*

Epithets - Adjective Phrases

One of the most apparent techniques of epic poetry is the use of Epithets. Epithets are adjectives, or adjectival phrases used to describe a person, object or place.

Prime examples of kinds of Adjective Phrases used by Virgil include;

- '*pious* Aeneas'

- '*Brave* Pallas'

- Mezentius, *scorner of the Gods'*

- '*Lausus, a tamer of horses'*

- '*Mighty* Troy'

These Epithets are used to describe some of the characteristics of a character, object or place and can vary or alter as the character, object or place changes. For example a simple adjective can change how we imagine the sea; the sea can be calm or it can be stormy – two very different states. Likewise Aeneas can be pious (*pietas*), but he can also be furious (*furor*).

Task: **Examples of Epithets in Book One**

Go through the Book One of the Aeneid

Identify at least three examples of Epithets in Book One

This is important as you can use these as examples of this feature of epic poetry in the exams.

Recycling of descriptive language

Also called *repetition*; Virgil does not use this as frequently as Homer, but it is still apparent in the *Aeneid*.

It is most commonly used at the level of scenes of action (mostly in battle) and includes certain stock phrases; heroes die graphically, covered in blood in the *Aeneid*; weapons are hurled with fury or thrust savagely into faces, throats and groins.

> *Task:* **Examples of Recycling of violent phrases in Book Two**
>
> *Go through the Book Two of the Aeneid*
>
> *Identify at least three examples of violent phrases or language*
>
> *This is important as you can use these as examples of this feature of epic poetry in the exams.*

Digression - Retardation of the plot

What is Retardation of the plot?

Retardation of the plot, also called a *digression or elaboration*, is another technique used by Virgil that he has drawn upon from Homer. This feature allows the epic poet to develop the interest of the narrative into a related anecdote, but still leaves room to return to the main story and plot. This digression is a common feature of epic and is used by Virgil to elaborate his descriptions of people and places.

Retardation of the plot is a strong feature of interaction between characters in the *Odyssey*. When characters they tell each other stories in the *Odyssey* they often digress. These digressions are sometimes allowed to go on at some length, but the main thread of the narrative is always returned to by the use of signals such as *'as I was saying earlier...'*

Retardation of the plot is now often described as *'ring composition'*. Ring composition is so called because the narrative returns to where it left off in a circular fashion.

Ring composition is a controlling feature of the oral poet that ensures that, despite the retardations, the main storyline still takes precedence and the direction of that is kept moving to its end.

Books Two and Three as digression

There are two prime examples of digression in the first three books of the *Aeneid*. Book Two and Three are both stories being told by Aeneas to Dido in Carthage. As such all the events contained within are plot retardations in order to tell the story to Dido (and therefore the audience of Virgil) of how Aeneas and his Trojans managed to arrive at Carthage. Other digressions occur with the tales of Hercules in Book Eight and the dilemma of King Latinus in Book Seven.

Task: Language and stylistic techniques in the Aeneid

Write a response to the following question;

To what extent do you think that Virgil's use of the language techniques described in this section will enhance or detract from the plot and story of the Aeneid?

Now that we have introduced several basic techniques we shall go into more detailed and complex techniques that are used by Virgil in the *Aeneid*.

Identifying Latin poetical techniques

What is more difficult to convey to a modern reader of Virgil in translation is his poetical innovation with Latin metre, however many translations in English attempt to convey some of this flavour with some success. One particular feature of Virgil's poetry in the *Aeneid* is his frequent use of *enjambment*, where the sense of a line of poetry runs over from one line to the next, rather than stopping at the end of every line with a sentence end. This has the effect of creating a more 'flowing' verse structure.

In keeping with the 'flowing' style of his verse, Virgil prefers to link clauses with lots of 'ands' rather than have lots of short sentences or subordinate clauses. This is a feature which can be more easily brought out in the English translation, and is something that you can look out for.

Virgil also makes frequent use of *alliteration* and *assonance*, in common with many other poets writing in Latin. This poetical effect can sometimes be successfully rendered in English. As you read the *Aeneid* try to identify alliterative effects, where the same letter is repeated many times in a line or sense unit, or assonance where the same sound is repeated.

Homeric and Hellenistic techniques

Virgil is also very fond of Homeric style *similes*. These are often extended similes, as in Homer, and are frequently comparisons to the natural world. We should notice lots of these similes when we start reading and we will explore similes in greater detail in the next section.

Virgil's skill as a poet lies in his ability to marry together two different kinds of poetry. On the one hand the grand sweep of Homeric epic and the personal or subjective Alexandrian poetry of the Hellenistic era on the other, which influenced another Roman poet, Catullus (who slightly preceded Virgil), very much indeed.

As you progress through the *Aeneid*, look out for the epic 'grand sweep' techniques that Homer uses in the *Iliad*. These can include the ebb and flow of the fighting in Book Eleven for example.

Virgil also uses personal or subjective techniques to create lines of subtle and beautiful poetry, such as we see in the interaction between Aeneas and Dido in Book Four as an example.

This last is something that Homer also achieved in the *Odyssey*, with its homeliness and deep felt relationships alongside its mythical majesty and scope.

This personal or 'subjective' slant to the *Aeneid* can be seen in the narrator's voice which is sometimes heard. A very famous example of this is well worth quoting in Latin:

sunt lacrimae rerum et mentem mortalia tangunt

Virgil. *Aeneid*, Book 1, line 462

This can be translated as;

'there are tears for things and mortal matters touch my mind'.

This is a line of great sadness and *pathos*, but it is also poetically very beautiful and reminds the reader that the *Aeneid* is not only about the epic story of the founding of Rome but is also about the personal tragedy and loss suffered by the Trojans.

Narrative Techniques

Virgil, like Homer, uses narrative techniques that are very familiar to us as a modern audience.

Like Homer's *Odyssey*, much of the *Aeneid* is told in flash-back (*analepsis*), and includes changes of narrative tempo and perspective. Virgil's narrative technique is likewise varied. Virgil also uses a technique of looking forward into the future (*prolepsis*).

Techniques such as changes of person and place are used in order to provide variety in the narrative and to create the 'cinematic' effect of which epic is capable; the 'grand sweep' or panoramic view, as well as the extreme close-up.

As you will see, Aeneas is not present in every scene, or indeed in every book. Book Eleven for example focuses on the Latins and most of the speakers and the focus of the action is based around Camilla, Turnus and King Latinus for example. In Book One Aeneas is a participant, but he also an observer of events. The focus of the narrative also often switches to the Gods as they discuss mortal affairs with varying degrees of compassion.

As you read Virgil, look out for changes of narrative pace, variation in perspective or person, location or time, though we will be examining these in closer detail as we progress in our analysis of the *Aeneid*.

A glossary of Language and stylistic techniques in Virgil's *Aeneid*

The following is a list of literary methods that we can identify in Virgil's *Aeneid*;

- *Allusion*

- *Analepsis*

- *Assonance*

- *Apostrophe*

- *Apotheosis*

- *Deus ex Machina*

- *Enjambment*

- *Epithet*

- *Intertextuality*

- *Metaphor*

- *Metonym*

- *Personification*

- *Prolepsis*

- *Simile*

- *Symbol*

Allusion - An *allusion* is a direct or indirect reference to other literary texts. In Virgil we can most easily identify allusions to the works of Homer.

Analepsis - *Analepsis* is a form of 'flashback'; a digression by the poet when they refer to events that have occurred previously. *Analepsis* can be either brief or extended. For example in book two of the *Aeneid* Virgil has Aeneas tell the story of the fall of Troy.

Apostrophe - An *apostrophe* is an address by a character to an inanimate object, or alternatively an address to a non-living form. In Sophocles' *Ajax* for example Ajax talks to his sword before falling upon it.

Apotheosis - *Apotheosis* is a literary device by which a character is transformed or elevated to a god-like status. At the end of Euripides' *Medea* for example Medea flies away in a chariot drawn by dragons, a clear transformation from her state at the beginning of the tragedy.

Assonance - where the same sound is repeated –so *meet, feet, greet.*

Deus ex Machina - A literary device used by poets, playwrights and authors to bring about a resolution of a conflict or situation through the deployment of the actions of a god, character or action that may seem otherwise unrelated to the story.

Enjambment - The sense of a line of poetry runs over from one line to the next, rather than stopping at the end of every line with a sentence end. This has the effect of creating a more 'flowing' verse structure.

Epithet – An *epithet* is a name bestowed upon a character which identifies a defining characteristic. For example in Virgil's *Aeneid* Aeneas is commonly referred to as 'pious' or 'dutiful' Aeneas.

Intertextuality - Often a writer or poet will make reference to the works of another writer or poet. For example it is often stated that Virgil makes direct or indirect references to the works of Homer.

Metaphor – A common literary device that is present in everyday usage by us all. A metaphor is a merging of two different elements or ideas. For example to say *'My head is spinning'* is a metaphor. Likewise Shakespeare famously used the metaphor *'All the world's a stage...'* in his play *'As you like it'*.

Metonym - A Metonym is the use of a part in order to represent the whole; the use of one item to stand for another for which it has been associated. For example in common usage the news channels refer to the UK government as *'Westminster'*. Another example is the presentation of a clock in film to represent time passing. A final example of a Metonym is to refer to the police as *'the long arm of the law'*.

Personification – Personification is when an inhuman object is given human characteristics.

Prolepsis - *Prolepsis* is a 'fast-forward'; a digression by the poet or writer when they refer to events that have occurred previously. Like *analepsis, prolepsis* can be either brief or extended. In book six of the *Aeneid* for example Virgil has Aeneas witness the parade of future great Romans.

Simile - A *simile* is a common literary technique that is a comparison of one item with another with which it intentionally similar. Generally speaking if something is like something else then this is a simile. So for example in Homer's *Odyssey* Menelaus likens Odysseus to a lion and the suitors to startled deer. Another example is to compare the love of a character to a beautiful flower such as a rose. As we shall see Virgil litters the *Aeneid* with similes like confetti at a wedding.

Symbol - A device used by writers and poets to substitute one thing for another. These symbols replace a word with an item associated with this word. So for example a Dove is commonly used as a symbol for peace. Red is a colour we commonly associate with danger and a snake is sometimes used as a symbol for temptation.

The difference between a metaphor and a simile.

A metaphor is a figure of speech that compares a subject to another which is otherwise unrelated. Saying your life is a journey is a metaphor for example.

A simile is not quite the same as a metaphor; it is introduced by a comparison word such as 'like' or 'as' or even 'just as'. The comparison is made but, unlike a metaphor the items of comparison are not identified with each other.

Task: Understanding key literary and linguistic devices

Below are some examples of text. Identify the techniques being used.

So for example – *'My love is a rose'* is a metaphor.

a) Messapus tamer of horses
b) The wine dark sea
c) The moon was a ghostly ship tossed about on cloudy seas
d) Man killing Hector

A passage from the *Aeneid;*

a) *"At that moment I seemed to see the whole of Ilium settling into the flames and Neptune's Troy toppling over from its foundations like as ancient ash tree high in the mountains which farmers have hacked with blow upon blow of their double axes, labouring to fell it..."*

Virgil *Aeneid* II. 625-628.

Now for a longer passage from the *Aeneid*, with multiple techniques.

b) *"Just as Mars, spattered with blood, charges along the banks of the icy river Hebrus, clashing sword on shield and giving full rein to his furious horses as he stirs up war, they fly across the open plain before the winds of the south and west, til Thrace roars to its furthest reaches with the drumming of their hooves as his escort gallops all round him, Rage, Treachery and the dark faces of Fear – just so did bold Turnus lash his horses through the thick of battle til they smoked with sweat, and as he trampled the pitiable bodies of his dead enemies , the flying hooves scattered a dew of blood and churned the gore into the sand."*

Virgil *Aeneid* XII.333-340

Language and stylistic techniques in Virgil's *Aeneid* influenced by Greek Tragedy

As mentioned earlier, Virgil was influenced by more poets and writers from the past than just Homer. For example. In Book Four of the *Aeneid* we can identify a strong tragic element that was influenced by playwrights such as Euripides. Dido in particular of the women in the *Aeneid* has been likened to Euripides' *Medea* in characterisation and in addition to this we can also identify some stylistic techniques used by Greek Tragedians in Virgil's work.

In particular these techniques include the following;

- *Agon*

- *Anagnorisis*

- *Catharsis*

- *Hamartia*

- *Kommos*

- *Peripeteia*

- *Rhesis*

A glossary of techniques influenced by Greek Tragedy in Virgil's *Aeneid*

Agon - An *agon* is as a set debate and is a common feature of Greek tragedy. In an *agon* a character presents his or her case, in a formal manner, and another character refutes the points made. It has the feel of the 'law-court' about it. The aim is to capture the audience through reasoned argument, and since tragedies often represent the clash of two opposing ideologies, there is much food for thought to be found in the *agon*.

Anagnorisis – Recognition (anagnorisis) is a change from ignorance to the awareness of a bond of love or hate. For example, in Sophocles' *Oedipus the King*, Oedipus has killed his father in ignorance and then learns too late of his true relationship to the King of Thebes. Recognition scenes in tragedy are of some horrible event or secret, like the realisation in Sophocles' *Ajax* that the eponymous hero has killed sheep instead of his supposed enemies in the Greek camp. Ajax realises he is now disgraced and doomed.

Catharsis - Catharsis gives us our word 'cathartic' which we use to refer to something with a great cleansing or purging power. The word in the context of Greek Tragedy refers to the effect a 'good' tragedy should have on the audience. It should purge the audience of its emotions, by inducing feelings such as pity, anger or fear and allowing the audience a safe place for the expression of them.

Hamartia - *Hamartia* derives from a Greek root word meaning 'to miss the mark' or 'to fall short'. In the context of Greek Tragedy, *hamartia* refers to a failing of the central character which brings about the catastrophe. It has sometimes been translated as a 'character flaw'; but this is to fall short of the true meaning of the word.

In fact, it is not so much an in-grained character fault as more an opportunity missed, or bad decision made which sets up the inescapability and inevitability of the tragic events which follow. Each tragedy possesses this 'falling short' or *Hamartia,* of a central character, and will be considered in our close reading of the text.

Kommos – A *Kommos* is a lament or grief stricken speech commonly found in a Greek tragedy. A *kommos* is often a lyrical exchange between characters or can be a standalone speech.

Peripeteia - Peripeteia refers to a (usually sudden) reversal or change of fortune of the central character. Again, like *hamartia* this is a typical feature of a Greek tragedy. The reversal can be from good to bad or vice versa. Aristotle considered the first, the change from happiness to misery, the more significant for tragedy.

Rhesis - A common feature of Greek tragedy, a *Rhesis* is the name given to a set speech by a character which is characterised by logical argument or ordered reasoning, yet may also include emotional appeal. It could be a monologue, where a character reflects on his opinions, feelings and motivations, or it could be part of a dialogue or argument.

1.5 Shaping meaning: The Simile

In this section we will;

- *Explore and understand some key linguistic and stylistic techniques used in Virgil's Aeneid*

- *Familiarise ourselves with the distinctive features of similes*

- *Identify the distinctive features of Virgilian style.*

- *Practise finding and analysing some of these linguistic features present in the Aeneid*

Introduction

In this topic we focus on some of the other linguistic and stylistic techniques of Virgil's *Aeneid*.

In particular we will focus on using Book Two of the *Aeneid* in order to demonstrate some of these techniques. By understanding these linguistic and stylistic features of the *Aeneid* at this early stage in the guide we will establish a sound basis of understanding of epic composition.

What is a Simile?

A *simile* is a common literary technique that is a comparison of one item with another with which it intentionally similar. Generally speaking if something is like something else then this is a simile. So for example in Homer's *Odyssey* Menelaus likens Odysseus to a lion and the suitors to startled deer. Another general example is to compare the love of a character to a beautiful flower such as a rose.

> **Task: Identifying Similes in the Aeneid**
>
> *Explore the books of the Aeneid that you have read so far.*
>
> *Try to find at least three good examples of similes.*
>
> *For each simile consider;*
>
> - *What is the nature of the comparison?*
>
> - *How effective do you think the simile is in conveying the ideas and/or attitudes of the writer?*

The difference between a metaphor and a simile.

A metaphor is a figure of speech that compares a subject to another which is otherwise unrelated. Comparing your life to a journey is a metaphor, or like Shakespeare in his play *'As you like it'*;

"All the world is a stage,

And all the men and women merely players;

They have their exits and their entrances"

A simile is **not** the same as a metaphor. Rather, a simile it is introduced by a comparison word such as *'like'* or *'as'* or even *'just as'*. The comparison is made but, unlike a metaphor the items of comparison are not identified with each other. Similes are typically determined and often use real-life comparisons. Virgil is particularly fond of comparing heroes like Aeneas and Turnus to feared hunting animals or the forces of the natural world, like storms. In this Virgil is clearly inspired by and is using the same techniques as Homer did in *Iliad* and *Odyssey*.

Likewise, Virgil, like Homer, compares or else references the type of experiences that would have been known to Greeks of his time. So, ships and sailing feature, as do activities such as cooking and hunting. The similes employed can at times even be humorous.

Task: Exploring a Simile

Below is a simile from the early part of the Aeneid.

"At that moment I seemed to see the whole of Ilium settling into the flames and Neptune's Troy toppling over from its foundations like as ancient ash tree high in the mountains which farmers have hacked with blow upon blow of their double axes, labouring to fell it..."

Virgil Aeneid II. 625-628

How effective do you think this Simile is in illustrating the fall of Troy?

The Homeric simile

Since Virgil drew extensively on Homer for inspiration, we shall take an example of a simile from Homer's *Odyssey*.

Below is a good example of the Homeric simile;

"The Suitors were scared out of their senses. They scattered through the hall like a herd of cattle that a darting gadfly had attacked and stampeded, in the spring-time when the long days come in".

Homer. *Odyssey* Book XXII.300-302

In this simile taken from near the end of the *Odyssey*, the suitors are being slaughtered by Odysseus and his allies in the Great Hall at Ithaca. It is clear through this simile that the suitors are clearly not putting up much of a fight; they are likened to a herd of stampeding cattle plagued to madness by insects.

Task: Analysing another Homeric simile

Read the following excerpt and the answer the questions below;

"Auburn haired Menelaus was hot with indignation. 'How disgraceful! He cried. 'So the cowards want to creep into the brave man's bed? It's just as if a deer had put her two little unweaned fawns to sleep in a mighty lion's den and gone to range the high ridges and grassy dales for pasture. Back comes the lion to his lair, and the fawns meet a grisly fate – as will the Suitors at Odysseus' hand."

Homer's Odyssey Book IV. 331-340

Ensure that you are able to write a brief response to the following questions;

- *What is the subject of the simile in this passage?*

- *What do you think the effect of this simile is here?*

- *How effective do you think it is in conveying an image to the audience?*

Menelaus' simile

The similes used by Homer are typically extensions of the previous sentence. In the above example, the simile serves to contrast between the bravery of Odysseus against the cowardly nature of the Suitors. The animal comparison between the predator; the lion, and the prey; the deer, is particularly apt. Odysseus is destined to hunt down the Suitors on his return to Ithaca and Menelaus assumes *will* happen and will take just revenge for their behaviour; as is appropriate for a Homeric hero to do.

1.6 The Epic Hero and Aeneas

In this section we will;

- *To investigate the similarities and differences between our concept of 'heroes' and those portrayed by Virgil*

- *To understand the concepts of Honour (timé) and Reputation (kleos)*

- *To begin to understand the Roman virtues of pietas, fides, mens*

- *Understand what is meant by furor*

Introduction to *time and kleos*

Key terms:

timé – The pursuit of honour and esteem.

kleos – Good reputation.

Two cultural concepts from Ancient Greece require some explanation before exploring the *Aeneid*. If you are studying Classical Civilisation at A Level it is very likely you have or will encounter these concepts in relation to Homer's *Odyssey* or *Iliad*.

Aeneas is a hero, and as such is expected to act in particular ways. In order to fit the mould of a hero; Aeneas needs to be brave, resourceful and at times violent.

The Ancient Greeks used two conceptual terms which were of specific concern to the Greek heroes; these concepts; Honour *(timé)* and Reputation *(kleos)* were an integral part of the makeup of the heroic characters in Homer's *Iliad* and *Odyssey*.

These conceptual terms are also present in Virgil's *Aeneid*. But as we shall see, Aeneas also exhibits other characteristics that make this hero fit into the Roman understanding of what it was to be a virtuous citizen.

What is a Hero?

The Hero can take many forms; from Superman or Spiderman with their superpowers to Bilbo Baggins from Tolkien's *The Hobbit* – In himself Bilbo has no special superpowers but his struggle and determination sees him through to success in the end.

Still other kinds of hero can be identified from real life; such as those that face dangerous illnesses with courage, raise money for charities or someone who rescues people from burning buildings.

Heroes can take many shapes and forms, but they do share many characteristics; they are brave, they may work as a force for good, they can be selfish or selfless and they more often as not win through in the end and triumph over the challenges that they are faced with.

The ancient Greek concept of the Hero: *timé* and *kleos*

The *Iliad*, more so than the *Odyssey*, the subject matter deals with what it is to be one of the hero class, such as an Achilles or an Agamemnon. It centred on achieving the value *timé* (honour or esteem).

Being a hero, or warrior, was a distinctly elitist pursuit, since only such men in the Homeric world have the nobility of mind to fight in battle (and the wealth to do so). This was paralleled to an extent in the Classical period, an individual's wealth determined their ability to fight, with the richest serving as cavalry, the middle classes serving as heavy armoured infantry (hoplites) and the poorer serving as light armed skirmishers, or excluded from fighting entirely.

Task: Identifying 'Heroic' traits

Think about the following well known characters from literature and from films - write a list of the traits and powers that make this character 'heroic'.

- *James Bond*
- *Harry Potter*
- *Wonder Woman*
- *Your own favourite "hero"*

An example of *timé* from the Iliad

"But powerful Diomedes froze him with a glance:

"Not a word of retreat. You'll never persuade me.

It's not my nature to shrink from battle, cringe in fear

With the fighting strength still steady in my chest.

I shrink from mounting our chariot – no retreat-

On foot as I am, I'll meet them man to man.

Athena would never let me flinch."

Iliad Book V, 278 – 284 (translated by R.Fagles).

Remember!
Kleos

kleos is renown. *Kleos* can also refer to praise poetry and this renown is most especially valued, as it is these deeds that can result in fame beyond death. Achilles for example is a Greek hero that sought (and found) immortality, due to his *kleos*.

Martial valour was a way for the elite of the Homeric world to ensure their *timé*, and thus to secure their *kleos* (good reputation: the things, good and bad, that people say about you) on the battlefield.

Not only was warfare a desirable pursuit of the elite, it was also their duty to fight when called upon in order to protect the palace and outlying territories which they ruled. A refusal to fight in these circumstances was a rejection of obligation. It was expected that a king or war leader should act in a heroic way, in return for which he received the loyalty of his subordinates and the dues from them necessary for his status as their leader. The world of Homer then was distinctly feudal in nature

Remember!

For Homer, the key to being a hero was the desire for *timé* and the concern for their future *kleos*.

An example of *kleos* from the *Iliad*

"Hector loosing a savage cry and flaring on like fire,

Like the God of fire, the blaze that never dies.

And the cry pierced Menelaus, deeply torn now

as he probed his own great heart: "What can I do?

If I leave this splendid gear and desert Patroclus-

Who fell here fighting, all to redeem my honour-

Won't any comrade curse me, seeing me break away?

But if I should take on Hector and Hector's Trojans

alone, in single combat – trying to save my pride –

won't they encircle me, one against so many?"

Iliad XVII, 100-107 (translated by R.Fagles).

In the example above Menelaus is concerned how it will look if he tries to protect the corpse of Patroclus against all odds or instead retreat and save himself to fight another day. In the event he makes a sensible decision and calls others to help him making demands of their own *kleos* (whilst maintaining his own good standing).

Heroes in the world of Homer value their honour and consequently their reputation or 'good name' more than any other concern. Through winning battles, fighting honourably; especially in single-combat and hopefully, victory ensures this. However, the negative aspects of *timé* and *kleos* lay in the ever-present reality of an early and untimely death in battle. This is what Achilles chooses when he sails to Troy, and his death ensures that his name will be preserved for eternity. This was the price paid by the hero in return for the only thing considered to be of any worth in the world of Homer.

Task: Identifying examples of timé and kleos in the Aeneid

As you read through the Aeneid it will be useful to consolidate your understanding of the concepts of timé and kleos by identifying two examples of each from across Virgil's poem

These examples can come from any character and from any point of the Aeneid.

Roman Virtues

Like any Imperial power in history, the Augustan regime in Rome wanted to extol specific characteristics that could be pointed to and claimed were the reasons why Rome was great and why Rome was justified in maintaining its imperial greatness. These virtues were also promoted during the difficult circumstances of the Punic Wars between Rome and Carthage.

These virtues included;

- *Mens*

- *Pietas*

- *Fides*

Mens: is translated from Latin to mean *'Composure'*, *'Resolution'* or *'clear headedness'*. This quality is ascribed to Aeneas in Virgil. The Roman dictator Fabius Cunctator (more on him in Book Six) built a temple to *Mens* during the Second Punic War.

Pietas: Is the recognition of and the discharge of an individual's duty to gods, country and family.

Fides: faithfulness. The Roman dictator Aulus Atilius Calatinus built a temple to *Fides* during the First Punic War in 249BC.

The Augustan regime had only recently emerged victorious from the period of Civil Wars that had been afflicting the Roman Empire since the 50s BC. We should not be too surprised to see that the same virtues that were promoted during the *creation* of the Empire during the Republican period were also being promoted to help *consolidate* and *maintain* the Roman Empire under Augustus and the imperial Principate.

Furor

Another term which we should familiarise ourselves with is *Furor*.

Furor is a Latin term from which the English words 'Fury' and 'Furious' originate. In the *Aeneid* Furor occurs when emotions or other violent urges are uncontrolled.

Furor is not a virtue, but rather an evil, a vice. We can identify this vice most easily in Turnus. Turnus wages war with fury – as the rampage through the Trojan Camp in Book Nine attests. However and more interestingly, Virgil has his paragon of virtue Aeneas also succumbs to *furor* on occasion.

In Book Two, Aeneas tries to kill the defenceless (though hardly blameless) Helen during the destruction of Troy. Again, Aeneas succumbs to furor in Book Ten when he learns that Pallas has been killed by Turnus. Finally and most disturbingly, Aeneas succumbs to *furor* at the end of Book Twelve when he slaughters the wounded and helpless Turnus.

In some translations of the *Aeneid* the word 'strife' is also used for *Furor*

Key term: Fate

The universal destiny of all. Even the gods are subject to Fate. To meet your fate usually means to die.

The Romans also used the word Tyche 'Fortune'. Fate was considered to be a goddess who can dispense both good and evil on mortals.

Key terms: Virtues and vices

Ensure that you are familiar with the meaning of the following;

- *Furor*
- *Pietas*
- *Mens*
- *Fate*
- *Fides*

As you study the Aeneid ensure that you can identify several examples of each – note the character and the episode and the context in which they are identified.

PART TWO: Historical context of the *Aeneid*

PART TWO

2.1 The Rise of Rome: An overview

2.2 The legacy of Julius Caesar

2.3 The Triumvirate and the rise of Augustus

2.4 The Battle of Actium and the aftermath

2.5 Virgil, Augustus, and the Roman Imperial tradition

2.1 The Rise of Rome: An overview

This section will help you to;

- *Understand the early history of Rome*

- *Begin to explore the wars and events through which Rome gained her Empire*

- *Consider whether Rome's acquisition of this empire occurred by accident or design*

Introduction

In this section we will explore in brief the history of Rome from its' semi-mythical establishment to the reign of Augustus.

It is strongly recommended that you read or research yourself the history of Rome. There are many books that you could consult, along with any good reference work on ancient history, and these will provide you with the background necessary to understanding some of the events that Virgil refers to in the *Aeneid*.

The Establishment of the Roman Empire

The Roman Empire was already extensive when Augustus rose to prominence. This Empire was acquired by Rome through a series of conflicts and acquisitions that saw the demise of rival tribes, city states, kings and empires. In this section we will consider some of these conflicts, to explore who Rome was competing against and when the territories that would become the Roman Empire were acquired by Rome.

In the early 2nd century AD the Roman Historian Tacitus recorded the following;

"When Rome was first a city, its rulers were kings. Then Lucius Junius Brutus created the consulate and free Republican institutions in general. Dictatorships were assumed in emergencies. A Council of Ten did not last more than two years, and there was a short lived arrangement by which the senior army officers….possessed consular authority. Subsequently Cinna and Sulla set up autocracies, but they too were brief. Soon Pompey and Crassus acquired predominant positions, but rapidly lost them to Caesar. Next, the military strength which Lepidus and Antonius had built up was absorbed by Augustus. He found the whole state exhausted by internal dissensions, and established over it a personal regime known as the Principate."

Tacitus, *Annals* 1.1

In this passage Tacitus refers to the following events;

- The legendary foundation of Rome in 753BC

- The expulsion of the kings by Lucius Junius Brutus in 510BC

- The Council of Ten from 451-449BC

- The consulships of the senior army commanders, in intervals between 444-367BC

- Cinna's four consulships 87-84BC

- Sulla's Dictatorship 82-79BC

- The Triumvirate of Caesar, Crassus and Pompey 60-53BC

- Caesar's Dictatorships 49-44BC

- The Triumvirate of Octavian, Lepidus and Antonius 43-31BC

- The Principate of Augustus 31BC-14AD

Tacitus' outline is brief and it is brief because he is concerned with other, later events, but Tacitus is also brief because much of the early history of Rome had been covered by the historian Livy, and also because Tacitus was no doubt aware that much of the early history of Rome was unclear and heavily reliant upon figures of myth and whose historicity was doubtful.

For the early history of Rome, we owe much of our understanding to the historian Livy. Other information of the early history of Rome comes from writers such as the poet Virgil in his *Aeneid*.

Both Virgil and Livy wrote their respective works during the period of Augustus' Principate. Both were part of a circle of writers close to Augustus himself. It is therefore important to appreciate the context in which these sources were written when considering their content.

Historian: Livy

Titus Livius was a Roman historian born in approximately 59BC and died around 17AD of Italian origin born in Patavium in Northern Italy.

Livy wrote a history covering the history of the city of Rome from the foundation of the city up to 9BC. This history chronicled the rise of Rome from city state to Empire. This history was comprised of 142 books of which only 34 survive (Books 1-10 & 21-45).

Aeneas and the mythical foundation of Rome

According to both Greek and Roman tradition, Aeneas survived the sack of Troy and led a group of survivors which eventually landed in Italy. On arrival in Italy, Aeneas allied with king Latinus, a local ruler, and after defeating other peoples in battle, settled in Italy, building a settlement called Lavinium.

Aeneas' son Ascanius founded a new settlement after the death of Aeneas and called it Alba Longa. According to Roman tradition, Ascanius' descendants gradually expanded the power and territory of their people (the Latins) and built a series of new settlements across the region of Italy in which the city of Rome now stands.

Although Roman mythical tradition does not ascribe the foundation of Rome to Aeneas and his son, it is these mythical figures who settled in the area of Rome, and from who the Romans could point to an even older mythical tradition; Troy.

Romulus and the mythical foundation of Rome

Romulus and his twin brother Remus, were born from the union of a Vestal Virgin called Rhea Silvia, who was descended from the line of Aeneas, and the God of War, Mars. According to the myth and Roman tradition, Vestal Virgins must always remain pure, and after she had given birth, Rhea was imprisoned at Alba Longa. The children were left to die in the wild.

However, Romulus and Remus did not die. They were found by a She-Wolf, who suckled the twins and kept them alive until they were discovered by a forester who rescued the twins and raised them as his own. In time the twins grew to adulthood and travelled to Alba Longa and helped king, Numitor secure his power.

Eventually, Romulus and Remus learned of their origins and determined to establish a new town on the site where they had been exposed. This site was the site that would become Rome. Romulus settled on the Palatine hill and Remus lived on the Aventine hill. As neighbours the brothers got on less well, and during a territorial dispute, Remus was killed and Romulus took possession of the whole, renaming it Rome. According to Roman tradition the date of this foundation was 753BC.

The semi-mythical kings of Rome (753-510BC)

The period between the establishment of Rome in 753BC and the establishment of Republican rule in 510BC was approximately 240 years. According to Roman early history, 7 kings ruled during this 240 years, which given the average age of a human being then and now is almost certainly unlikely.

More plausible are;

a) Either there were more kings covering this period of time.

b) The period of time is much shorter.

Little is known about the kings of Rome and what is recorded in Livy's earlier books. Livy records these kings' names as;

1. Titus Tatius

2. Numa Popilius

3. Tullus Hostiius

4. Ancus Marcius

5. Tarquinius Priscus

6. Servius Tullius

7. Tarquinius Superbus

According to Livy, the last king, Tarquinius Superbus, was driven out by a group of senators called Lucius Junius Brutus after the rape and subsequent suicide of a noble born daughter, Lucretia, by a son of the king. Once Tarquinius was driven into exile, Brutus and his conspirators declared Rome a Republic.

Task: The foundation of Rome

According to the Roman tradition outlined above, it is Romulus who is accredited with the foundation of the city of Rome.

Write a response of 1-2 paragraphs long to the following questions;

Why do you think Aeneas is included in the foundation myth?

Look at the Tacitus quote above again;

Why do you think Tacitus begins his account of the rise of Augustus with the establishment of the Republic and not the foundation of the city?

Carthage

Carthage was a large and prosperous city state situated in North Africa (the modern Tunis) and peopled by inhabitants of Semitic origin from the coasts of the Levant. Carthage was principally a trading city; her ships dominated the Western Mediterranean for centuries and her navies allowed Carthage to establish trading centres in Sicily, Corsica, Sardinia and the Iberian Peninsula (Modern Spain).

The 1st Punic War 264-241BC

The first war between Rome and Carthage lasted for 23 years and is known as the 1st Punic War. It began because of an internal dispute in an independent city state on the island of Sicily. During the course of this dispute, one side seized power and ousted the other. Both sides called in assistance from Rome and Carthage respectively. Carthage had trading colonies in Western Sicily, but Rome had no direct involvement in Sicily at all at this point.

Carthage and Rome both sent armed forces to the island. The leading city of Sicily was Syracuse, and this Greek city initially sided with Carthage, but after a siege, in 262BC allied itself with Rome. The same year saw another ally of Carthage; Acragas was captured and sacked by Roman forces. A Carthaginian army was also defeated in battle, but the strength of Carthage was in her navy. Unless Rome could defeat the Carthaginians at sea, the war would likely be prolonged and produce stalemate.

Rome built several navies, but it was not until 260BC when, with the aid of a new boarding ramp, the Romans were able to defeat the Carthaginians at sea, first in 259BC and again in 256BC. Rome seemed to be winning; however a Roman army that landed in North Africa was crushed in a battle by the Carthaginians, led by a Spartan mercenary general in 255BC.

Further setbacks for Rome occurred. Two Roman fleets were destroyed in storms with huge loss of life. Carthage managed to land a large army of mercenaries in Sicily and for the next 10 years, inconclusive warfare continued. Both sides were exhausted, but the war continued. In 243BC the Romans managed to raise a new fleet which they used to apply pressure on the Carthaginians in Sicily and restrict supplies to them. A final Carthaginian fleet was sent to Sicily in 241BC; this fleet was met in battle and defeated.

While both sides were exhausted, it was the Carthaginians that desired peace more. Negotiations opened and a peace was made. Carthage was to pay a large fine, evacuate her armies from Sicily and relinquish her assets in Sicily (and later in Corsica and Sardinia, when Carthage found herself in a war with her own former mercenaries). These islands were the first overseas provinces controlled by Rome.

The extent of Roman control c.218BC

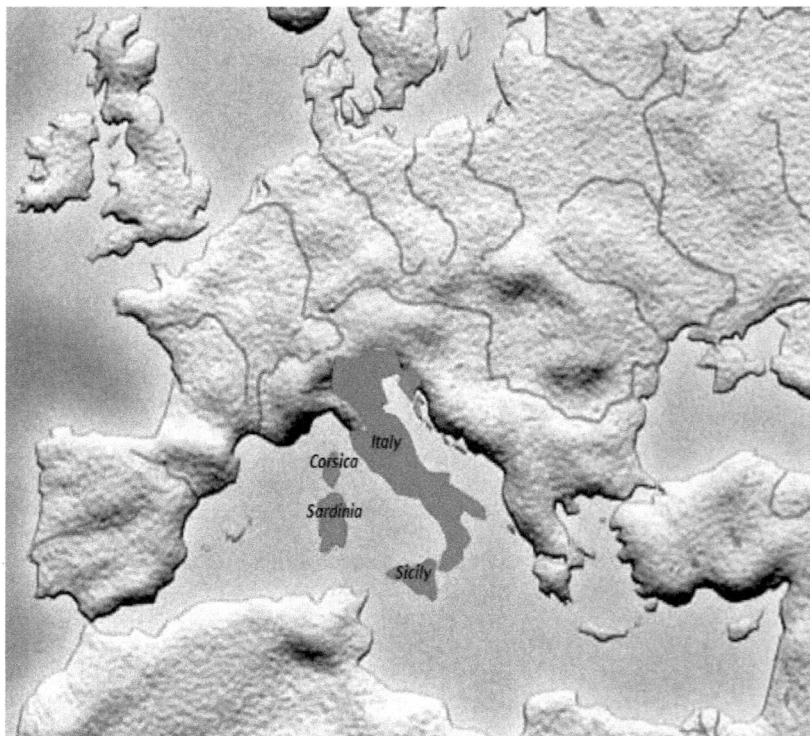

The Second Punic War 218-201BC

Deprived of access to Sicily, Sardinia and Corsica as a result of the 1st Punic War, Carthage needed to seek out new markets. A Carthaginian expeditionary force was sent to Spain. Spain was wealthy in mineral wealth, particularly silver, and the Spanish tribes were populous and fierce in war. Such a combination of resources would enable Carthage to be even stronger than before.

The Carthaginian forces in Spain were led by Hamilcar Barca, a veteran of the 1st Punic War and an enemy of Rome. He established a Carthaginian foothold in Spain – a new city was established called 'Carthago Novo'; New Carthage (the modern Cartagena) and the Carthaginian rule in Spain began to draw wealth and manpower from the resources of Spain.

In 219BC Hannibal, the son of Hamilcar Barca, determined to challenge Rome. Hannibal sacked the city of Saguntum and eliminated Rome's potential foothold in Spain. Wasting little time and eager to prevent Rome from attacking him in Spain, Hannibal determined to keep the initiative and led an army northwards, famously crossing the Alps and invaded Italy.

Fighting numerous battles, the Romans were almost completely out-generalled by Hannibal, in 218-216BC a succession of battles resulted in victories for Hannibal culminating in the battle of Cannae, where tens of thousands of Romans were slaughtered by a smaller Carthaginian army. However, although some Italian cities joined Hannibal, he could not detach the Latin cities from Rome, nor could he capture Rome itself. He simply did not have the resources to do so. Neither would Rome consider peace.

The Romans adopted new strategies. Roman armies were sent to Spain to defeat the Carthaginians there. The Roman army in Italy would hamper Hannibal's movements, but it would not fight him. Another army was sent to Sicily to deal with Syracuse, which had joined Hannibal, and another potential ally for Hannibal, Philip V, king of Macedon, was dissuaded from sending forces to help Hannibal.

These changed tactics bore fruit. Tarentum, a major ally of Hannibal in Southern Italy was captured in 212BC and in 211BC Syracuse was captured and sacked. Carthage sent periodical assistance to Hannibal in Italy, but this help was limited by the Roman navy, which had the edge over the fleets of Carthage. Hannibal was increasingly confined to the southern regions of Italy.

Meantime in Spain, the Roman armies defeated numerous Carthaginian forces and captured Carthago Novo in 209BC. Hannibal's brother, Hasdrubal, escaped from Spain and followed in his brother's footsteps by crossing the Alps, intending to join Hannibal in Italy. This second invasion was met by Rome before the brothers could reunite and Hasdrubal was defeated and killed in 207BC.

The victor of Spain, Scipio, now determined to end the war. He invaded North Africa in 204BC and attacked Carthage and her cities there. Under pressure, Carthage summoned Hannibal to their assistance and he withdrew from Italy. In 202BC the two generals met in battle. At Zama Hannibal was defeated and his army crushed. Realising that all was lost Hannibal advised Carthage to surrender.

The Third Punic War 149-146BC

Despite being confined to North Africa, Carthage continued to remain prosperous. She paid of the huge war indemnity owed to Rome after the Second Punic War, but had troubles with the neighbouring tribes and kingdoms of North Africa. Faced with a threat from the neighbouring Numidian kingdom, Carthage decided to re-arm.

Rome viewed this rearmament with suspicion. Refusing to consider that this rearmament was directed anywhere other than at Rome, it was decided to deal with Carthage once and for all. A Roman invasion force rapidly besieged Carthage itself and after a three year siege the city was captured and destroyed. The surviving Carthaginians were sold off into slavery. Carthage was no more. Its land became Roman land, the province of Africa.

The expansion of the Empire 146-100BC

In 146BC Carthage was destroyed. Also in this same year the Greek city of Corinth also attempted to throw off Roman control. Corinth was destroyed as a demonstration that Rome would not tolerate insubordination in those under her *imperium*. If it had not been clear previously, it was now clear that Rome was not prepared to accept anything but submission from those under her control. Perhaps realising this and fearing for the consequences, the Greek king Attalus III bequeathed his kingdom in Asia Minor to Rome in his will when he died in 133BC. Others did the same.

In North Africa the Numidian kingdom of Jugurtha was acquired by Rome after a long campaign that followed on from a challenged succession 118-105BC. Jugurtha had hoped that he could buy Rome off and allow him to keep his realm. He was wrong. In 104BC Rome's attention shifted towards the North when a huge German invasion attacked Northern Italy. Thereafter Rome would be increasingly involved north of the Alps.

By 100BC, the Roman Empire then was already large. In another century, the Roman Empire would be much larger. But as the conquests continued apace, competition amongst the Senate for command of these glorious (and lucrative) campaigns would result in increasing competition in the Senate, this competition would led to turmoil and turmoil to civil war.

The extent of Roman control c.100BC

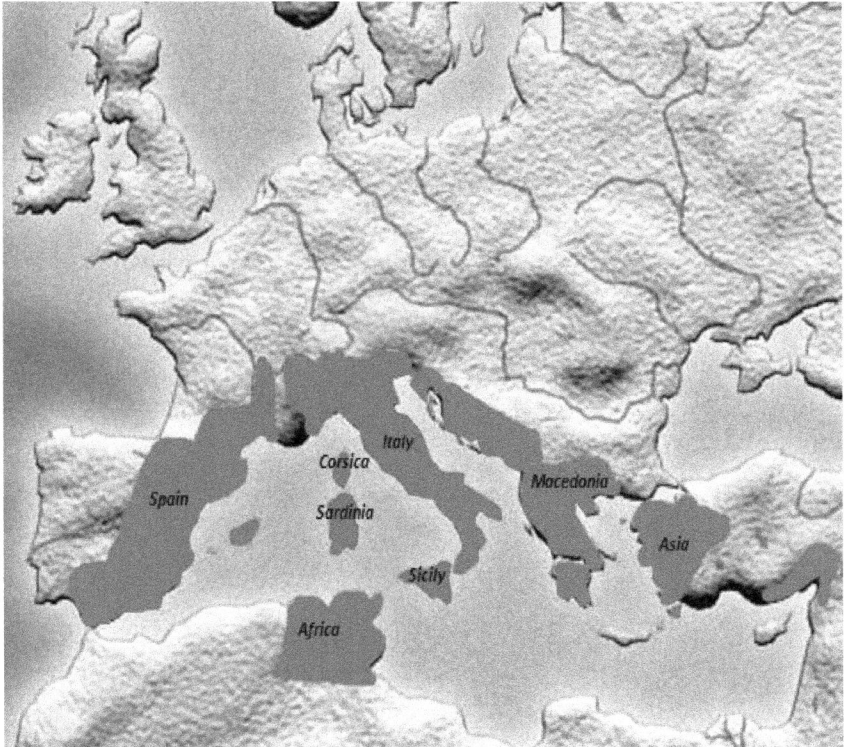

> **Imperium**: 'Supreme Power' Imperium was a term used to describe a Roman politician or military commander's authority and ability to carry out their commands.

2.2 The legacy of Julius Caesar

This section will help you to;

- *Understand the importance of Julius Caesar in establishing the Principate of Augustus*

Introduction

Julius Caesar is one of a relatively select group of individuals of historical importance from the ancient world who has recorded his own motives and actions in his own words. In 49BC Julius Caesar effectively declared war on his political enemies by marching on Rome. In the following passage he explains why;

> *"As for myself", he said, "I have always reckoned the dignity of the Republic of first importance and preferable to life. I was indignant that a benefit conferred on me by the Roman people was being insolently wrested from me by my enemies".*

Julius Caesar *Civil War I.9*

The Civil War of 49-46BC was according to Julius Caesar then a war to safeguard his own position and dignity. It resulted in an autocracy and in 44BC Caesar's assassination by those who thought they were Caesar's equals.

The final years of Julius Caesar

Caesar had become a prominent leader of Rome after 63BC by using a combination of political alliances with men like Crassus and Pompey, outright bribery and manipulation of his religious office of *Pontifex Maximus*, Caesar became Consul in 59BC and secured the command of Narbonese Gaul as his province. Once in his province, for the next eight years Caesar consistently exceeded his magistracy and waged a series of wars against the tribes of Gaul and their neighbours, even twice invading Britain. These conquests were launched often on the slightest pretexts, and provided Caesar with both wealth and fame.

As Caesar's popularity swelled among the people of Rome and amongst his own soldiers, he attracted increasing hostility and jealously from the Senate in Rome. However Caesar's political alliances fragmented with the death of Crassus in 53 BC. Pompey became increasingly distant to Caesar after the death of his wife (who was Julius Caesar's daughter) and eventually joined the bulk of the Senate in opposition to Caesar.

In order to avoid prosecution for exceeding the bounds of his governorship, Caesar required a new magisterial post, preferably the Consulship. But in order to become Consul, Caesar had first to surrender his governorship and stand for election in person. Caesar wanted to stand for election whilst still in office, a position the Senate refused to ratify. Caesar's political allies who represented his interests, were assaulted in Rome and forced to flee. Caesar felt that his only option was to march on Rome with part of his army.

Surprised by Caesar's actions, Caesar's opponents fled Rome before gathering an army in Greece. Pompey's forces were smashed in battle in 48BC at the battle of Pharsalus and in a whirlwind campaign Caesar secured Egypt in 48/47BC, Syria shortly after and then defeated Scipio and Cato in North Africa in 46BC. Caesar then returned to Rome to celebrate a triumph over his enemies.

Caesar became *Dictator* and used this position to ensure that he had total control over the Roman Senate. However, unlike other Romans such as Sulla and Marius who had seized control of Rome before, Caesar opted to be lenient towards his political opponents. This policy of clemency allowed Caesar's opponents to surrender and return to Rome with no loss of property or risk of loss of life. Some of Caesar's opponents, such as Cato and Scipio, opted instead to commit suicide rather than accept what they saw as surrender.

Caesar's policy of clemency also caused resentment amongst some of Caesar's supporters who had hoped to profit by the defeat of their opponents, but now saw these same people back in Rome and being allocated positions of prestige. Caesar's social policies were wide ranging and included the reform of debt laws as well as unpopular laws (unpopular with many of the political elite) which confiscated large areas of land which Caesar needed to settle his veteran soldiers on.

This antagonism was increased when Caesar was offered and accepted the title of *Dictator perpetio* (Dictator for life). Caesar also accepted calls for the establishment of a priesthood dedicated to worshipping himself; Julius Caesar. These actions combined with those above were too much for the more conservative sections of the Senate. A conspiracy of Senators was formed, including former supporters of Caesar who felt overlooked, and Caesar was stabbed to death on the Ides of March (15th March) 44BC by senators led by Brutus and Cassius in the theatre of Pompey.

The murderers of Caesar saw themselves as tyrant killers (Tyrannicides) and proclaimed the restoration of the Republic, yet they failed to consolidate their position by eliminating Caesar's supporters (notably Marcus Antonius) and by seeking the support of the Plebs. Marcus Antonius managed to rally his supporters and the murderers of Caesar were driven from Rome within weeks of Caesar's murder.

Task: Researching Julius Caesar

Although the focus of this study guide is not Julius Caesar, you will find it extremely valuable if you spend some time researching Julius Caesar's life and in particular his final years of 49-44BC.

You may wish to read the following ancient sources;

- *Julius Caesar Civil Wars*

- *Suetonius' life of Julius Caesar*

- *Plutarch's life of Julius Caesar*

Reading these sources will give you a good background to Caesar, the events of the Civil war and the events leading up to his death.

The extent of Roman control c.44BC

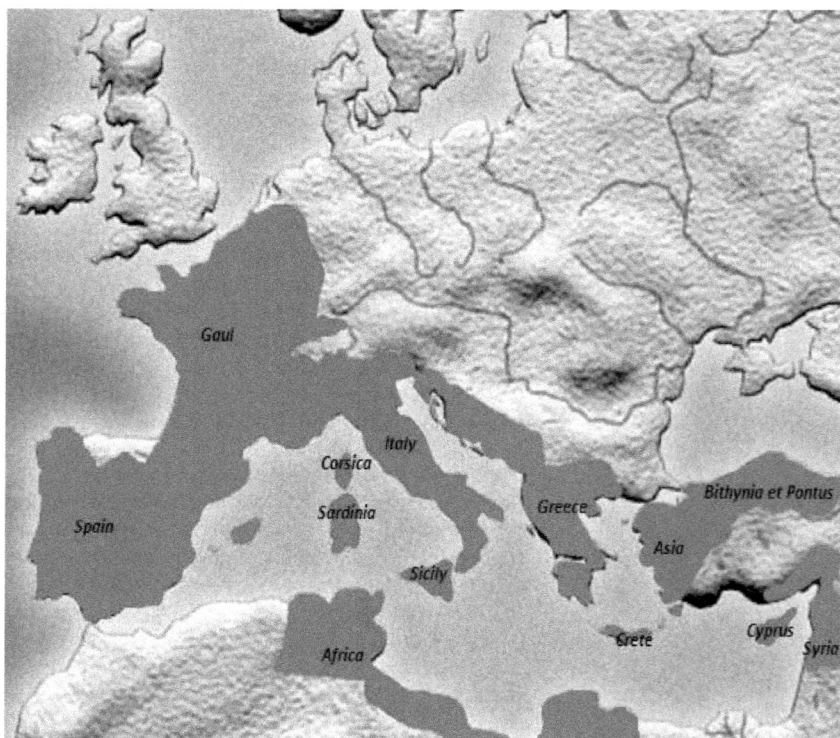

2.3 The Triumvirate and the rise of Augustus

This section will help you to;

- *Understand the steps taken by Octavian to gain power*

- *Understand the key participants of the triumvirate*

- *Consider the changing nature of the alliance between Antonius, Lepidus and Octavian*

- *Understand the background of key participants in the triumvirate*

- *Consider the reasons for the collapse of the triumvirate*

The Rise of Augustus

The future Augustus, Octavian was born in 63BC, the son of Marcus Octavius, a rather middling Roman Senator and Atia, the niece of Julius Caesar. Marcus Octavius died in 59BC. In 46BC, Octavian, aged 17 was permitted by his uncle Julius Caesar to join him in his Triumphal procession. However, it appears to have come somewhat as a shock to all concerned when Caesar's will was read and it was announced that Caesar had named Octavian as his heir. At the time of Caesar's assassination, Octavian was not present in Rome. He was in the province of Illyria training to serve in one of Caesar's armies, but on receiving word of Caesar's death Octavian hurriedly returned to Italy.

Money and Vengeance

On his return to Italy, Octavian had two aims. One was to avenge the murder of Julius Caesar. The other was to secure his inheritance. Caesar had left Octavian money and land, and in order to inherit this wealth, Octavian needed to both be in Rome and also to ward off other possible rivals for the wealth of Caesar. Brutus for example could declare Caesar a tyrant and all his possessions confiscated. Antonius and Lepidus could also be a problem; both were senior members of Caesar's party and established politicians in their own right. They had not been named in Caesar's will, but if the will remained unclaimed, they could be in a position to oversee and administer the wealth of Caesar as they saw fit.

Octavian determined to act decisively. As he journeyed back to Rome through Italy, Octavian recruited many of Caesar's former army veterans, who were angered by the death of their beloved Caesar and saw in Octavian a chance to exact their revenge, but also to obtain further wealth by supporting his claims. By the time he reached Rome, Octavian had accumulated two legions; some 10,000 men.

Meantime, at Rome, the murderers of Julius Caesar had been forced to leave Rome by a combination of Antonius, Lepidus and hostility of the people of Rome. One of these men had taken refuge in Mutina, a city in Northern Italy and was besieged there by Antonius.

Influenced by Cicero, the Senate declared Antonius an outlaw and an army led by the Consuls of 43BC Aulus Hirtius and Gaius Pansa was to march on Antonius. At Cicero's insistence, Octavian was granted the powers of a Praetor and permitted to attach his legions to those of the Consular army. At the same time, Octavian was recognised as Caesar's heir and hailed as 'Caesar' himself.

Antonius was defeated at Mutina and driven into Gaul where he joined Lepidus, who had also been outlawed by the Senate. However, both Consuls died in the battle at Mutina and Octavian was the senior Roman commander left with the army. In addition to his own legions, he now commanded both the consular armies. At the age of twenty, Octavian marched his armies back to Rome and demanded the Consulship, a position he was in no way qualified for according to the *Cursus Honorum*.

The combination of the threat of Octavian's army, as well as the concern that Caesar's assassins, Brutus and Cassius, were recruiting armies in the East, as well as the nearer threat of Antonius and Lepidus, pressurised the Senate to make Octavian Consul. Cicero, who was prominent among the Senate at this time, perhaps felt that Octavian could be controlled and guided. He was wrong.

Octavian marched north in autumn 43BC to confront Lepidus and Antonius. What he did when he met them, took Cicero and the Senate totally by surprise.

The Cursus Honorum

The Cursus Honorum was the career path of a Senator, whereby in order to proceed to a senior office, a Senator had to have served previously at a lesser office. So in order to be eligible to be a Consul, a Senator must have been a Praetor for example.

The basic progression up this path was;

- *Quaestor*

- *Praetor*

- *Consul*

Several prominent Romans did not adhere to the Cursus Honorum and the result was often conflict, Pompey for example became Consul without holding a junior office, Octavian entered the Senate as a Praetor at the age of 19 and became Consul at the age of 20.

The Triumvirate of Octavian, Lepidus and Antonius

In the autumn of 43BC, Octavian, Lepidus and Antonius in Northern Italy and reached an agreement that they would work together. Each man had brought several legions with them and these armies would enforce the united will of the three men. The agreement made, Octavian, Lepidus and Antonius marched on Rome.

On the 27th November 43BC, A Roman law, the *Lex Titia* appointed Antonius, Lepidus, and Octavian *"triumviri rei publicae constituendae consulari potestate"*. It established a three man commission (Octavian, Lepidus and Antonius) responsible for reorganising the constitution and state of Rome over five years.

The proscriptions of the Trimvirate

One of the initial acts of the Triumvirate was to bloodily remove their political enemies amongst the Senators and Equites. Lists were made of individuals who were to be proscribed. Their wealth and lands were confiscated and anyone who killed the individual named would be rewarded, whilst anyone who helped someone on the list was liable to suffer the same fate. The numbers of Senators killed entered the hundreds, those of the Equites numbered in the thousands. Amongst the many killed was Cicero. Some managed to escape with their lands and wealth confiscated, including a brother of Lepidus. Still others managed to escape with their lives and fled either to Brutus and Cassius in Asia, or Sextus Pompeius in Spain.

The historian Dio wrote;

"And while the people were still in this state of mind, those murders by proscription which Sulla had once indulged in were once more resorted to and the whole city was filled with corpses. Many were killed in their houses, many even in the streets and here and there in the fora and around the temples; the heads of the victims were once more set up upon the rostra and their bodies either allowed to lie where they were, to be devoured by dogs and birds, or else cast into the river. Everything that had been done before in the days of Sulla occurred also at this time, except that only two white tablets were posted, one for the senators and one for the others."

Dio XLVII.3

Eliminating the opposition

By conducting the proscriptions the triumvirate eliminated political opposition in Rome and they acquired great wealth through confiscation. In addition to the proscriptions, the triumvirs were responsible for appointing all magistrates and dealing with the state and Empire as they saw fit. Opposition in Rome might have been quelled, but political opponents remained in Asia and Syria (Brutus and Cassius) as well as in Spain (Sextus Pompeius).

It was decided that Lepidus would remain in Italy and perhaps negotiate with, or maintain a watch on, Sextus Pompeius. Antonius and Octavian meantime would move with the bulk of the army to confront Brutus and Cassius, who had also gathered an army and were marching towards Italy. No doubt both Antonius and Octavian were united in their desire to avenge Julius Caesar; certainly this argument would have been compelling propaganda with which to inspire their army.

Antonius and Octavian met Brutus and Cassius in battle at Philippi in Greece in 42BC. Both Cassius and Brutus were killed.

The Triumvirates then determined to divide control of the Empire amongst themselves. Antonius took the eastern provinces and Octavian the western provinces. Lepidus appears to have been side-lined in the aftermath of the battle of Philippi. Perhaps he was under suspicion for negotiating with Sextus Pompeius, but eventually Lepidus was given a large military command and became responsible for the African provinces.

The Lex Titia was to expire in 38BC, however once this was reached and the Triumvirs continued to act as before, it became clear that the triumvirate was to continue. No opposition to the triumvirate emerged in 37BC and it was decided to extent Lex Titia, and continue with the triumvirate for a further 5 years.

The Perugia affair

Almost immediately Octavian faced a serious threat to his position. Marcus Antonius' brother, Lucius Antonius who was Consul for 41BC attempted to force Octavian out of Italy. With Marcus Antonius' wife Fulvia and the eight legions that he commanded, L. Antonius seized Rome for a time before Octavian managed to drive him out. L. Antonius and Fulvia took refuge in the Italian city of Perugiua which Octavian forced to surrender in 40BC. Lucius Antonius and Fulvia seem to have acted without Marcus Antonius' knowledge and he did nothing to support his brother. Once Octavian forced the surrender of Fulvia and Lucius Antonius, he seems to have borne L. Antonius no ill will but appointed him as a provincial governor in Spain. Marcus Antonius received his wife back, but Fulvia soon died.

Reconciliation

Octavian had resisted the threat of L. Antonius and Fulvia. Lepidus was allocated a command in Africa with a substantial force. Octavian and Antonius met at Brundisium in 40BC and their alliance was cemented by a marriage between the recently widowed Antonius and Octavian's' sister Octavia. When Antonius' legate died in post in Gaul, it was Octavian that appointed a successor. Clearly it was felt that Antonius was to concentrate on the Eastern provinces, whilst Octavian took responsibility for the Western.

Octavian was kept at Rome on other business. The men of the armies that had fought at Philippi were returning to Italy and as they were demobilised, they required land and money with which to pension them off. Octavian spent the year's 42-40BC in Italy, trying to find land and money for approximately 100,000men. Antonius meantime travelled to the East where he faced the large task of reorganising the provinces there and also dealing with an invasion of Syria and Asia Minor by the Parthian Empire.

Antonius in the East

Whilst Octavian was so engaged against Sextus Pompeius and Lepidus in the West, Antonius spent the year's 42-40BC conducting a tour of the Eastern provinces. The provinces in the East had been exploited in the Civil Wars for wealth and manpower and were in a state that required attention. The Parthian Empire also was seeking to exploit the turmoil of the Civil Wars and profit by attacking Syria and Asia Minor. It was in Asia Minor that Antonius first met with the Egyptian Queen Cleopatra. Despite being married, (first to Fulvia and then to Octavia) Marcus Antonius got Cleopatra pregnant, but did not see his new family for several years.

The Parthian Empire had invaded the Eastern provinces and captured large areas of territory. By 40BC a Parthian army, led by a renegade Roman, Labienus had penetrated into Asia Minor but was defeated by a lieutenant of Antonius. in 39BC. The next few years were spent in preparation for a great invasion of Parthia.

In 36BC Antonius invaded Parthia through the highland regions of Armenia with 60,000men. The campaign was not a success. Antonius advanced for a time but was forced to withdraw after having lost over 20,000 men. Despite the failure of the campaign, Antonius had secured the important buffer kingdom of Armenia through the use of a client king. Antonius now returned but not to Rome. Instead he went to Cleopatra.

2.4 The Battle of Actium and the aftermath

This topic will help you to;

- *Understand the events that led to the final confrontation between Octavian and Antonius*

- *Consider Octavian's position after the death of Antonius*

Recommended Readings for a historical overview

- *Cassius Dio 50*

- *Horace Epodes 9*

- *Propertius Elegies 4.6*

- *Res Gestae 25*

- *Suetonius Augustus 17-18*

- *Virgil Aeneid 8.675-728*

The break with Antonius

> *"The Roman people had been robbed of their democratic form of government, but had not become a monarchy in the strict sense of the term; Antonius and Caesar still controlled affairs on an equal footing, having divided by lot most of the functions of government between them, and though nominally they considered all the rest as belonging to them in common, in reality they were trying to appropriate it to themselves, according as either of them was able to seize any advantage over the other."*

Cassius Dio Book L.1

News of the breach between Octavian and Antonius reached Rome in 33BC. On the one side Antonius' supporters tried to defend his actions whilst Octavian portrayed Antonius as a slave of Cleopatra; a *'fatale monstrum'* according to Horace. Also in 33BC the Triumvirate came to its' legal end. Antonius offered to surrender his powers and position if Octavian would do likewise. Octavian, was unwilling to renew an alliance with a man who had rejected both himself and his sister and who had also presented himself more as a Hellenistic monarch than a Roman citizen. Octavian rejected Antonius' overtures but honoured the end of the Triumvirate.

At Rome the Consuls of 32BC were supporters of Antonius. They tried to defend Antonius by attacking Octavian in the Senate, but Octavian had widespread support of the Plebs and their attempts failed. Admitting defeat, the Consuls and some 300 Senators abandoned Rome and joined Antonius in Egypt, who had officially divorced Octavia and in doing so severed all links of friendship with Octavian. Octavian retaliated by seizing Antonius' Will and reading it out to the Senate. In the Will was damning proof that Antonius was seeking to aspire to a monarchy; an Empire independent of Rome for his children.

In this Will, all of Cleopatra's children were to be legitimate and recognised as Roman citizens (including Julius Caesar's biological son Caesarion). Whilst Caesarion was to succeed to the kingdom of Egypt, Antonius' and Cleopatra's children were to rule parts of the East as their own personal kingdoms. Antonius was also to be buried not in Rome, but alongside Cleopatra and in the manner of Egyptian royalty. The threat then was twofold. If this Will was enforced not only would Rome lose significant portions of the Empire to Antonius' children, Caesarion, as a recognised son of Julius Caesar which would undermine Octavian's position in that respect.

Octavian played the situation to its fullest potential. Antonius was declared un-Roman, a traitor to his own people and a threat to the existence of Rome.

Actium

In the *Res Gestae* Augustus outlines the popular support he had against Antonius and Cleopatra;

> *"The whole of Italy voluntarily took oath of allegiance to me and demanded me as its leader in the war in which I was victorious at Actium. The provinces of the Spains, the Gauls, Africa, Sicily, and Sardinia took the same oath of allegiance. Those who served under my standards at that time included more than 700 senators, and among them eighty-three who had previously or have since been consuls up to the day on which these words were written, and about 170 have been priests."*

Res Gestae 25

The Senate appointed Octavian as Consul and Antonius declared an enemy of the state, simultaneously declaring war on Cleopatra. Reports reached Rome that Antonius was marching on Italy with his army and a fleet largely composed of Cleopatra's forces was supporting and supplying them.

As well as some 300 Senators, Antonius had 30 legions and a fleet of 500 ships. Their intention was to destroy Octavian, who was coming to meet him with his own forces.

The two sides met in Greece. Cleopatra's presence was both a blessing and a curse for Antonius. A blessing because she was paying for and feeding Antonius' soldiers as well as providing much of the fleet, but a curse because her very presence gave ammunition to the Octavian's claim that Antonius was a slave to her and that Rome was to be ruled by a foreign tyrant if they succeeded. Another problem for Antonius was that Cleopatra was unpopular with the Senators that had fled Rome. Desertions began.

Octavian left his friend Maecenas in charge at Rome and with his fellow consul Agrippa confronted Antonius. Agrippa commanded the Roman fleet and he succeeded in cutting off the supply route from Egypt and blockading Antonius' fleet at Actium. Antonius rejected suggestions that he confront Octavian's army and instead attempted to break the naval blockade. Antonius' fleet failed to break out and was forced to retire, but Cleopatra's squadron broke clear and set sail for Egypt. Antonius followed in his ship and abandoned his army. The campaign was over and Antonius' army and the remainder of his fleet surrendered.

Octavian sailed after Antonius and reached Egypt in 30BC, where Antonius had been deserted by his few remaining soldiers, realising they were defeated both Antonius and Cleopatra committed suicide. Whilst Octavian was mostly merciful towards the rebel Senators and the children of Antonius and Cleopatra, but he considered Caesarion (the son of Cleopatra and Julius Caesar) and Antonius' eldest son (by his 1st wife Fulvia) as potential rivals. They were killed.

Egypt was seized, not as a province, but as the personal possession of Octavian. An Equestrian, Gaius Cornelius Gallus was appointed as Prefect responsible for the administration and control of Egypt.

Octavian 30-27BC

In 30BC as the leader of the Caesarian party, Octavian had effectively eliminated all existing political rivals. He had command of scores of loyal legions and any opposition that still existed amongst the Senators had been forced to flee to Antonius and had subsequently been defeated and discredited.

Octavian however was faced with a dilemma. Quite simply the Empire was too large to run for a single person. If he delegated his powers, Octavian had to be careful that those he appointed were trustworthy. If Octavian decided to retire into private life, he might well find himself the victim of the next person to take power. If, on the other hand, Octavian determined to act without the Senate, as might a monarch, he could suffer the same fate of Julius Caesar.

Acta: *literally means 'things done'. It can also be explained as laws, or the proclamations and enactments of the Emperor which have been approved in the Senate under oath.*

Octavian then had to carefully decide his next step. In the immediate term he was protected to some extent by holding the Consulship, and this he did successively from 31-27BC. Octavian ensured that the other Consul was a loyal supporter who remained in Rome. Perhaps being absent from Rome might help and so Octavian elected to remain in the provinces in 30-29BC touring the East and reorganising the situation there if he found it necessary to do so. Whilst absent, Octavian was honoured at Rome with celebrations and honorifics. The Senate in 29BC also voted, whilst he was still absent to confirm all of Octavian's *Acta*.

Return to Rome

Octavian returned to Rome in 29BC and celebrated his triumph over Antonius and Cleopatra. Octavian made lavish use of the wealth of Egypt to gift the Plebs, as well as to introduce a building programme. The doors of the temple of Janus were closed, symbolising peace throughout the Empire and Octavian also began to demobilise the legions that he no longer found a need for. Over 100,000 veterans (the equivalent of about 20 full strength legions) were to be pensioned off and settled in 28 new veteran colonies in Italy as well as in provinces such as Africa and Syria. The expense of this was vast and cost both Octavian and the State hundreds of millions of sesterces, but the needs and demands of the veterans could not be avoided without causing further instability.

The first settlement

When Gaius Caesar had established the peace and re-imposed order in the provinces, he was given the cognomen Augustus. The sixth month, Sextilis, was re-named August in his honour.

Summary of Livy Book 134

In 27BC Octavian appeared before the Senate in Rome and offered to lay down all his powers and reinstate the magistracies and constitution to the Senate and the people of Rome. Augustus himself writes of this event in the Res Gestae that in 28/27BC;

Key terminology

Imperium

Means supreme power. This supreme power was bestowed upon certain magistrates of Rome in their dealings with others. Imperium also permitted magistrates to exact obedience from those subject to the power and authority of the magistrate.

"In my sixth and seventh consulates, after putting out the civil war, having obtained all things by universal consent, I handed over the state from my power to the dominion of the senate and Roman people. And for this merit of mine, by a senate decree, I was called Augustus and the doors of my temple were publicly clothed with laurel and a civic crown was fixed over my door and a gold shield placed in the Julian senate-house, and the inscription of that shield testified to the virtue, mercy, justice, and piety, for which the senate and Roman people gave it to me. After that time, I exceeded all in influence, but I had no greater power than the others who were colleagues with me in each magistracy."

Res Gestae 34

In addition to the honours mentioned in the Res Gestae, at the Senates' behest, the month of Sextilis was renamed 'August' and awarded the title of Princeps Senatus. Octavian was also offered and accepted a new command. This command was of the provinces of Gaul, Spain, Egypt and Syria and was to last for 10 years. The awards granted to Octavian in 27BC are known as the 'First Settlement'.

On receiving these honours, Augustus elected not to remain in Rome, but instead travelled out to take command of his provinces in person and remained absent from Rome from 27-24BC. Augustus travelled to Gaul and Spain to reorganise and inspect his provinces. In this time fought a campaign in what is now Northern Spain against the Celtiberian tribes.

After another brief return to Rome, Augustus recovered from an illness that nearly killed him and set off to the East in 22BC. He would tour the eastern provinces for nearly three years.

Virgil would also journey out to accompany Augustus for part of his return journey and it was on this return journey that Virgil died in 19BC.

Upon his return to Rome in 19BC, supporters of Augustus would now claim that;

The civil wars had been brought to an end in their twentieth year, foreign wars were laid to rest, peace recalled, and the din of arms everywhere silenced, validity was restored to the laws, authority to the courts, precedence to the senate, while the powers of the magistrates were reduced to their ancient limits; except that to the eight praetors were added two more. With the recalling of the old, time honoured pattern of the commonwealth, the land was once more cultivated, religion honoured, men given security, and guaranteed possession of their property.

Velleius Paterculus II.89.3

Task: Compare and contrast the actions of 'Octavian and Augustus'

Consider the actions of the Triumvirate Octavian in 43/42BC and the actions of Augustus after Actium

In each case, what problems were faced and with what methods were used to solve these problems?

Why poets such as Virgil might be deployed to promote the image of 'Augustus' rather than 'Octavian?'

2.5 Virgil, Augustus and the Roman Imperial tradition

This section will help you to;

- *Understand how important the influence of Augustus was in composing the epic*

- *Explore the links connecting the Emperor Augustus to Aeneas in Roman tradition*

- *Understand the role and importance of Aeneas*

Introduction: The importance of Aeneas in Rome's imperial destiny

Several questions may be best answered here before we proceed to looking at the actual *Aeneid.*

How does Aeneas relate to Rome's foundation myth? Why would this mythical figure be of value in forging Rome's Imperial destiny?

How does Aeneas relate to Rome's foundation myth?

By choosing Aeneas as the hero, Virgil provides himself with a monumental opportunity to carve out a legend and a fresh status for Rome, and for Augustus, the emperor of the world empire that is Rome.

Aeneas possesses all the right qualifications for promoting Rome and also for promoting Augustus;

- *A divine parent*

- *A reputation of faithfulness, loyalty and piety*

- *A brave and experience warrior able to go against the very best of the opposition*

- *A destiny to fulfil*

- *An established mythical tradition that goes as far back as is possible in the human experience*

- *Links to Rome and Greece in tradition*

Aeneas also came with the potential for rewriting the Trojan War. The history of the world had been generally accepted (for Romans and the inhabitants of much of Mediterranean) to have been written by and directed by the affairs of Greece. Greece had been the victors over Persia and Alexander the Great had conquered and shaped much of world events for centuries. Now though was Rome's turn.

Aeneas gave Virgil the opportunity to tell a story not of Greek triumph, but Trojan triumph and through Aeneas' efforts, the race who were to become the contemporary Romans, who now dominated the affairs of the world.

Thus, the eventual success of the Trojans as led by Aeneas is their quest to start again; to found a new Troy. The story of Aeneas is thus a story of old wrongs being righted. Although the Greeks may seem to have been the victors, it is really the Trojan (Romans) who are to be the true victors.

Virgil's relationship to the regime of Augustus

Unlike Homer, whose patronage and earlier influences (if he or they had any) is largely unknown, Virgil's *Aeneid* is very much dependent on some understanding of contemporary Roman thought and history. Contemporary politics are important to understanding Virgil's message, in a way that is not so important in Homer. We shall see this in action as we explore the *Aeneid* in greater detail.

The family tree of Aeneas, who was thought to be the direct ancestor of Julius Caesar gives you some idea of how closely linked the legend of Aeneas was with the history of Rome contemporary to Virgil;

Family tree connecting AUGUSTUS to AENEAS and the GODS VENUS and JUPITER

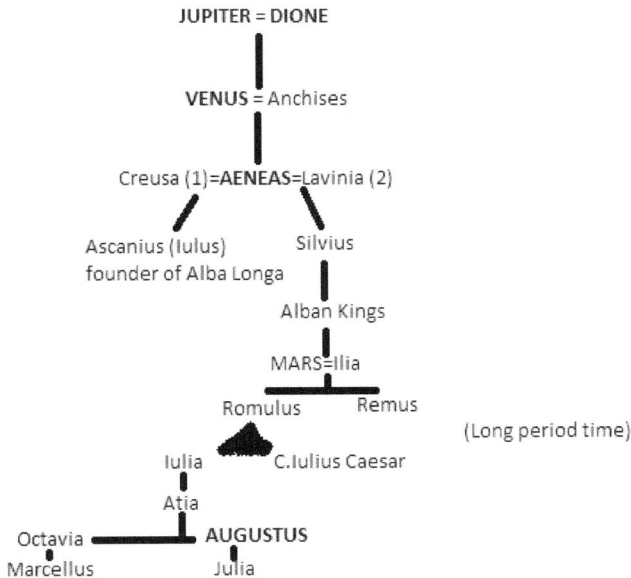

Virgil as noted above died a very wealthy man; it is difficult to think that there was any alternative way for Virgil to amass such wealth unless he was directly patronised by, and had the favour of the elite of Roman society – especially the support of Augustus.

There is then a political slant to Virgil's career. Unlike Homer, who composed within the framework of inherited mythology and legend for the entertainment and enjoyment of his art (as well as in all probability employment) Virgil's motivations when he wrote the *Aeneid* were, to a great extent, to support Augustus' efforts to weld Rome into the forefront of a nascent world empire and Augustus' own central role in this effort.

To do this Augustus required a substantial founding myth that he could be associated with, and a sense of the destiny of Rome and the god-ordained right of its position at the forefront of that very empire. By telling the legend of Aeneas, loved by Venus his mother and fated to build a new and greater Troy from the shattered ruins of the old on the shores of Italy, credence is given to his 'ancestor', Augustus, who was contemporary Rome's modern-day Aeneas.

The choice of Aeneas should come as little surprise when we know that Augustus' own adopted father, Julius Caesar, had a deliberate policy of associating himself with the Goddess Venus. In this Caesar was not unique. Other Romans of prominent status had associated themselves with various gods and goddesses previously. In addition to this link through Caesar, Augustus seems to have favoured the God Apollo as his personal patron deity, but Apollo did not provide such a convenient mythical link for Virgil as did Aeneas and his mother Venus.

Creating a new Imperial destiny out of the mythical traditions of the past

Though Rome did possess immense power, it had not all been plain sailing. Virgil had lived through many traumatic events in recent Roman history. The Republic of Rome had witnessed many years of squabbling over power within government, and this had led to a weariness and dissatisfaction with political leaders amongst men of Virgil's generation. Those that survived, that is.

The city of Rome had survived a series of ruinous civil wars and the latest victor in these civil wars, Augustus, was also determined that he would survive and that there would be no more dissension in Rome. He was in control and was determined to remain that way. The regular citizens of Rome and idolised Augustus' adopted father Caesar and Augustus too drew upon their support in turn for adulation in turn. Many in Rome hoped for a strong and god-guided leader who would be the one to lead Rome into a period of peace and prosperity. In short, a saviour figure. Augustus was determined to be this saviour.

It must have seemed to Virgil and some of his contemporaries higher up in Roman society that in Augustus they may have found their saviour anew: a man who could keep the peace both in Rome and in the Provinces; that Augustus could re-establish *'romanitas'* ('Roman-ness') in a type of moral 'back-to-basics' campaign to counteract the perceived degeneration of contemporary Roman society. To Virgil's original audience, the parallels between Aeneas on the one hand with Caesar and Augustus on the other, as leaders who all forged concord out of turmoil and war would have been very clear indeed.

The dangers of being seen to be a king

However, Augustus had a very recent warning from history about how not to proceed. His own adopted father Julius Caesar had been murdered by his political rivals in the Senate in 44 BC precisely because they feared his power and his strong leadership, especially worried that he would be granted the title of 'king'.

The title of king *'Rex'* was difficult for Romans to swallow, despite the yearnings for an end to fear and political wrangling over power. They had been highly suspicious of kings ever since Tarquin Superbus in the 5th century BC was ousted as the last king of Rome. He had abused his position, murdered rivals and stolen wealth. The suspicion that Caesar was to be granted the title of king was enough to see him murdered.

Augustus himself would do much worse and crueller things than Tarquin Superbus had ever done during the proscriptions and the civil wars, but so long as he did these terrible acts in a way that was at least officially sanctioned through the existing government institutions of Rome; the Senate and the laws like the Lex Titia, then he could not only get away with them, but extend his own power and authority.

Augustus as the nephew and heir of Caesar, managed to successfully established himself as the *'first amongst equals'*, or emperor, without use of the title 'king' which Romans feared as an end to their political freedoms.

Virgil's task

With the benefit of hindsight, it must have seemed to Romans of Virgil's day that Rome was always fated or destined to wield great power. How else could anyone explain its military success and genius, combined with a fair dose of good fortune since it seemed to come from nowhere to dominate its rivals? For many Romans the only explanation could be that the gods were guiding Rome in its destiny, and that Rome had for its ancestors the direct descendants of gods.

Virgil's task of promoting the regime of Augustus was far from easy. Despite the desire of the Roman elite for peace, stability and a period for clear direction after the chaos of the civil wars and the proscriptions. Virgil had to negotiate the boundary between promoting Augustus as a strong and confident leader of men, but not to be a king, which to the Roman mind unacceptable.

The association of Augustus with Aeneas then as a legendary founder of a new city emerging from the ruins of a city destroyed by war and turmoil was then a clever one. Aeneas was so far removed in the past that he could tell his story with great flexibility in order to best complement Augustus in a more subtle way that promoted the personal efforts and personal sacrifices of one man alone in order to establish a city of peace, prosperity and unrivalled splendour that benefits all.

Task: The presentation of Augustus in Virgil's Aeneid

Ensure that you have access to the following passages of Virgil's Aeneid;

- *Book 1. 257-296 – The prophecy of Jupiter*

- *Book 6. 752-892 – The Parade of future Romans*

- *Book 8. 671-731 – The Shield of Aeneas*

Questions

a) *Read Virgil's Aeneid Book 1. 257-296. How well does this passage portray Augustus as a bringer of peace and justice?*

b) *In what ways does Virgil represent Augustus as the culmination of Jupiter's prophecy in all of these passages?*

PART THREE: Books One to Three of the *Aeneid*

PART THREE

3.1: Book One: Aeneas arrives at Carthage

3.2: Book Two: The Fall of Troy

3.3: Book Three

3.4: Presentation of character: Aeneas and Anchises

3.5: Homeric Influences in Books I-III

3.6: The Supernatural in Books I-III

3.1 Book One: Aeneas arrives at Carthage

This section will help you to;

- *Understand the content of the proem of the Aeneid*

- *Understand the events and structure of Book One*

- *Begin to explore the characters of Aeneas and Dido*

- *Understand the importance of Carthage to the development of the Roman Empire*

- *Consider how Carthage is portrayed in Book One*

Introduction

Media Res

Virgil elects to begin his poem *Media Res* – this means that the audience enters the story part way through.

This section will help you to understand the first book of the *Aeneid*. Here Virgil introduces his audience to the story of Aeneas and the Trojans that have survived the fall of their ancestral city. The story commences *Media Res*, with the Trojans now close to achieving their destiny of settling in Italy where in time, their descendants will found Rome and achieve the Imperial destiny that has been established and confirmed by Virgil's contemporary ruler Caesar Augustus.

In Book One of the *Aeneid*, Virgil introduces many of the central themes of Virgil's *Aeneid* that will be developed throughout the epic. In addition to introducing his audience to Aeneas and the core aspects of his character, Virgil introduces other important themes such as the Imperial destiny of Rome, the role of the Gods and the portrayal of the ideal Roman. Virgil also firmly establishes the *Aeneid* in the world of the hero in Book One, and in doing so clearly demonstrates the influence of Homer in providing the background and inspiration in the creation of his own story.

Media Res

Like Homer in the *Iliad* and the *Odyssey*, Virgil elects to begin his poem *Media Res* – this means that the audience enters the story part way through. Virgil could have started with the sack of Troy, or he could have commenced his story with the Trojans setting sail just after the fall of Troy. Instead, Virgil begins his story with the Trojans almost at Italy and the storm that scatters the Trojan fleet just when they are so close to landing in Italy. By doing so, Virgil can refer back to events that have passed since the fall of Troy at another point.

Book One Synopsis

Virgil introduces his epic poem. The introduction reveals that this poem is the story of Aeneas, a Trojan hero who, escaping from the destruction of Troy, is destined to travel to Italy and found a city. Aeneas however will only achieve this destiny after many hardships, battles and after experiencing many losses. Virgil also explains in this introduction that Aeneas will suffer at the hands of the Goddess Juno, who has a personal grudge against Aeneas and the Trojans.

Virgil then goes on to describe a city – but this city is in Africa, not in Italy. This city, named Carthage, is a city of great wealth that would in time become Rome's greatest enemy. Carthage is beloved of the goddess Juno and Carthage is the city that Juno hopes will rule the earth; that is if Rome does not overcome Carthage first. This is one reason why Juno is hostile to Aeneas and the Trojans. Virgil also gives additional reasons for the hatred of Juno for the Trojans; Ganymede and Paris were two Trojans who had previously incurred the wrath of the goddess.

Having set out the reasons for his epic, and the role of the Goddess Juno, Virgil now introduces the Trojans. They are on a journey, sailing in twenty ships from Sicily towards Italy. Juno however spots them and decides to cause mischief. Juno calls on another God, Aeolus, the king of the winds and persuades him to unleash strong winds that will wreak havoc on the Trojan fleet. A storm engulfs the fleet.

Virgil now shifts attention briefly to Aeneas who witnesses the onset of the storm in horror and despair before going onto describes the impact of the storm. The storm begins to claim the Trojan ships; some are thrown onto rocks, others founder in the heavy seas and men are thrown overboard. The Trojans appear doomed until another god notices and intervenes. The God of the Sea, Neptune drives the winds back to Aeolus and with the assistance of other sea Gods, the Trojans escape from disaster.

Aeneas and some of the Trojans in seven ships reach land – but the fleet is scattered and Aeneas has no knowledge of the fate of the other vessels. As the Trojans set up camp Aeneas goes exploring and hunting and returns to camp with food and words to encourage and lift the morale of the Trojans.

Virgil shifts the scene now to a Council of the Gods. Venus, the Goddess of Love and mother of Aeneas, appeals to Jupiter to show mercy to Aeneas. Other Trojans managed to escape the sack of Troy and settle in new homes in peace; why cannot Aeneas?

Jupiter reveals the fate of Aeneas, who is destined to settle in Italy and in time from the Trojans will a new city rise and eventually rule the world. This city will be Rome. Virgil has Jupiter pronounce that in time Rome will produce a leader destined to lead this great city to everlasting glory. For the moment though, Aeneas is in Africa and

Mercury is sent to Carthage to ensure that he will receive a warm welcome in that city.

Virgil now returns to the Trojans. Aeneas and his comrade Achates head out exploring again. They soon encounter Venus in disguise. Aeneas' mother explains where Carthage is and advises that Aeneas go directly to Carthage. Venus also explains the origins of this new city and its' queen Dido. Aeneas then reveals who he is and where he is from. Venus tells Aeneas that other Trojans survived the storm and have now reached Carthage. Venus now departs, but not before Aeneas recognises that she is his mother.

Aeneas and Achates are enveloped in a cloud and reach the city hidden from view. They witness the establishment of Carthage and the construction of its walls, towers and other buildings. The pair pay particular attention to a temple to Juno embellished with scenes from the tale of Troy and the Trojan War. Queen Dido is described and she is welcoming the Trojans who survived the storm. Having seen that his comrades are safe, Aeneas emerges from the cloud to the astonishment of all.

Dido welcomes Aeneas and a feast is prepared. Aeneas in turn sends to his ships for gifts and also for his son Ascanius. Venus however steals Ascanius away and replaces him with Cupid in disguise, with the aim of making Dido to fall in love with Aeneas and his son. Book One then ends with a request for Aeneas to tell the story of how he escaped from Troy and arrived in Carthage.

Task: Comprehending Book One

Read Book One of the Aeneid

Once you have, write brief responses to the following questions;

- *How has Virgil chosen to start his work?*

- *What do you think Virgil has focussed on in Book One?*

The structure of Book One

- *Proem (lines 1-11)*

- *The Anger of Juno (lines 12-49)*

- *The Storm (lines 50-169)*

- *Aeneas makes land (lines 170-222)*

- *The Council of the Gods(lines 223-305)*

- *Aeneas and Venus (lines 306-409)*

- *Carthage (lines 410-579)*

- *Aeneas revealed (lines 580-end)*

The Proem of the Aeneid

These first lines of the *Aeneid* are called the *'proem'*, which comes from the Greek word *'proemium'*, which simply means 'the introduction'. The first ten lines of the *Aeneid* are noticeably different from the rest of Book One. Unlike the rest of the Book One, these initial lines take the form of a prayer or invocation to the Muse.

The Muses were the Ancient Greek goddesses of the Arts. Poets and other artists called upon to help them craft their poems, sculptures and plays. Since Virgil is writing an epic poem in the tradition of Homer and utilising myths and stories that relate back to Homer, it is fitting then that Virgil should seek to begin his story in the same vein of tradition.

As the daughters of Zeus, the Muses could also punish those who attempted to create artistic products without first offering prayers or seeking the assistance of the Muse. Incidentally, the word 'Museum' comes from the name of a holy site that was dedicated to the Muses.

As well invoking the assistance of the Muse; the proem sets the scene for the rest of the *Aeneid* without giving too much of the story away to the audience. A modern equivalent to the proem could be a film trailer that shows just enough of the film to appeal to potential audiences, without giving away the plot or the spectacle.

In his proem Virgil is to tell the story of Aeneas; a man beset by challenges and troubles brought upon him by the anger of Juno. However in the proem Virgil also provides hope. It is Aeneas' destiny to establish a city for the Trojans in Italy. This city, Lavinium, will in time result in the foundation of another, greater city, the City of Rome, which in Virgil's time and, according to him, will rule the mightiest Empire before or since.

The Anger of Juno

Task: The anger of Juno

To what extent do you think that Juno's anger against Aeneas is justified as explained by Virgil in Book One?

Ending the *proem* Virgil now elaborates on the anger of the Goddess Juno. Why does she hate the Trojans so? Virgil explains in lines 11-33 that Juno hates the Trojans because their descendants are destined to destroy her favourite city; that of Carthage. This is a reference to Rome's historical past.

From 264BC to 146BC Rome and Carthage fought three exceedingly bloody and long lasting wars for domination of the Western Mediterranean. These Punic Wars saw Rome almost destroyed and Italy devastated by the armies of the Carthaginian Hannibal during the Second Punic War 218-201BC. It was not until the Third Punic War 149-146BC that Rome finally managed to utterly destroy Carthage and yet it was through these very same wars that Rome was able to take the first steps on the path to her Imperial destiny and Empire.

Virgil however also makes reference to other reasons why Juno was angered by the Trojans. Juno is motivated by personal jealousy. She lost out to Venus in myth due to the judgement of Paris and also Juno was jealous of the attentions that her husband Jupiter lavished on Ganymede.

The Storm

Having established the reasons why Juno was angry with the Trojans Virgil now directs our attention to an act of punishment. Juno summons the winds that are under the guardianship of the God Aeolus from their home under the mountains of Central Greece (Aeolia) and orders Aeolus to release the Winds so that they can shipwreck the Trojan fleet. In return she promises Aeolus marriage to her servant; the nymph Deiopea. Aeolus agrees.

The winds are released and batter the Trojan fleet. Aeneas is now introduced into the narrative and his first words take the form of a lamenting prayer; he declares that he would have been better to die at the hands of the Greek hero Diomedes rather than suffer this fate.

The Trojan fleet is scattered; three ships are driven onto a hidden reef known to the Romans as 'The Altars' another three ships are driven onto a sandbank at the mouth of the River Syrtes. These locations were known locations to the Romans of the 1st century BC and as we shall see as we progress through the *Aeneid*, Virgil litters his poem with reference to actual physical locations which add a touch of realism to his audience.

By doing so, Virgil allows Aeneas to depart from his mythical past and to enter the known historical world of the Romans. This is important as he needs Aeneas to become a historical rather than mythological character in order to successfully link Aeneas to

Augustus; the Emperor of Rome and establish in turn Augustus' own divine origins.

Just when all seems lost, another God intervenes. Neptune sees the devastation wrought on the Trojan fleet and calms the seas and drives the winds away. Other sea gods move to the assistance of Aeneas and his men. The ships are rescued and re-floated, however the fleet is scattered.

Aeneas makes landfall

The Trojans make land, anchoring off the coast of North Africa. Aeneas is now brought centre stage by Virgil and his first thoughts are not for himself, but for his men. Aeneas ensures that his men are settled and fed, eating the remainder of their corn supply, taking care to honour the Goddess of corn Ceres first. Aeneas then goes hunting and quickly demonstrates his hunting skills by bringing down three great stags and a deer for each ship's crew in addition. Aeneas then makes a morale raising speech in order to lift the spirits of his men in lines 199-209, which understandably have taken a shock by the disasters of the sudden storm and the fears they have for themselves and the grief of their supposedly lost comrades.

The Council of the Gods

Having ensured that the Trojans have reached shore, Virgil shifts the focus of the narrative to the Gods. Venus appeals to Jupiter for mercy on her son. This appeal closely mirrors that of Athena to Zeus on behalf of Odysseus in the *Odyssey* in Book One. In this council Virgil makes clear that other Trojans escaped the sack of Troy and managed to establish new homes in peace and safety. Reference is made to Antenor; a Trojan Elder and Counsellor to King Priam mentioned in the *Iliad* (III.178). Antenor's sons Acamas and Archelochus were comrades in arms of Aeneas during the *Iliad* (III.930-934); but both are killed in battle later on in the *Iliad*. Antenor has escaped and managed to establish a city in Northern Italy and here Virgil uses a real city – Patavium (the modern Padua near Venice in NE Italy).

Virgil has Jupiter reveal something of the destiny of Aeneas in this council. He will establish a city in Italy called Lavinium (a city South of Rome) and his son Ascanius will in turn establish a city on Alba Longa – a dormant volcano some 13 miles South East of Rome today, which was a centre of some historical and religious importance to the Latin peoples of Italy in antiquity. The foundation of myth of Rome is alluded to as it the career of Augustus' adoptive father Julius Caesar.

In doing this at such an early stage Virgil is integrating his epic poem into the mythical and historical past of Italy and subtly transforming established myths in order to fit his intended narrative and into his ambition to ensure that his epic poem helps to legitimise the power and authority possessed by the contemporary Augustus by linking Augustus to the established traditions of Italy.

Aeneas and Venus

Aeneas heads out exploring once more, accompanied by Achates, and the pair soon encounter Venus. Venus is disguised as a girl or nymph out hunting. She is dressed exotically; like a 'Spartan Girl'. In antiquity the Spartans were considered unusual in many ways by their fellow Greeks. In particular the girls and women of Sparta were considered to be treated with a greater degree of freedom than many other Greek women. They could own property and exercise in public for example. In Rome, a woman was expected to stay out of public view, remain in the home and work on producing textiles.

Aeneas soon perceives that the girl he has encountered is a nymph or goddess. He does not however realise that it is actually his mother. He mistakes her for Diana; the goddess of Hunting. Venus explains in a digression both where Aeneas is but also the nature of Carthage and the story of how Dido came to North Africa.

Venus asks Aeneas to introduce himself – which he does, but he is angered when he realises that the girl is actually his mother. Venus never reveals herself directly to Aeneas in Virgil's story; even when she is helping him. It is a complicated relationship; even though Aeneas receives divine help, he rarely seems to obtain this assistance in a straightforward way from his own Mother. It almost seems to Aeneas that his mother's love is as cruel as it is caring;

'Why am I never allowed to take your hand in mine, to hear your true voice and speak to you as you really are?' (*Aeneid* I. 408-409)

We should not be too surprised that these words by Aeneas are not responded to by the Goddess. Aeneas does have the support of his mother, but Virgil is keen to ensure that Aeneas is a man that achieves his own destiny primarily through his own efforts and not handed everything he is destined to achieve on a plate; as has been set out in the *proem*.

Carthage

Aeneas and Achates reach the city of Carthage and wonder at the sights and activity that they witness. The scene presented is a snapshot of the foundation of a new city. All is activity; walls and a harbour are under construction as is a theatre. Laws are being established and a government organised. Virgil employs a detailed simile to illustrate this activity; the Carthaginians are likened to bees. The first simile in the *Aeneid* is presented in lines *149-158*.

'busy in the sunshine all through the flowery meadows, bringing out the young of the race, just come of age, or treading the oozing honey and swelling the cells with sweet nectar…'

Aeneas witnesses this sight and Virgil has his hero rejoice at the sight, but with a slight tinge of jealousy;

'Their walls are already rising!'

The attention of the Trojans is now directed towards a temple dedicated to the Goddess Juno. Virgil describes this grand structure in some detail, in particular the scene depicted in the stone work. Stonework, incidentally, in which Aeneas can also identify himself.

What follows is a digression on the Trojan War – events that are originally found in the *Iliad* at recalled including the death of Rhesus (from the Iliad Book X) and the deaths of Troilus (Iliad Book XXIV) and Hector (from the Iliad Book XXII). Once again, Virgil is keen in these early stages of his story to inter-textualise his work with that of the existing great epics.

The characters of Memnon and Penthesilea are not in the *Iliad* and come from a later (and lost – but not in Virgil's day) epic called the *Aethiopois*. The *Aethiopis* epic told the story of events after the death of Hector. Memnon was an Ethiopian Warrior and son of the Goddess of Dawn whilst Penthesilea was an Amazon warrior Queen. Both fought bravely against the Greeks at Troy before being killed in battle.

Virgil makes reference to the harbour under construction at Carthage. This was important because Carthage was famed in antiquity for its great harbour and ship building facilities. This harbour was the source of Carthaginian might, and Carthage's efforts to improve its harbour prior to the third and final war between Rome and Carthage (The 3rd Punic War 149-146BC) were viewed as an act of aggression by the Roman Senate.

In Virgil's and Augustan's time the city of Carthage was re-founded as a colony for retired military veterans. The visit of Aeneas to Carthage could therefore be seen as an allusion to Rome's permanent control and mastery of Carthage now during the reign of Augustus.

Aeneas revealed

Virgil delays the appearance of his chosen hero in Carthage and we may wonder why. Why is Aeneas obscured in a mist before suddenly appearing in the midst of a city he has been told will be friendly to him and his followers?

One answer could be that Virgil wants to heighten the suspense for his audience. The Roman audience knew Carthage as an implacable enemy that was overcome after over a century of almost constant warfare. The Trojans however are not Romans just yet and the relations between Carthage and Rome have yet to become hostile.

A better reason however is that Virgil wants to delay the appearance of his hero until Aeneas knows that his men are safe and that the fame of the hero Aeneas has been established. Once it becomes clear that Dido is not hostile; she is welcoming and hospitable towards the Trojans and with this hospitality granted, Aeneas can now safely reveal his presence and be presented to the Carthaginians without asking for help directly.

Dido is stunned by the appearance of Aeneas and interestingly Virgil chooses to characterise Dido as 'doomed' (lines 713 and 748) and 'unfortunate', this foreshadows events in Book Four. She comes good on her earlier promise to offer hospitality to the Trojans.

Task: Presentation of character in Book One

How is Aeneas portrayed in Book One?

How is Dido portrayed in Book One?

Explore the language used by Virgil to portray these characters.

How does he want his audience to feel about them?

The Judgement of Paris

This mythical story originates in an epic poem called the Cypria. According to this story Paris was herding animals on Mount Ida when he was visited by the God Hermes (Mercury) and three goddesses; Hera (Juno), Athena (Minerva) and Aphrodite (Venus). Hermes presented Paris with a golden apple and told Paris to settle an argument among the three goddesses; which of the three was the fairest? Each goddess offered Paris a gift if they would pick them;

- *Hera offered Paris great wealth and kingship of a kingdom*

- *Athena offered Paris unparalleled wisdom*

- *Aphrodite offered Paris the most beautiful wife*

According to this story Paris already had a wife (a nymph) but nevertheless chose Aphrodite as the most fair and his reward was Helen (already married to Menelaus). This led to the hatred of Athena and Hera for Paris, the Trojan Wars and Paris' eventual death.

> ### Ganymede
>
> *In Greek myth Ganymede was the son of a Trojan king called Tros. Ganymede was so beautiful that he was desired by Zeus (Jupiter). Zeus abducted Ganymede and made him his immortal cupbearer on Mount Olympus and also his lover. As a result Ganymede was greatly resented by Hera (Juno).*

The Carthaginian foundation story

In a small digression in Book One Venus tells Aeneas a story of the foundation of the city of Carthage. According to Venus in lines 337-370;

- Dido escaped from Tyre and the rule of her brother Pygmalion

- Dido was married to a man called Sychaeus who was killed by Pygmalion in order to seize his wealth

- Dido was told by Sychaeus' ghost where to find this gold

- Dido and her followers escaped from Tyre and reached North Africa

- Dido and her followers purchased a piece of land from local North African rulers called the *'Byrsa'*

The Carthaginian foundation myth that is told by Virgil in the *Aeneid* is loosely based on other traditions that circulated. Although no contemporary Carthaginian account of this foundation myth survives, the Sicilian-Greek historian Timaeus wrote an account of Carthage's origins in the late 4th-early 3rd century BC. His outline of it is as follows;

A Tyrian king called Mattan died and divided his kingdom between his son and daughter who were called Pygmalion and Elissa. Pygmalion refused to share power with Elissa and in order to remove a source of opposition killed Elissa's husband Acherbas; the High priest of Tyre's patron god Melqart. Elissa fled the city; but not before she had fooled Pygmalion. Elissa pretended to agree to return to Tyre and move into the palace and bring the wealth of her husband with her. However Elissa then fooled Pygmalion's servants who were sent to escort Elissa back to Tyre by pretending to throw sacks of gold into the sea. These servants then joined Elissa in her flight from Tyre as they feared the consequences of returning without the expected gold. Elissa and her followers went to Cyprus, collected more followers and then sailed to Africa.

On arrival in North Africa the Tyrian exiles purchased some land from the Libyan king Hiarbus; but only enough that could be covered by the hide of an oxen; a *byrsa*. The Tyrians however cut the ox hide into very thin strips and covered a much greater area. This then was subsequently known as the Byrsa. The Phoenician word *Byrsa* however could also mean 'fortress or high point'.

Elissa was soon pressurised into a marriage with Hiarbus who threatened war if the marriage did not go ahead. Elissa however came up with a final ploy. She agreed to marry Hiarbus, but asked to build a huge bonfire to appease the spirt of her dead husband first. When the fire started Elissa avoided the marriage by jumping into the fire and stabbing herself to death.

Carthage: A brief overview

Carthage was a city that was situated on the coast of North Africa in what is now the country of Tunisia. The city was established by colonists from the Phoenician city of Tyre. According to tradition the date of establishment of this new city was 814/3BC – but the earliest archaeological evidence so far unearthed seems to place the earliest phases of the city from around 750BC.

Carthage was a city whose lifeblood was trade. It was Carthage's control of the sea lanes of the Western Mediterranean that brought the city prosperity and power. In time Carthage would establish its own colonies and settlements in Sardinia, Corsica, Sicily and Spain.

Carthage traded heavily in metals such as gold, silver and tin from Southern Spain and exported foodstuffs and ceramics around the Western Mediterranean. When military power was called for the Carthaginians used its tremendous wealth to employ thousands of mercenaries to serve in its armies.

From around 600BC Carthage was in conflict with Greek cities in Sicily and sometimes found allies in Italy; Etruscan cities of central Italy and also seems to have had a treaty of friendship with Rome in 508BC which was renewed in 348BC. During these centuries the cities of Rome and Carthage seem to have avoided any entanglements in the other's perceived areas of influence. So Carthage kept out of the mainland of Italy, whilst Rome kept out of the affairs of Sicily, Sardinia and Corsica. This relationship deteriorated rapidly in the first part of the 3rd century BC as these areas of influence began to coincide. A dispute over mutual interests in Sicily led to a long and devastating war fought mostly in Sicily and at sea.

> **Task: The presentation of Carthage in Book One**
>
> *How is Carthage and it people portrayed in Book One?*
>
> *Explore the language used by Virgil to portray this city*
>
> *How do the Carthaginians compare to the Trojans in Book One? In what ways are they similar and in what ways are they different?*
>
> *How does Virgil want his Roman audience to feel about Carthage?*

The Wars of Rome and Carthage

Carthage and Rome fought three wars; known as the Punic Wars (so called from the Latin word for Phoenicians – *Poeni*);

- *The First Punic War (264-241BC)*

- *The Second Punic War (218-201BC)*

- *The Third Punic War (149-146BC)*

These wars have already been discussed briefly in Part Two.

The story of the foundation of the Roman Empire is therefore deeply entwined with the fate of Carthage. Without the wars against Carthage, Rome may never have developed beyond an Italian regional power. Had Carthage defeated Rome then the future history of Europe and Africa may have been very different indeed.

3.2 Book Two: The Fall of Troy

This section will help you to;

- *Understand the importance of storytelling in the Aeneid*

- *Understand the events and structure of Book Two*

- *Continue to explore the character of Aeneas*

- *Begin to understand the importance of the influence of Homer on Virgil*

Introduction

Virgil takes the opportunity to tell the story of the fall of Troy from the Trojan perspective in Book Two. This is interesting as the might of Imperial Rome suffered very few military setbacks during the Augustan period (at least that it publically acknowledged). The Roman audience would have been used to hearing stories of Roman soldiers sacking and destroying other towns and cities, such as the conquests of Julius Caesar in Gaul. To hear of what it would be like to on the side the lost would be unusual for a contemporary Roman audience of Virgil.

In the *Iliad*, Homer never actually describes the sack of Troy, or the story of the Trojan Horse. These stories came from other epic poems in the Trojan cycle; the so called 'Little Iliad' and the Sack of Troy. Both of which epics do not survive in themselves; but are preserved in other later writings.

The Trojan Horse was the famous stratagem that finally ended the Trojan War. Whilst a Greek would celebrate this event, for a Trojan on the losing side, the experience was utterly different and in this episode Virgil artfully explores this traumatic event for his chosen hero.

From Aeneas' perspective, the Trojan War was both his personal tragedy (since many of his friends and family were killed by Greeks during the sack of the city) and his public tragedy, since he witnessed the destruction of the city of Troy and all it represented. However, without Troy and the destruction of that city; the Roman Virgil would not be able to link the mythical past to the historical past of Rome and the future destiny of Rome as a great Empire; experiencing its apogee under Augustus.

> ### Key Terms: Analepsis and Pathos
>
> **Analepsis** - *Analepsis is a form of 'flashback'; a digression by the poet when they refer to events that have occurred previously. Analepsis can be either brief or extended.*
>
> **Pathos** – *a literary technique designed to evoke pity or sympathy in the audience that has its root in Greek Tragedy.*

Synopsis of Book Two

Virgil now has Aeneas take up the narrative of the story for the next two books of the *Aeneid*. Aeneas introduces his own story in a kind of proem that sets the tone and establishes the events to be told; the final hours of the city of Troy.

The Greeks have failed in all their efforts to capture Troy up to now. Now however, the Goddess Athena helped the Greeks to build a giant Wooden Horse. This they filled with warriors as the rest of the Greek take to their ships and pretend to flee back to their homes. Instead the Greeks hide only a short distance off shore at the island of Tenedos.

The Trojans emerge from their city and begin to explore the Greek camp. As they do, they discover the Wooden Horse. Most of the Trojans desire to bring the structure into the city – but others disagree. On Trojan in particular, Laocoon, comes close to discovering the truth of the matter; that the Wooden Horse is full to capacity with fully armed Greek heroes. Here Virgil has Laocoon speak the infamous words;

> *'I am afraid of Greeks, particularly when they bring gifts'.*

> Virgil. *Aeneid* II.49

Laocoon then throws his spear at the Wooden Horse – and the hollow structure booms. However, the Greeks remain undiscovered.

Virgil now has Aeneas tell of a Greek prisoner who is bought before the assembled Trojans. This Greek is Sinon, a man who has been left behind by the Greeks in order to ensure that the Wooden Horse is taken into the city of Troy and also to release the Greek warriors contained within when the Trojans are asleep. Sinon now tells his own story in an extended digression. Sinon was a friend of a Greek named Palamedes who was falsely killed by the other Greeks. Sinon also tells how he in turn fell victim to a plot concocted by Ulixes (Odysseus) and Calchas, the Priest of Apollo. Sinon claims that he is a scapegoat and was to be sacrificed in order to ensure that the Greeks could safely sail away. Sinon managed to escape from this fate and hid until the Greeks departed.

Sinon is granted refuge in Troy by the Trojan king Priam. Sinon then instructs the Trojans to bring the Wooden Horse within the city walls; the Greeks constructed it to appease the Gods as compensation for their violation of the stolen Palladium. Sinon's words are endorsed by an omen from the Gods; the punishment of Laocoon.

Laocoon is the priest of Neptune and as he is preparing a sacrifice the Goddess Athena sends two giant serpents to kill him and his young sons. The serpents swim from Tenedos and snare Laocoon's children in their coils. As Laocoon tries to intervene and save his children, he too is taken by the serpents and slain. The Trojans mistakenly interpret this terrible deed this as a punishment for Laocoon striking the Wooden Horse.

Persuaded, the Trojans bring the horse into the city and begin to celebrate their salvation from the Greeks who seem now to be finally defeated. As the Trojans celebrate the Greek fleet begins to return from Tenedos in preparation for the surprise attack. As the city sleeps Sinon opens up the Wooden Horse and the Greeks within emerge and seize the city gates.

Aeneas now brings himself into the story (so far he has been absent). Aeneas is visited in a dream by the ghost of Hector, who urges Aeneas to flee; in time he will establish a new city. Aeneas does not immediately obey and instead Aeneas dresses for battle and joins the fight to save the city. Gathering a few comrades Aeneas battles his way through the city and makes his way towards the palace of Priam. The Trojans defeat a party of Greeks and take their shields and disguise themselves as Greeks. For a time this ploy is successful; Aeneas and his men wreak havoc, but then get caught up in a major battle where all is confusion. Some Trojans even attack them in this battle Aeneas witnesses Cassandra being seized and the death of her new husband as he tries futilely to save her.

Aeneas reaches the palace of Priam and begins to defend the place but is unable to save Priam and his son Polites from dying horrifically at the hands of Achilles' son Pyrrhus (also called Neoptolemus). The battle continues and most of Aeneas' comrades die in the resultant battle. When Aeneas sees Helen trying to hide, he gets carried away by his passions and the situation he finds himself in and tries to kill her. He is only prevented in this when Venus directly intervenes and commands his to leave the city.

Aeneas now realises that his own family is in danger and returns home. He gathers his family and sets out to leave the city as instructed. Aeneas' father Anchises at first stubbornly refuses to abandon his home and in despair Aeneas contemplates joining the battle once more. However Aeneas' wife Creusa and an omen involving Aeneas' son Iulus, persuade both Anchises and Aeneas to flee. Aeneas gathers the household Gods (Penates) and Trojan survivors and heads out of Troy unimpeded by Greeks carrying on his shoulders his father Anchises.

All does not go well however. Creusa goes missing and is lost in Troy. Once Aeneas has led the others to safety at the sanctuary of Ceres, he returns to Troy to search for his missing wife. Virgil uses this opportunity to describe the final destruction of the city of Troy. Eventually Aeneas is visited by the ghost of his wife Creusa – how she died is not known; Creusa tells Aeneas to go to the land of Hesperia (Italy) and there found a new city. A new wife also awaits Aeneas there as well. Aeneas returns to the sanctuary of Ceres and is joined by other survivors from the destruction of Troy.

The style of Book Two

The use of story-telling by Virgil in Book Two is a conscious imitation of Homer; just as Odysseus tells the Phaeacians about his adventures in Books Nine to Twelve of the *Odyssey*, so Virgil provides Aeneas his chosen hero with the opportunity to re-tell his Carthaginian hosts of his own sufferings and also to allow Aeneas speak in his 'own' voice, which enables Virgil's audience in turn to experience *pathos* for Aeneas and the Trojans through the description of the terrifying experience of the destruction of Troy.

The overall presentation of the destruction of Troy is one of great sadness and tragedy. This *pathos* is also generated as we see the comparison between the actions of the Trojans and the Greeks. The Greeks are presented negatively throughout Book Two. They are liars, deceptive and cruel. But they are ultimately victorious in sacking the city of Troy. The Greeks do not win by physical prowess alone; they have to resort to cunning and deceit (Virgil is keen to promote that these characteristics are presented as 'un-Trojan' or 'un-Roman' qualities) in order to achieve victory. There is also tragedy in the fact that it was the inexorable will of the gods that caused Troy to be destroyed that no human hand was able to prevent.

The structure of Book Two

- *Aeneas' Proem (lines 1-12)*

- *Greek gifts (lines 13-57)*

- *Sinon's digression (lines 58-199)*

- *The punishment of Laocoon (lines 200-269)*

- *Battling through the streets of Troy (270-468)*

- *The death of Priam (469-558)*

- *Helen and Venus (lines 559- 633)*

- *The escape from Troy (lines 634-end)*

Greek gifts

In Book Two Virgil has Aeneas consistently portray the Greeks are deceptive, sacrilegious, sneaky and cruel. The Wooden Horse for example is a deceptive trick that enables the Greeks to overcome the Trojans, not through battle, but through subterfuge and deception - in battle the Trojans have held their own against the much more numerous Greeks for almost ten years.

Laocoon's famous speech in Book II lines 40-49 clearly warns the Trojans of the dangers of accepting the Greek offering;

'Do you seriously believe that your enemies have sailed away? Do you imagine Greeks ever give gifts without some devious purpose? ...Whatever it is, I am afraid of Greeks, particularly when they bring gifts.'

Task: Questions on Sinon

Try to answer these without looking at the text.

a) Describe three of the lies that Sinon tells the Trojans, before he gains the sympathy of King Priam.

b) As a result, what does King Priam do for Sinon?

c) Describe three of the lies Sinon tells the Trojans about the reasons for the construction of the wooden horse.

Sinon's Digression

'Listen to this story of Greek treachery, and from this one indictment, learn the ways of a whole people'.

Virgil. *Aeneid II*.55-58

Task: Sinon's Story

How is Sinon portrayed in Book II?

What does Virgil want his audience to view the Greeks in comparison to the Trojans?

Why might he do this?

Sinon is an interesting character and his stories occupy much of Book II. Sinon tells an extended story that details how he comes to be left behind by the Greeks, the political infighting that divides the Greeks and the nature of the Wooden Horse as an effort by the Greeks to atone for their sacrilegious crimes. Sinon's story is compelling and detailed. Unfortunately for Aeneas and the Trojans, Sinon's story is a complete lie from start to finish.

Virgil presents the Trojans as somewhat naïve in their approach to Sinon; as a people that are honourable and valiant; it would never occur to the majority of the Trojans that other people (such as these perfidious Greeks) could think and act in such a way. Sinon himself says of himself that;

'Fortune may have made Sinon an object of pity, but for all her malice, she will make him a cheat or a liar'.

Virgil. *Aeneid II*.80

Having claimed (falsely) that his story is true and that he deserves mercy, Sinon now tells his tale. He details how he fell victim to a plot by Ulixes (Odysseus), who persecuted him and his friend Palamedes. The tale is detailed and utterly convinces the majority of the Trojans. In a nice touch, Virgil even has Sinon break off his narrative in order to encourage the Trojans to beg him to tell them more of his story;

'...but why do I waste time? Why go over this sordid story to no purpose?

Virgil. *Aeneid II*.101-102

Sinon artfully presents Ulixes as spiteful, manipulative and vindictive in a way that contrasts sharply with the presentation of Odysseus in the *Odyssey* and the *Iliad*. The Wooden Horse he says is reparation for the Greeks' violation of the Trojan Palladium.

Task: The death of Laocoon

Read Virgil's Aeneid Book II, lines 200-228

From 'And now there came upon this unhappy people another and yet greater sign,

To... and under the circle of her shield.'

"How effectively does Virgil portray the horror of the events of this passage?"

Remember to explore both to the language used and the events described.

The punishment of Laocoon

This is a very famous episode in the *Aeneid*, and reminds the audience of the inevitability end of the city of Troy. Along with Cassandra, who also predicted the treachery of the Greeks and the trick of the wooden horse, Laocoon is here presented by Virgil as a potential saviour of the Trojans. However, because Troy is doomed and because of the hatred of Athena for the Trojans, Laocoon is not permitted to prove that the Wooden Horse is in fact a deadly trap for Troy.

The punishment of Laocoon by Athena is swift and brutal. Twin sea serpents make straight for Laocoon, and Virgil's description of them as horrific monsters using lines such as *'coil upon measureless coil'* reminds us of their monstrous size, as do the references to *'their blood stained crests'* remind the reader of their monstrous nature.

That there are two of them is deliberate, since they each have a mission; Laocoon's two small sons. This is savage as the small boys are clearly not a threat to anyone. They are innocent victims of Athena's wrath, and Laocoon himself suffers a grim death as he tries desperately to save his sons.

All three Trojans are embroiled in the serpents' coils, and Laocoon is covered in *'gore and venom'*. There is a Homeric-style simile to finish off this brutal picture: Laocoon cries like *'the bellowing of a wounded bull shaking the ineffectual axe out of its neck as it flees from the altar'*.

This is a powerful simile indeed: the image of the bull reminds us that, in a way, Laocoon is also a sacrificial offering. He must be slaughtered to appease Athene and also to satisfy the grim fate of

The story of the Palladium

The Palladium was according to myth a sacred cult object dedicated to the Goddess Athena. The myths of Troy claimed that Troy would never be captured whilst the Palladium was within Troy. So Odysseus disguised himself and managed to enter the city and with the help of Helen managed to escape from Troy carrying with him the Palladium.

Troy, which is to be destroyed by the Greeks. The horror of the simile is also plain, and brings vividly to mind the terrible cries of a wounded animal who cannot really understand why it is suffering, just like Laocoon's young sons.

That the two serpents crawl away to seek shelter under Athena's shield (also called 'Pallas, the Tritonian goddess') in her temple reinforces the idea that the tragedy of Laocoon, and the wider fate of Troy, is fated.

The punishment of Laocoon

Task: War and battle in Book Two

How is war and battle portrayed in Book II of the Aeneid?

Battling through the streets of Troy

Virgil elects to have his first battle scene a defeat for the Trojans. Despite the heroics of Aeneas and his men, their efforts are ultimately futile. Men are killed in brutal ways, guts are speared and heads are crushed. The Greeks have been portrayed through Sinon as deceptive. Now it is the turn of the Trojans to practice a clever deceit; they swap their shields and armour with fallen Greeks and attack with some success. However the deceit also turns on the Trojans. In the confusion of battle the Trojans are attacked by other Trojans and also the Greeks become wise to the trick.

The death of Priam: Pyrrhus; a savage warrior

Pyrrhus, also known as Neoptolemus, was the son of Achilles. After the death of Achilles before Troy the Greeks brought his son to fight at Troy. The presentation of Pyrrhus by Virgil in Book Two is an interesting contrast to Sinon. Whilst Sinon is a sneaky liar, Virgil presents Pyrrhus as a savage and uncompromising warrior who has no mercy or pity. Like Sinon though, Pyrrhus is also presented as sacrilegious and no respecter of religion.

Task: Pyrrhus

How is Pyrrhus (Neoptolemus) portrayed in Book II?

What does Virgil want his audience to view the Greeks in comparison to the Trojans?

Why might he do this?

Pyrrhus is described by a detailed simile; Pyrrhus is a snake; a terror to the Trojans just like his father;

'He was like a snake which has fed on poisonous herbs and hidden all winter in the cold earth...'

Virgil. *Aeneid* II.471

Having established Pyrrhus' credentials so to speak, Virgil now justifies this portrayal. Pyrrhus violently breaks into the palace of Priam and leads the Greeks in slaughter through the halls of the Trojan king.

Pyrrhus slaughters the king of the Trojans in a particularly cruel way. Virgil tells how Priam arms himself for battle; but his bodily strength is not equal to the courage of his spirit. He nonetheless determines to face Pyrrhus in battle. But first Pyrrhus must kill Polites.

Polites, one of the youngest sons of Priam, is wounded and trying to flee from the clutches of Pyrrhus. Virgil has Polites run to seek help; and like many sons in trouble, Polites seeks the sanctuary of his father. The effort however is futile, and Pyrrhus kills him before the horrified eyes of his parents.

Now it is Priam's turn. He scolds Pyrrhus and compares him unfavourably to his father. Even Achilles showed respect to the pleas of Priam (as told in the *Iliad*, Book XXIV). Pyrrhus however is unmoved and unrepentant. His words are cruel and taunting towards Priam who he is about to kill;

'In that case you will be my messenger and go to my father, son of Peleus. Let him know about my wicked deeds and do not forget to tell him about the degeneracy of his son Neoptolemus. Now, die.'

Virgil. *Aeneid* II.548-549

Pyrrhus then drags Priam to the altar of his own household gods and there runs him through with his sword. Priam's corpse is also further desecrated by being beheaded.

Pyrrhus of Epirus

Pyrrhus of Epirus (319-272BC) was a Greek king from the western regions of what is now mainland Greece and Albania. Pyrrhus invaded Italy in 280BC when Tarentum; a city of Greek origins in southern Italy appealed for help against Rome. Pyrrhus invaded Italy with an army of nearly 30,000 men and included Elephants. Pyrrhus defeated a Roman army at Heraclea in 280BC and again at Ausculum in 279BC. Both victories however came at heavy cost to Pyrrhus' army.

In 275BC the Romans managed to defeat Pyrrhus at Beneventum and Pyrrhus abandoned Italy. These costly battles are the root of the common phrase 'Pyrrhic Victory' (to win but at such a great cost that you end up losing).

Analysis of excerpt - examination style response

Read the passage and answer the questions.

'As soon as [Polites] reached his father and mother, he fell and vomited his life's blood before their eyes. There was no escape for Priam. Death was now upon him, but he did not check himself or spare the anger in his voice. 'As for you,' he cried 'and for what you have done, if there is any power in heaven that cares for such things, may the gods pay you well. May they give you the reward you have deserved for making me see my own son dying before my eyes, for defiling a father's face with the murder of his son. You pretend that Achilles was your father, but this is not how Achilles treated his enemy Priam. He had respect for my rights as a suppliant and for the trust I placed in him. He gave me back the bloodless body of Hector for burial and allowed me to return to the city where I was king.' With these words the old man feebly threw his harmless spear. It rattled on the bronze of Pyrrhus' shield and hung there useless sticking on the surface of the central boss. Pyrrhus then made his reply. 'In that case you will be my messenger and go to my father, son of Peleus. Let him know about my wicked deeds and do not forget to tell him about the degeneracy of his son Neoptolemus. Now, die.' As he spoke the word, he was dragging Priam to the very altar, his body trembling as it slithered through pools of his son's blood. Winding Priam's hair in his left hand, in his right he raised his sword with a flash of light and buried it to the hilt in Priam's side. So ended the destiny of Priam. This was the death that fell to his lot. He who had once been the proud ruler over so many lands and peoples of Asia died with Troy ablaze before his eyes and the citadel of Pergamum in ruins. His mighty trunk lay upon the shore, the head hacked from the shoulders, a corpse without a name. Then for the first time I knew the horror that was all about me. What was I to do? There came into my mind the image of my own dear father, as I looked at the king who was his equal in age breathing out his life with that cruel wound. There came into my mind also my wife Creusa whom I had left behind, the plundering of my home and the fate of young Iulus.'

The Aeneid, translated by David West, Penguin Books (1990) 2.530-564

The question is in the spirit of the examination; it is a chance for you to gather your thinking on the Odyssey and the Aeneid, and to practise making cross-links, comparisons and contrasts between the two books.

Section A

a) How effectively does Virgil create sympathy for Priam in this passage?

Write this response in no more than 500 words

Section B

b) To what extent does this passage of the Aeneid provide a damning indictment of war?

Write this response in no more than 750 words

Aeneas, Venus and Helen

Virgil has presented his hero Aeneas as surrounded by the chaos and trauma of battle and slaughter. Aeneas has witnessed the death of his comrades, his friends and his king. It should come as no surprise then that Virgil presents Aeneas with a human failing in Book II. He tries to kill a defenceless woman.

Aeneas sees Helen, the cause of the Trojan War and the cause of all the deaths that Aeneas has witnessed. Seeing her alone and hiding, Aeneas sees a small way in which he can make the Greeks suffer as he and the Trojans are suffering;

'I shall win praise for blotting out this evil and exacting a punishment which is richly deserved. I shall also take pleasure in feeding the flames of vengeance and appeasing the ashes of my people.'

Virgil. *Aeneid* II.587-588

These words are uncharacteristic of Virgil's hero and almost present Aeneas as acting in a similar way to Pyrrhus. However, whereas Pyrrhus is unrestrained in his savagery and cruelty, Aeneas is restrained. His mother Venus intervenes in the most direct way in order to stop her son from acting in a way that is unbecoming.

Venus reveals herself in all her godhood to her son; no disguises are used. Venus brings Aeneas back to his senses and directs his attention to the fate of his family; Aeneas cannot prevent the destruction of Troy; he cannot kill Helen and he cannot save Priam and his family. He can however save himself and he can bring his family and household gods out of the destruction.

Aeneas now realises that the Gods are participating in the destruction of Troy and that the city is fated to burn. Virgil uses another simile to describe this realisation of the fall of Troy; the city is like an ash tree that is being felled by farmers. Not matter how mighty this tree, it cannot resist the axes of the farmers.

Aeneas and his family

Aeneas now has the challenge of bringing his family out of Troy and to bring them to safety. But this is not straightforward. Anchises; Aeneas' father is reluctant. He would prefer to die with his city. His words cause more indecision in Aeneas who once again contemplates a futile death in the streets of the city. However, Creusa and Iulus both manage to persuade Aeneas. Creusa uses words and reminds Aeneas of his duty;

'If you leave us here, what fate is waiting for little Iulus, for your father and for the woman who used to be called your wife?'

Virgil. *Aeneid* II.678-679

As will be seen throughout the *Aeneid*; Duty is a key driver of Aeneas and is vital in driving the plot of Virgil's story forward. On several occasions Aeneas makes several hard choices, overcoming his personal desires by knowledge of his duty. The realisation of this duty is confirmed by the Gods as well. Jupiter sends a pair of omens; a flame appears atop the head of Iulus and is followed in short order by the peal of thunder and the sight of a shooting star.

Aeneas' mind is made up and the family escape from Troy; with Aeneas carrying his father on his back. This bearing of his father from Troy is one of the earliest stories of Aeneas and was portrayed in art for centuries before Virgil came to write the *Aeneid*.

All does not go smoothly for Aeneas however even now. His wife Creusa is lost in the escape from Troy and Aeneas is distraught. He heads back into the city and searches for Creusa in vain until her ghost is revealed to him. Creusa cannot make the journey with Aeneas. She is his past and Aeneas now needs to look to the future. A new bride awaits Aeneas in a new country where he will found a new city.

Task: Comparing Book II to events in the Odyssey.

How does the narrative of Book II of the Aeneid compare to the following episodes in the Odyssey;

- *Helen's portrayal of Odysseus' antics in Troy (Odyssey. Book IV.270-296)*

- *Menelaus and Odysseus in the Trojan Horse (Odyssey. Book IV.302-324)*

- *Demodocus' Song and Odysseus' reaction (Odyssey. Book VIII.541-610)*

3.3 Book Three: The Wanderings of Aeneas

This section will help you to;

- *Understand the importance of storytelling in the Aeneid*

- *Understand the events and structure of Book Three*

- *Continue to explore the character of Aeneas*

- *Continue to understand the importance of the influence of Homer on Virgil*

Introduction

This topic focuses on the *Aeneid* Book Three, which is not part of the set texts to be studied at A level, though it is still important to read for knowledge of how the plot develops.

In some ways Book Three is Virgil's version of the *Odyssey*. It details Aeneas' journey from Troy to Carthage; a journey that has taken seven years. But Virgil takes inspiration for the contents of Book Three from texts other than just Homer's *Odyssey*. The influences of other epics are detectable in Book Three as are stories and characters from Greek Tragedy.

Book Three Synopsis

Apollonius Rhodius: An epic poet

Apollonius of Rhodes lived in the 3rd Century BC and was the poet of an epic story of Jason and the Argonauts.

His 'Argonautica' was a four book poem that heavily influenced later writers, including Virgil.

The Trojans first port of call once they leave their ancestral homeland is Thrace; a region in modern Northern Greece. Here Aeneas quickly sets about building a new city named Aeneadae. This establishment however is a failure. Whilst digging into a heavily vegetated mound Aeneas is horrified to discover that the earth is bleeding. Unwilling to at first accept this bad sign, Aeneas struggles with a well rooted shrub and hears a voice from beneath the earth.

The voice is that of Polydorus; a Trojan prince and son of Priam. Polydorus was sent to Thrace for his own safety. However, his host murdered him for the wealth that he brought with him. The decision is made by the Trojans to abandon Aeneadae and seek a new home. Polydorus is given a second, decent burial.

The Trojans abandon Aeneadae and continue their journey. The Trojans reach the island of Delos in the central Aegean Sea. Delos was an island sacred to the God Apollo and by the 1st Century BC was a thriving commercial centre and slave trading port. The Trojans receive hospitality from the local king, named Anius and receive an oracle from the God Apollo to seek out their home in the land of the Trojan forefathers. Aeneas' father Anchises interprets this oracle to mean the island of Crete.

Occupation of Crete is made possible because the Greek king Idomeneus who ruled Crete and who had played a prominent role in the Greek army during the Trojan War has recently deserted the island. The way therefore is clear for the Trojans to take up residency in the island.

The Trojans reach Crete and establish a new city named Pergamea. However the oracle has been misinterpreted; the city is a false start and the Trojans are afflicted by plague and hunger. Anchises instructs Aeneas to return to Delos and consult the oracle of Apollo again. Before he can do so however, the Trojan Household Gods (The Penates) advise Aeneas in a dream that Crete is the wrong place for the Trojans. The Trojans need to go to Italy (called Hesperia). Once this is understood by the Trojans, they set sail again.

The Trojans set sail but are soon lost in a storm that blows them westward. In time the Trojans reach the islands of the Strophades. The Strophades are the home of mythical creatures; Harpies. According to Virgil the Harpies themselves are refugees like the Trojans; they were defeated by Jason and the Argonauts and took refuge on this island.

According to Virgil, the Harpies are part woman, part bird and are ruled by Celaeno and have a loathsome appearance;

'They are birds with the faces of girls, with filth oozing from their bellies, with hooked claws for hands and faces pale with a hunger that is never satisfied.'

Virgil. *Aeneid* III.217-218

The Trojans and Harpies soon clash and engage in a battle as the Harpies raid the Trojan's feast. The Harpies are driven off but the Harpy Queen Celaeno prophesises that the Trojans will not build a city in Italy until they *'eat their own tables'*. With this troubling predicting, the Trojans continue their journey.

The Trojans take to sea once more and head past the islands ruled by Odysseus without landing. They do land on the Western coastline of mainland Greece at the site of what will be Actium. The Trojans celebrate the Trojan Games at Actium and Aeneas dedicates here a shield seized in battle from a Greek warrior during the Trojan War. After departing from Actium the Trojans reach the city of Buthrotum. Here they encounter a welcome surprise; they meet Trojans. Andromache the widow of Hector and Helenus, a son of Priam famed for his knowledge of prophecies. These Trojans were captured in the fall of Troy, but are now rulers of the city of Buthrotum.

Helenus has succeeded to the throne of Pyrrhus – the son of Achilles who was bloodily encountered in Book II. He is dead, killed by Orestes, the son of Agamemnon over who should marry Hermione; daughter of Menelaus and Helen. On the death of Pyrrhus, Helenus then married Andromache. Virgil reveals in an ironic twist that Pyrrhus was slain by Orestes on an altar; just like Pyrrhus had done to Priam.

Helenus gives Aeneas detailed advice. He predicts that the Trojans will reach Italy but will also need to visit the Underworld first. The city that Aeneas is destined to found should be done at a site where Aeneas finds a sow with a litter of thirty piglets. Southern Italy is populated by Greeks and should be avoided; nonetheless the Trojans need to appease the Goddess Juno when they see Italy in a new way.

Before the Trojans land in Italy they should beware of the dangers of the sea monsters Scylla and Charybdis. Finally, once the Trojans reach Italy Aeneas should seek the prophetess of Cumae. This priestess, known as the Sibyl will lead Aeneas to the Underworld.

Once this advice is given the Trojans prepare to depart. Helenus and Andromache provide their guests with valuable gifts and they continue on their journey. Aeneas and his followers skirt the coast of Italy and obey the instructions of Juno in praying to the Goddess in the new recommended fashion. The Trojans see Sicily but are driven by the tides to the lands of the Cyclops. Here the Trojans witness the volcano of Etna and retrieve a Greek who has been abandoned by Odysseus. This Greek warns the Trojans of the dangers of the Cyclops and is taken with them when they leave; witnesses to these monsters, but not affected by them. The Trojans finally reach Sicily and the city of Drepanum. Here the Trojans are safe but Anchises dies (we are not told of what). From Sicily the Trojans are then struck by the storm referenced in Book One and then reach Carthage.

The structure of Book Three

Book Three can most easily be divided into the following episodes;

- *The attempt to found Aeneadae (lines 1-69)*

- *The attempt to found Pergamea (lines 70-192)*

- *The Harpies (lines 193-277)*

- *Andromache and Helenus (lines 278-508)*

- *The Cyclopes and arrival in Sicily (lines 509-end)*

Task: Echoes of Homer

As you read Book Three identify as many echoes as you can of the Odyssey and the Iliad.

Also consider how Virgil changes or adapt these echoes to fit his own narrative.

In Book Three, Aeneas undertakes his own *'Odyssey'* similar to the obstacles encountered by Odysseus in Books Nine-Twelve of the *Odyssey* in that there is a strong element of the supernatural, for example:

- *The bleeding bush*

- *Delos and the oracle of Apollo*

- *Crete and the plague*

- *Aeneas' vision of the household gods*

- *The Harpies and the three-day darkness*

- *Helenus and Andromache*

- *The meeting with Achaemenides*

Physical locations mentioned in Book Three

> **Actium:** A headland at the entrance to the Ambracian Gulf on the West coast of mainland Greece. Actium was the site of a temple to Apollo from at least the 6th century BC and games were known to be celebrated in association with this site. More famously Actium was the site of the decisive naval victory of Octavian (the future Augustus) over Marcus Antonius and Cleopatra. Shortly after this victory; both Marcus Antonius and Cleopatra committed suicide and Octavian established a city at the site called Nicopolis (Octavian's 'Victory City') Octavian also embellished the sanctuary to Apollo and formally adopted Apollo as his patron God.

> **Delos:** Delos is a small island in the Cyclades island group in the central Aegean Sea. Delos is positioned between the islands of Mykonos and Rheneia. Delos was in legend the birthplace of the Gods Apollo and Artemis and a cult centre to Apollo had been established there in the 8th century BC.

> **Sicily:** Sicily is the large island just off the 'toe' of Italy and part of the modern country. Early historical traditions of Sicily claim that the original peoples of Sicily came from Spain (Sicans), Italy (Sicels) and Troy (Elymians).

> The Elymians were the main inhabitants of western Sicily and inhabited cities such Drepanum and Eryx – both of which are mentioned in the *Aeneid*. The island was bitterly fought over in both the 1st and 2nd Punic Wars and subsequently Sicily became the first Roman province.

Mythical people and beings mentioned in Book Three

> **Andromache:** Andromache was the mythical wife of Hector; the principal defender of Troy. According to the myth their son Astyanax was killed after the sack of Troy by the Greeks and Andromache became Neoptolmenus' slave. Andromache is a character in several extant Greek tragedies including Euripides' Andromache and *Women of Troy*.

> **Helenus:** A Trojan Prince, brother of Hector and mentioned in the *Iliad*. Helenus was in myth a priest of Apollo.

> **Polydorus:** A Trojan Prince, brother of Hector and mentioned in Greek Tragedy.

> **Cyclops:** Mythical creatures mentioned in the *Odyssey*. They are giants with a single eye, herders of livestock and will eat men if the opportunity arises.

> **Harpies:** Mythical creatures. They were encountered by the Argonauts on the island of Salmydessus off Thrace. They had been sent here to plague a blind seer named Phineus. The Argonauts

agreed to drive away the Harpies in return for guidance. After the Harpies were driven away, they took refuge on the Strophades islands (where they were encountered by Aeneas).

Task: Comparing Book III to the Odyssey

Please note that you will need to have read Homer's Odyssey in order to respond to this question.

Write a response to the following question;

'To what extent do you agree with the view that it is inaccurate to compare Book Three of the Aeneid to Books Nine to Twelve of Homer's Odyssey'?

3.4: Presentation of character: Aeneas and Anchises

This section will help you to;

- *Understand how Virgil presents the character of Aeneas in Books One to Three*

- *Explore the language used by Virgil to describe character in Books One to Three*

- *Understand how Virgil presents the character of Anchises in Books Two and Three*

Introduction

In this section we will explore the presentation of the characters of Aeneas and Anchises by Virgil in Books One to Three.

The portrayal of Aeneas in Book One

Aeneas is presented as an energetic leader in Book One. He gets his men onshore after the storm. He scouts the local area; he ensures they have food to eat and a fire to dry themselves by. Aeneas also seeks to rouse the morale of the Trojans with a speech – suppressing his true feelings and hiding his worries from his men;

'These were his words, but he was sick with all his cares.

He showed them the face of hope and kept his misery deep in his heart'.

Virgil. *Aeneid* I.208-9

Aeneas is placing his own fears and desires as secondary to those of his men and his country; a key virtue for Romans in the 1st century.

The portrayal of Aeneas in Book Two; Obedient to the gods or a failure as a Hero?

In Book One we see Aeneas as a leader of his people, caring for their welfare and safety. In Book Two Virgil presents us with different aspects of his personality; Aeneas is a skilled warrior, able to stand in battle against almost any Greek hero, more importantly however, we see Aeneas battling his own conscience in a different kind of conflict; whether to go with the Heroic tradition of *timé* and *kleos* (honour and reputation) and seek a glorious death in battle, or to fulfil his duty to the gods and his loyalty to his family (*pietas* and *fides*) and save them.

In Book Two Virgil reinforces Aeneas' reputation as a brave warrior and leader of men. Aeneas arms for battle and heads out into the streets of Troy. As he does he gathers together a band of likeminded Trojan warriors. But Aeneas is clearly seen by all as the leader. He harangues the Trojans giving them an open and honest assessment of their situation and character;

'You are the bravest of all our warriors, and your bravery is in vain.

If your desire is fixed to follow a man who fights to the end, you see how things stand with us.'

Virgil. *Aeneid* II.349-350

Aeneas then leads these men into battle. Greeks are encountered and dispatched mercilessly. The Greeks have used trickery to enter the city; the Trojans now use a little piece of deception themselves; they take the shields of the Greeks and so disguised can wreak more havoc on the invaders who do not realise who they are until it is too late.

And yet there is a major problem in Aeneas' actions in the sack of Troy that conflicts heavily with his honour and reputation as a Homeric style hero; he abandons the city and survives. Virgil is aware of this and so too it appears is his character Aeneas;

'I call to witness the ashes of Troy. I call upon the flames in which my people died.

In the hour of your fall I did not flinch from the weapons of the Greeks or from anything they could do.

***If it had been my fate to fall**, my right hand fully earned it.'*

Virgil. *Aeneid* II.431-434

By surviving the sack of Troy when all the men who initially accompanied him died in battle obviously does not sit well with Aeneas. Virgil is making Aeneas aware of the possible implications of his survival on his heroic reputation. If he survived when all the other Trojans with him died in battle and futile defence of Troy; does this make Aeneas a coward?

Virgil also has Aeneas recount an episode that presents Aeneas in another difficult moment. He contemplates and then tries to murder an unarmed woman in a fit of anger. Aeneas spots Helen, the wife of Menelaus and the lover of Paris (and subsequently his brother Deiphobus) hiding in a corner of the centre of Troy. Helen was perceived to be the author of all the troubles of Troy and so on one level Aeneas could be justified in killing her. Helen's death during the sack of Troy would rob the Greeks of their greatest prize.

However, Helen was widely considered in antiquity to be a victim of the Gods and a vehicle for their designs to bring Troy to ruin. Helen had been chosen by Aphrodite/Venus to be the reward given to Paris for choosing that goddess in a beauty pageant. Aeneas does not consider this though. He is carried away by the horrific experience he is immersed in and it is only the direct intervention of Aeneas' mother that prevents him from murdering Helen. Whether

Aeneas would be justified in killing Helen is irrelevant when we consider how this episode portrays Aeneas as a Hero.

What keeps Aeneas alive in Book Two and potentially forces him to compromise his Heroic reputation is his destiny, obedience to the will of the Gods and concern for the safety of his family.

The portrayal of Aeneas in Book Three

In a shift from the presentation of Aeneas as a Hero (albeit with a reputation that is slightly tarnished) Virgil now presents Aeneas as primarily a pious man, obedient to the will of the Gods. It is *pietas* which is the primary characteristic of Aeneas in Book Three.

There are several reasons to make this claim;

- Aeneas sets out on his journey carrying with him the Gods of Troy and his own Household Gods.

- Aeneas ensures that the body of Polydorus is given a decent burial.

- Aeneas consults the God Apollo and acts upon the advice.

- Aeneas obeys the will of the Penates when they tell him to abandon Crete.

- Aeneas adopts a new way of prayer.

- Aeneas performs the Trojan Games and sacrifices to Jupiter at Actium.

- Aeneas receives more advice from Apollo through his priest Helenus and acts upon it.

- Aeneas tries to placate the anger of Juno by sacrificing to her on arrival in Italy.

- Aeneas worships the gods on arrival in Sicily.

Aeneas is consoled by the Penates in a dream. On awakening he is quick to offer prayer (III.173-175) and give thanks for these instructions that save him the need to retrace his steps.

Aeneas' *piety* is also exhibits by his reaction to misinterpreting the oracles of the Gods and the idea of impious acts. For example; Aeneas is horrified by the foul murder of Polydorus. Virgil uses a metaphorical phrase that is repeated or recycled in a similar way on several occasions in the *Aeneid*;

'*My hair stood on end with horror and the voice stuck in my throat*'.

Virgil. *Aeneid* III.49

Virgil used this metaphorical phrase in II.773 when Aeneas encounters the ghost of his wife Creusa. This phrase hair standing on end has continued into modern a trope with the idea surviving in the horror genre.

Aeneas is also very obedient of his father in Book Three. Anchises is at the very least joint leader of the Trojans on their journey. Aeneas consults with and obeys the advice of his father Anchises at all times. Virgil gives Anchises the title *'Father'*.

This title will later be extended and granted to Aeneas and looks forward to 2BC when Augustus will be granted the title *'Pater Patriae'* (Father of the Fatherland). This of course was after the death of Virgil so he could not know that this title would be granted to Augustus. The title had been granted though to Cicero in the 60sBC and Julius Caesar in the civil wars of the 40sBC for saving the state so perhaps Virgil expected this title for Augustus at some point.

The role and presentation of Anchises in Books Two and Three

Anchises' first appearance in the *Aeneid* is a contrast to his son. Whilst Aeneas has been traversing the streets of the fallen Troy, Anchises has stayed at home. Anchises is both elderly and according to myth (but not mentioned in the *Aeneid*) either blind or lame in one leg as a result of a punishment from the Gods for boasting that he had produced a son with the Goddess Venus.

Virgil presents Anchises as a stubborn old man in our first encounter with him in Book Two. He does not want to leave Troy and would prefer that he (and by extension the whole family) are killed in the sack of the city. These words drive Aeneas to despair and the hero almost heads back into the streets to seek a futile death.

However, Anchises is if anything even more pious than his son. In the *Aeneid* he never disobeys or shows reluctance to follow the will of the Gods once it is made known to him. He reacts to omens that are witnessed and interprets the will of the Gods for the most part accurately. For example, Anchises interprets the sign of the flame on young Iulus' head (II.680-690) and his request for confirmation is granted by the sign of a thunderbolt and the sight of a meteor.

In Book Three Anchises acts first and foremost as a priest. But he also seems to be joint leader of the Trojans along with Aeneas. It is Anchises that bids the fleet to set sail (III.9) and Anchises is consulted by Aeneas on several occasions in the journey from East to West. The Trojans find welcome at Delos partly through the friendship that Anchises has with the local king named Anius (III.80). Anchises interprets the oracles of Apollo at Delos; however he makes an error in the interpretation and advices the fleet to sail to Crete and not Italy. This is rectified and Anchises then realises the error in mixing up the Trojan ancestors Teucer and Dardanus. Anchises also interprets the promise of war in Italy by the sight of white horses (III.540-541).

Anchises dies in Sicily shortly after their arrival. This is necessary for the plot of the *Aeneid*. If Anchises had not died, then Aeneas would not be the undisputed leader of the Trojans and could not fully develop as their heroic leader if he was always deferring to his father.

'Father'

Anchises' death signals the beginning of Aeneas as the *'Father'* of the Trojans and a founder of the Roman race. In Book Three Anchises is often described as 'Father Anchises'. Later on in the *Aeneid* Aeneas will in turn receive this sobriquet. In early Rome the title of the heads of the patrician families was *'Patrés' 'Father'* and the deliberate choice of this word is used by Virgil in order to associate Aeneas as the first head of the first Trojan patrician family in Italy.

3.5: Homeric Influences in Books One and Two

This section will help you to;

- *Compare the proem of the Aeneid with those of Homer*

- *Explore and compare the language used by Virgil and Homer*

Introduction

In this section we will begin to consider how much Virgil is influenced by the epics of Homer.

Intertextuality in the *Aeneid*

It is fair to say that intertextuality of Homer's epics in the *Aeneid* is intense. Intertextuality means to create links through common references, background, structure and use of language. It could attempt to link language, a shared character, a common mythical background or tradition.

A cursory view of the *Aeneid* and the epics of Homer for example include the following connected links;

- A shared hero in Aeneas
- A shared background in the Trojan War
- A similar structure in the formation of the epics
- A similar style of language in certain places (i.e. battles, storms)
- A similar style of language techniques in the use of digression and repetition

Homeric influences in Book One

References to Homer's poems litter the *Aeneid*. For Virgil it is essential for his own story to establish at an early stage that although the *Aeneid* is a story of a Trojan Hero whose descendants will in time be responsible for the establishment of the greatest empire the World has ever seen (According to his Roman audience in any event), it is nonetheless the story of a hero that first came to prominence in the *Iliad*. This tradition needs to be respected by Virgil and the material contained in the poems of Homer and other epics is also used to enrich the *Aeneid*.

Task: Comparing the proems of the Aeneid, Iliad and Odyssey

Read the proems of all three epic poems (the proems of Homer are below). What is similar and what is different in the proems of Virgil and Homer

The proem of the Iliad translated by R. Fagles;

'Rage — Goddess, sing of the rage of Peleus' son Achilles,

murderous, doomed, that cost the Achaeans countless losses,

hurling down to the House of Death so many sturdy souls,

great fighters' souls, but made their bodies carrion,

feasts for the dogs and birds,

and the will of Zeus was toward its end.

Begin, Muse, when the two first broke and clashed,

Agamemnon lord of men and brilliant Achilles.

What god drove them to fight with such a fury?

Homer Iliad I.1-9

The proem of the Odyssey translated by R. Fagles;

Sing to me of the man, Muse, the man of twists and turns

driven time and again off course, once he had plundered

the hallowed heights of Troy.

many cities of men he saw and learned their minds,

many pains he suffered, heartsick on the open sea,

fighting to save his life and bring his comrades home.

But he could not save them from disaster, hard as he strove —

the recklessness of their own ways destroyed them all,

the blind fools, they devoured the cattle of the Sun

and the Sungod blotted out the day of their return.

Launch out on his story, Muse, daughter of Zeus,

start from where you will — sing for our time too.

Homer Odyssey I.1-12

In addition to the *proem* – which as we have already explored established Virgil's intent to create and Epic poem in the heroic tradition of Homer, there are several other references to the mythical traditions first established by Homer.

The Greek hero Achilles who is the leading character in the *Iliad* is mentioned on several occasions in Book One including lines 31-2, lines 99-100 and in particular in the description of the temple of Juno. The Fate of Little Ajax (the son of Oileus) is a story initially told in the *Odyssey* (Book IV.560-573). Virgil recycles this story in the *Aeneid* Book One lines 40-50.

There are several references to Diomedes in Book One. Diomedes was one of the greatest Greek warriors in the *Iliad*; and importantly for Virgil's narrative, Diomedes was also a survivor of the war and the aftermath and returned to Greece relatively trouble free. In the *Iliad* Diomedes wounds several Gods in battle including Aphrodite/Venus (Aeneas' mother) and Ares/Mars (the God of War). One individual to have a lucky escape from the rampaging Diomedes in the *Iliad* is Aeneas himself. Although Diomedes plays no direct role in the *Aeneid*, his name is used as a kind of hovering threat over the head of Aeneas.

Virgil also is influenced by the *Odyssey* in other parts of Book One; whilst the God Aeolus is visited by Juno in Book One, the same God was visited by Odysseus in the *Odyssey* (Book X). There are many storms in the *Odyssey* (Books V/IX and X) and therefore Virgil too uses a storm in order to direct the flow of his narrative. However in the *Aeneid* the god that saves Aeneas and his men from the storm is Neptune (Poseidon) and in the *Odyssey*, it is Poseidon who whips up a storm to torment Odysseus in Book V. both Juno and Poseidon in the *Aeneid* and the Odyssey respectively use a storm primarily to delay the hero from their respective destiny. For Odysseus on the one hand to return home, for Virgil to land in Italy and establish the Roman race.

As the audience proceeds further into Book One, more references to Homer's poems reveal themselves which hint at future events to be told in turn in the *Aeneid*. For example Aeneas' speech to his men (lines 199-209) refer to the perils avoided by the Trojans on their journey; the monsters of Scylla and the Cyclops. These monsters will be encountered by Virgil's audience in Book Three but both of these perils were encountered earlier – in Homer's *Odyssey* by Odysseus.

Homeric influences in Book Two

It is clear that Book Two is perhaps the most 'Homeric' of all the *Aeneid*. Virgil is keen to link his story with that of the mythical traditions of Troy if he is to establish his story of Aeneas coming to Italy. Before Aeneas can arrive in Italy, he needs to leave Troy.

The result then is Book Two; the final destruction of Troy by the Greeks. Virgil utilises the established mythic traditions to the full in Book Two. The Wooden Horse, the prophetic warnings of Laocoon and the slaughter of the final remnants of the Trojan royal family are all illustrated graphically by Virgil.

The battle scenes are also Homeric. The fighting in the streets and the palace of Priam are explicit and bloody. Men die in terrible ways.

We can compare a few examples. First from the *Aeneid*;

'Coroebus was the first to die. He fell by the right hand of Penelaus and lay there face down...' (II.424)

And Polites for example;

'fell and vomited his life's blood' (II.532)

and now with the *Iliad*;

(Diomedes) 'killed Astynous, then Hypiron, a frontline captain.

One he stabbed with a bronze lance above the nipple, the other his heavy sword hacked at the collarbone... (Iliad V.160-162)

and

'Odysseus plunged a spear in his back between the shoulders –

Straight through his chest the shaft came jutting out

And down Socus crashed'. (Iliad XI.527-529)

Task: Homeric Similes in Book One and Two

Identify a Homeric Simile in Book One and another in Book Two.

What is the context and subject matter of these similes?

What language and phrases are used by Virgil in these similes that you find most appealing?

How effective do you find these similes? Do you think they add or detract from the narrative of the Books?

Task: Virgil and Homer

Which of the following statements do you think has more weight?

Virgil uses Homer and Greek myth as a springboard to launch his own epic, but his story is primarily an Italian one.

Virgil first and foremost wants the Aeneid to fit into the mythical tradition of Homer.

Use evidence from the Aeneid and from what you know of Virgil and Homer to support your reasoning.

3.6: The Supernatural in Books One and Two

This section will help you to;

- *Understand the supernatural elements in Book Two*

- *Consider the role of Gods and prophetic warning in Books One to Two*

- *Explore and compare the language used by Virgil to describe the supernatural*

- *Consider the importance of disguise and recognition in Book One*

Introduction

In this section we will begin to the important themes of the supernatural in Books One to Two.

The role of Gods and prophetic warnings in Book Two

Book Two is littered with supernatural events by Virgil. This deliberate decision fits in well with the epic tradition in which he desired the *Aeneid* to be considered and establishes for the audience that just as the destruction of Troy is predestined. So too the audience can look forward to another destiny being fulfilled; that of Aeneas leading the Trojans to Italy to establish in time a city that links Rome to the mythical Troy.

The Gods in Virgil's *Aeneid* are, like those portrayed in Homer, anthropomorphic (human-like) and because they are human like their actions and behaviours are similar to our own. The Gods of both Virgil and Homer feel jealousy, love, anger and the desire for revenge. This makes them dangerous, unpredictable and far from trustworthy allies for mortals.

The Gods have the impulse to engage in human-like behaviours, though they are exempt from the dangerous consequences that afflict mortals and give mortals caution and concerns, such as death and tragedy. They can therefore afford to treat human affairs as something of a game, despite the fact that many of them have family connections to the mortals involved in these games – who suffer accordingly.

The gods are ultimately beings apart, living free from the personal experiences of hunger, disease and death. The gods' interventions in Book Two are typical of their wider behaviour. They can be cruel and deeply unfair, bearing grudges for slights that mortals are not even aware that they have committed – such as that of Laocoon by striking the Wooden Horse.

Although Troy *is* fated to be destroyed, some gods continue to favour the Trojans while others are set against them. This raises the stakes of their involvement even further, since the gods who are anti-Trojan, Juno and Athena especially, are intent on causing the utmost damage despite the ultimate futility of them doing so, since fate/destiny cannot be changed – even by the Gods.

Task: The role of gods in Books One and Two

Write a response to the following question;

To what extent do you agree with the view that Aeneas has little or no control of events in Books One and Two?

Venus in Book Two

The Goddess Venus intervenes in Book II. She not only saves Aeneas; but she also saves Helen. Both of these individuals are beloved of Venus and both are fated to survive the destruction of Troy; Aeneas to journey to Italy and establish a city; Helen is to return to her original husband Menelaus and live out her mortal days in Sparta. Virgil needs to abide by these mythical traditions in order for his epic poem to fit alongside those of Homer's credibly.

Venus ensures that Aeneas can escape from danger and return back to his family in order to lead them to safety. She needs to console her son in this traumatic time. Venus makes clear that the destruction of Troy is predestined and nothing can stop it. Not even the gods. Aeneas now sees this truth and Virgil illustrates this realisation with the detailed simile of a tree being felled in Book Two lines 623-633.

Prophetic warnings in Book Two

There are several prophetic messages contained in Book Two;

- **Laocoon** tries to warn the Trojans about the dangers of the Wooden Horse – but his fate is to be killed by serpents sent by Athena before he can convince them.

- **Hector** warns Aeneas that Troy had been overrun, so he was entrusted with the household gods, including Vesta, Goddess of the Hearth, who will come to hold a position of great importance in the Roman Forum.

- **Venus** directs Aeneas to escape, and she makes it clear that the gods are behind the overthrow of Troy. There is no hope of saving it, so Venus gives Aeneas safe passage out of the battle.

- **Iulus** An omen of a flame on the head of Aeneas' son and then another of a thunderbolt and a shooting star from Jupiter strengthen Aeneas' conviction that the only possible course of action is to leave Troy.

- **Creusa** The ghost of Aeneas' first wife, Creusa, tells Aeneas that he must sail to Italy (called Hesperia) to the River Thybris (Tiber) where he will find a new wife, who has been chosen by the gods. This is an important early taste of his future destiny.

Disguise and recognition in Book One

The Trojan elder Ilioneus makes his sole appearance into the *Aeneid* at this point. Ilioneus appeals to Queen Dido for sanctuary for the Trojans and asks for assistance. Ilioneus does not know whether Aeneas is alive or dead but his lengthy speech (lines 520-560) establishes;

- Who the Trojans are

- The Trojans are not a threat to Carthage

- The Trojans are seeking Italy

- The Trojan leader is Aeneas but he is missing in the storm

- The Trojans need help

Dido offers assistance to the Trojans and it is now time for Virgil to reveal the presence of Aeneas.

Task: Disguise and recognition in Books One and Two

Write a response to the following question;

To what extent do you agree with the view that disguise and recognition is the most important theme in Books One and Two?;

You should aim to:

- *Explore episodes in Book One and Two were disguise and recognition are important.*
- *Evaluate the importance of these episodes in relation to other questions.*

PART FOUR: Books Four to Six of the *Aeneid*

PART FOUR

4.1: Book Four: The tragedy of Dido

4.2: Morality, women and family in Book Four

4.3 Book Five: The Funeral Games

4.4 Book Six: Aeneas and the Underworld

4.5 Book Six: Aeneas and Rome

4.1: Book Four: The tragedy of Dido

This section will help you to;

- *Understand the content of Book Four of the Aeneid*

- *Understand the events and structure of Book Four*

- *Continue to explore the characters of Dido*

- *Continue to explore the importance of Carthage to the development of the Roman Empire*

Introduction

In Book Four Virgil focuses the attention of his audience on the story of Queen Dido of Carthage. If in Books One through Three Virgil has been influenced by the epic poetry of Homer, then Book Four is more in the form of a Greek Tragedy.

Task: Rapid comprehension questions

a) In conversation with Dido, what does Anna tell her sister about why she thinks the Trojans have arrived in Carthage?

b) Does Anna support Dido's love for Aeneas?

c) What does Anna suggest Dido should do?

d) How does Dido die?

Synopsis

Book Four begins with a discussion between Dido and her sister Anna. Dido admits to Anna that she is obsessed with Aeneas. Not since Dido lost her husband Sychaeus has Dido felt this way about a man. Anna is sympathetic. Dido has rejected the kings and princes of Libya and Tyre and on a more practical level, an alliance with Aeneas and his Trojans will help to keep Carthage safe from North African tribes such as the Gaetulians and Numidians; these tribes were historical tribes of North Africa and possessed a fearsome warrior reputation. Having reached this decision to try to persuade Aeneas to stay with her, Dido makes a tour of the religious sanctuaries of Carthage in order to illicit the support of the Gods.

In order to persuade Aeneas to remain in Carthage, Dido takes Aeneas on a tour of the city, demonstrating its wealth and regularly feasting. This obsession with the Trojan has led to Dido no longer providing the city with the leadership it needs. Building projects come to a halt and the people cease to work or train and become idle.

Virgil then shifts the scene from Carthage to the Goddesses Juno and Venus. Juno seeks Venus' help. They should work together to bring the Trojans and Carthaginians together in an alliance. Juno hopes this way to prevent the Trojans from reaching Italy, and also to save Carthage from future destruction by the Romans. Venus however is not deceived and knows that Jupiter has already pronounced that the Trojans are destined to reach Italy.

Despite Venus' concerns the two goddesses arrange for Dido and Aeneas to be forced together into a form of marriage. A hunt is arranged and Virgil describes the attendants carrying hunting spears and nets, Dido is richly attired in Phoenician clothes – purple dyed and embossed with gold. Aeneas also is richly clothed and his son Ascanius (Iulus) is riding carefree amongst herds of deer and goats. He ignores these creatures and seeks more dangerous prey.

A storm hits and the hunting party is scattered. Dido and Aeneas take shelter in the cave and the pair consummates their passionate desire. Dido deludes herself that she and Aeneas are now married and for a time, Aeneas seems to go along with this view. The news of this 'marriage' is not well received however and Virgil describes how the personification of Rumour wreaks havoc in Carthage and neighbouring areas.

Rumour reaches Iarbus, a Libyan king. Iarbus is the son of Jupiter and is angered that his own marriage proposal to Dido was rejected, but Aeneas (the son of a lesser God to his eyes) has been successful. He protests to his father.

Jupiter responds to Iarbus' prayer and sends Mercury to tell Aeneas that Carthage and Dido are not his destiny, he must leave. Mercury finds Aeneas working on a building project in Carthage; he is dressed like a Carthaginian princeling and seems to be content to remain in Carthage with Dido. When Mercury orders Aeneas to continue his journey to Italy, Aeneas is horrified when he realises that he is defying the will of the Gods and putting his own needs before the needs of his Trojan people. He at once plans to leave Carthage and calls on the Trojans to prepare the fleet.

Dido learns of Aeneas' preparations and angrily confronts Aeneas. Dido begs Aeneas to stay and reminds him of their marriage. This marriage has damaged both of their reputations among the Carthaginians and their neighbours. Aeneas replies that they were never married and reminds Dido that his first responsibility is to the Trojans and achieving their destiny of reaching Italy;

'It is not by my own will that I still search for Italy'

Virgil. *Aeneid* IV.361

This response does not appease Dido. She calls Aeneas a traitor and reminds him of all the assistance she has given him and the Trojans.

As Aeneas and the Trojans prepare to leave, Dido sends Anna to appeal to Aeneas for one final time; but Aeneas is deaf to Anna's appeal. In despair and realising that her reputation has been ruined, Dido prepares herself for death. Dido keeps her plans secret but instructs her sister to build a pyre on which she says she will burn all the memories of Aeneas.

Aeneas prepares to set sail and is hastened in his departure by another visitation by Mercury. Dido, seeing that the Trojan fleet has departed now decides on death. She laments her loss of Aeneas and predicts that this abandonment will cause eternal hatred between Carthage and the Trojans. She also prays that the Trojans encounter war and bloodshed once they reach Italy. Dido grabs a Trojan sword and leaps onto the pyre and with a final curse for the Trojans, Dido stabs herself and dies in the embrace of her sister, her spirit released at last by Juno who feels pity for the queen.

Task: Dido's prayer

Read Virgil Aeneid IV.622-629

What is the content of this prayer?

Why might a Roman reader find this prayer a poignant one?

How effective do you think is the language used by Virgil in this prayer?

Dido and Carthage

Whilst Virgil makes reference to other epic poems throughout the *Aeneid*, he also makes a few original inventions of his own. The Aeneas-Dido romance was one of the original innovations by Virgil.

The city of Carthage was re-established by Augustus in the 20s BC as a Roman colony. With Dido and Aeneas being presented by Virgil as the respective founders of Rome and Carthage, Virgil describes in Book One the foundation of Carthage. In a nice twist (I.142-149) Virgil has Aeneas witness this foundation. When we consider that Virgil knew that Augustus had ordered the reconstruction of Carthage he is also bringing an end to the enmity between Rome and Carthage which is first caused by the breach between Dido and Aeneas and is heralded by Dido's prediction.

Virgil presents his readers with a new twist to the relationship between the cities; a shared enmity caused by a failed relationship. For the Roman audiences of Book Four they are aware that a great conflict will occur between Rome and Carthage.

Virgil provides his audience with a *'What if'?* Scenario; what would have happened to Rome, history and the world if Aeneas had chosen to never leave Africa?

Dido is not Roman; however in a reversal of character traits in Book Four, Dido is pious, charitable, honest and hardworking. She is given by Virgil the Roman characteristics that are normally attributed to Aeneas. In Book Four on the other hand, the Trojans are the ones presented as impious and deceitful by Dido (IV.305-310).

Aeneas and Dido Mosaic

4.2: Morality, women and family in Book Four

This section will help you to;

- To read the Aeneid Book Four

- To analyse further the character of Dido

- To examine the historical and political background to Book Four

- To consider the moral undertones of Book Four

Introduction

This section focuses on the *Aeneid* Book Four, and on moral values and the roles of family and women in Virgil.

The sadness and difficulty of the situation that Virgil has placed Aeneas and Dido in (Aeneas must leave her for Italy and his future destined bride) allows Virgil to visit that familiar motif, the wronged lover and to squeeze all the *pathos* he possibly can from the scenario. Thus, Dido does not accept Aeneas' need to leave with grace. Instead, she argues powerfully, using a variety of reasons as to why he should stay.

> **Task: Presentation of character: Dido**
>
> *Consider again the character and behaviour of Dido in Book Four.*
>
> *Do you sympathise with her?*
>
> *Is it difficult to understand Aeneas' actions here, or do you think that what he does is justified?*

Dido

Dido is the principal character in Book Four. So far in the *Aeneid*, Dido has been the compliant audience to Aeneas' stories of suffering and adventure as is recounted in Books Three and Four, and has fallen even more deeply in love with Aeneas.

However, Dido's passion for Aeneas is certainly not straight-forward. Dido is a conflicted woman; Dido is a widow, and has already sworn her fidelity to her first husband Sychaeus, promising never to marry again.

The status of the *univira* or *'one man-woman'* had much social capital with the Roman elite, who idealised the woman who only married once and stayed faithful to the memory of her partner should she outlive him. However, Augustus issued new laws that encouraged women to re-marry and to bear children.

Virgil has Dido torn between the moral propriety of being a *univira* and between the advice of her sister Anna, who seems to speak from a common-sense, pragmatic approach. In effect, Anna advises Dido to pursue Aeneas. Her advice is that since Dido is still young, she shouldn't waste her life in perpetual mourning.

Neither Dido nor Anna seems to have understood the key motivational drive in Aeneas' life, which is not love and marriage, but his *duty* towards his people and *destiny*. Aeneas *must* found Rome. Aeneas cannot get avoid this fact, no matter what his own personal desires are. As such Aeneas cannot be permitted to have a happy life with Dido in Carthage.

So, Dido is a character worthy of a Greek tragedy caught between two opposing and irreconcilable forces: her god-inspired love for Aeneas and the god-driven destiny of Aeneas, which must propel him towards Italy.

The Hunt and the Cave

How much Dido misunderstands Aeneas is the depicted in the hunt scene. The goddesses Juno and Venus; respectively the goddesses of marriage and sexual love and desire concoct a plan to 'set up' Dido and Aeneas.

The imagery is clear: just as hunted animals are prey, so are Aeneas and Dido. In the cave, there are many features of a typical Roman wedding, which would have been easily recognised by a Roman audience, and approved by Augustus, who was keen to promote the institution of marriage. There are hymns and torches are lit, whilst the ceremony is presided over by the goddess of marriage herself, Juno.

The Romans actually had different types of marriage, which included different levels of commitment or with different levels of legal binding.

Task: Should he stay or should he go?

Make a list of the reasons that Dido presents to Aeneas as to why he should stay.

- *Which reasons do you think are effective ones?*

- *Which reasons do you think are least effective?*

Book Four as a Greek Tragedy

From reading the *Aeneid* it is clear that Virgil had a good knowledge of, and possibly a passion for, Greek Tragedy. Book Four could be viewed as homage to a Greek Tragedy. It has been argued that Book Four bears some resemblance to Euripides' play *Medea*.

Virgil was aware that any good Geek Tragedy required the following features;

- A lead Tragic figure

- A Supporting character sympathetic to the lead character

- An Agon (a set debate or trial)

- Hamartia (fatal law)

- Peripeteia (reversal of circumstance or change in fortune)

- A Kommos (a lament)

- Anagnorisis (recognition of disaster)

Task: Book Four as a Tragedy

Virgil was aware that any good Geek Tragedy required the following features;

- *A lead Tragic figure*

- *A Supporting character sympathetic to the lead character*

- *An Agon (a set debate or trial)*

- *Hamartia (a term which means a fatal law or fault in the tragic figure)*

- *Peripeteia (a term which means a reversal of circumstance or change in fortune)*

- *A Kommos (a lament)*

- *Anagnorisis (recognition of the situation in which the tragic figure finds themselves in)*

Using the above list – read Book Four once more and try to identify these features of Greek Tragedy in Book Four.

Marriage in Rome

Marriage in Roman society was primarily enacted in order for procreation of children. But there were several kinds of marriage available. Marriage had to be between Roman citizens or between those who had the right of marriage (*conubrium*) and the minimum marriageable age for males was fourteen and females was twelve.

A formal marriage was recognised by the ceremonies of *confarreatio* and *coemptio* (respectively sharing of tasting spelt grain and a pretend sale of the bride to the husband). However a marriage could also be recognised through *usus* – a year of cohabitation of the man and woman which created a lasting union (*affectio maritali*).

If she had any, a wife could either surrender control of her property to her husband or keep it for herself. To transfer the control of the wives' property to her husband was to have a marriage with *manus*. However, this was not mandatory.

Divorce was a relatively simple matter – if you were the husband. No formal notice was required to divorce a wife, unless the wife had bought property into the relationship which had been transferred in *manus*. In this case, it was expected that the husband would return the property in question before the divorce could take place. The question of whether this 'marriage' in the cave is really a genuine one is crucial. Clearly, there could be some room for misunderstanding since there were different types of marriage. In this way a note of doubt creeps into the proceedings: Dido clearly harbours some guilt over what she has done, and the outcome of her relationship with Aeneas is rumour and discord.

Mercury's message to Aeneas is designed to force him to leave behind the mess that has been created in Africa by this 'marriage'. Aeneas is not meant to be in Carthage when there is a destiny to achieve. Besides her passion and intense emotional nature, Dido is unable to understand Aeneas' destiny.

Reasons Dido presents include;

- Aeneas should wait for the good weather rather than leave immediately.

- Aeneas loves her; so why is he leaving?

- Dido will die if Aeneas does not stay with her.

- They are married (or are they?)

- Dido has sacrificed her good reputation for the sake of this relationship.

- Aeneas, as a guest, should behave courteously.

- Dido will be alone and in danger if Aeneas leaves since she has many enemies.

- Dido does not even have a child by him, which would at least provide her with some comfort.

Dido reproaches, blames and recriminates Aeneas as well as pleading with him to stay in a scenario of emotional intensity. The reasons that Dido presents are very far from logical or unemotional statement of her case, quite the opposite.

Aeneas certainly does not come across all that well in Book Four. Aeneas' arguments in response to Dido's seem to be almost exactly what she does not want to hear. Predictably, these excuses serve only to enrage and enflame Dido's already heightened emotional state. The request that Dido should be happy for him with his new kingdom and new bride is particularly cold and calculating. He has been ordered by fate and the Gods and must obey; Dido's love for him does not matter at all.

In Aeneas' defence, however, he has made it very clear in his re-telling of the fall of Troy how he has been singled out by the gods for a destiny which has the power to overpower any and all obstacles. It is just Dido's tragedy that she only realises the full truth of this, too late.

Preventing war through marriage: The Treaty of Brundisium

In 40BC the Triumvirs Octavian, Lepidus and Antonius arranged a meeting at Brundisium that renewed the alliance between them and averted a new civil war for a time. In return for an arranged marriage, Antonius was confirmed as ruler of the Eastern provinces, Octavian as ruler of most of the Western provinces and Lepidus kept control of Africa, but only for a short time.

Octavia

Octavia was Augustus' sister. She was married several times. First of all to Claudius Marcellus who died in 40BC. Despite this, Octavia was soon married to Antony in order to seal the treaty of Brundisium.

In 37BC Octavia helped to renew a pact between Antony and Octavian, but in 35BC Octavia was not permitted to join Antony (on his orders) in the East. Octavia returned to Rome and was officially divorced by Antony in 32BC. This divorce was used by Octavian to great propaganda effect and helped him to discredit Antony at Rome. After Antony and Cleopatra committed suicide after the debacle at Actium in 31BC, Octavia elected to raise Antony's children by his other wives.

Octavia was praised in Rome as an ideal Roman matron and died in 11BC.

Political marriages under Augustus

Roman women from elite families were often treated as chess-pieces to be moved around in suitable alliances, with little, if any thought for the personal wishes of those women (who did not, of course, have equal rights to men) or for matters of love or desire.

Two notorious casualties of this in Augustus' own family were Tiberius, his adopted son, who was forced to divorce a woman he loved greatly in order to marry Augustus' only biological daughter

Julia. Julia herself had three political marriages. Julia was eventually banished in disgrace for sexual immorality by her own father, as a sad consequence of his unbending attitude to Rome, the role of women and a strict code of sexual morality.

In this context, divorce for political reasons was acceptable (as was divorce because of a wife's infertility, since securing a male heir was vital) and it would have been viewed as noble to put aside political duties for love. Augustus' close friend and ally Vipsanius Agrippa married three times with each marriage linking him more closely to Augustus;

- 37BC Caecilia Attica (resulting in two daughters)

- 28BC Marcella (Augustus' niece and resulted in a daughter)

- 21BC Julia (Augustus' daughter and resulted in three sons and two daughters)

Had Aeneas chosen to stay in Carthage with Dido, he would have been choosing love rather than political duty. This was not a virtuous decision to the Romans, and not only that but he would have been rejecting his *pietas* and *fides* (the love of the gods and the great responsibility they have given him to found Rome). Aeneas therefore has no choice: he must leave Dido.

Antonius and Cleopatra

The relationship between Dido and Aeneas works well purely as drama on its own merits, but for a contemporary Roman reader there would have been an obvious historical connection to be made; the relationship of Antonius and Cleopatra.

After Fulvia died, Antonius married again. His second wife was Octavia, Augustus' sister. She was portrayed as a model of the ideal Roman *matrona* (matron, or married older woman). Octavia appears to have been loyal, loving, dutiful, and faithful.

She ran a well-managed household for Antonius. This was the type of social role for women that Augustus was keen to promote, and so Antonius's tempestuous affair with the exotic and mysterious Queen of Egypt Cleopatra represented to Augustus a betrayal on many levels. Not only was it a betrayal of Augustus and a rejection of the delicate political alliance between the pair, it also represented a betrayal of the 'family values' Augustus was keen to promote and also a betrayal of Rome, since Cleopatra represented the power of Egypt, potentially a second 'Carthage'.

Antonius married Cleopatra whilst on duty in the East and they had several children together. These children would certainly not have been recognised in Rome, where Antonius' legal wife was still Octavia.

The parallel to Dido is now clearer: Dido represents the exotic, beautiful but ultimately dangerous foreign wife, who rules a foreign kingdom with huge wealth and resources which was a potential threat to Rome. Aeneas, like Antonius, faces a choice; to put the interests of his people first or his own desires. Augustus wanted people to think that Antonius had placed his own desires first; to the resultant danger to Rome and it is this danger that Aeneas narrowly avoids.

A modern audience may find Dido a highly sympathetic character, it is important to remember that this contrasts with the 'Roman' audience. Political and dynastic marriages such as that of Octavia and Antonius were common, and this one was designed to seal the treaty of Brundisium between the two men and maintain the fragile peace that it marked. To break the treaty meant to break this peace and declare war.

Task: Written Response

Write a response to the following question;

'To what extent does Virgil try to present Dido and Aeneas as a parallel to Antony and Cleopatra?'

Consider if there is anything which these couples have in common, or are they completely divided by their differences?

4.3 Book Five: The Funeral Games

This section will help you to;

- *Understand the events and structure of Book Five*

- *Consider the cultural and mythical relationships between Troy, Rome and Sicily*

- *To consider the similarities and differences between Virgil and Homer.*

- *Explore the role and portrayal of women in Book Five*

Introduction

Book Five is not a set text for study at A level. Nevertheless, this topic explores the content, language and structure of this part of the *Aeneid*.

Book Five Synopsis

Book Five should be considered a continuation of Book Four. The Trojans have set sail and, leaving Carthage, are heading towards Italy. However they are faced with uncertain weather and the Trojans decide to head to Sicily instead. Aeneas makes the decision to travel to the city of Eryx, where King Acestes rules. Acestes is of Trojan blood and welcomes their arrival.

Since it has been a year since Anchises has died, Aeneas now calls for funeral games in honour of his father. Aeneas prays to his father and witnesses the sign of a snake that emerges from Anchises' tomb in order to taste the offerings, before retiring back.

The funeral games begin with a race between four ships from the fleet. Virgil vividly describes this race in a lengthy section; he describes the tension of the race, the calls and taunts of the competitive captains and the comedy of laggard helmsmen being thrown overboard.

The second contest is a foot race in which Trojans and Sicilians compete. Again there are mishaps described. One runner slips in the dung and gore of a sacrificed animal whilst leading the race.

The third contest is a boxing match between a Trojan warrior and a local veteran from Eryx. The fight is ferocious and Aeneas has to intervene before the boxers end up killing each other. The elder of the pair, Entellus from Eyrx kills an ox with a single punch in order to demonstrate his true prowess; having done so Entellus retires from boxing for good.

The fourth competition is an archery contest. When King Acestes arrow is transformed by the gods and Aeneas is quick to honour the King of Eryx after witnessing this sign.

The games are now turned into a performance by the young Trojans who parade their horses and show off their equestrian skills before fighting a mock battle. Ascanius leads the Trojan youth in this performance and here Virgil is recounting one of the highlights of Imperial Roman pomp and splendour (the Trojan Games).

The games are noticed by the goddess Juno and she decides to intervene. Juno sends the messenger goddess Iris is sent to cause chaos. Iris visits the Trojan women and disguises herself as one of them before convincing them to burn the ships. Do this and the Trojans will have to settle in Sicily.

Madness takes possession of the women and they try to carry out their arson attack. The Trojan men however see what is occurring and led by Aeneas and his son Ascanius they rush to the scene. The women still possessed, flee to the hills and forests.

The ships are saved by the intervention of the god Jupiter. A storm and a downpour is sent and douses the ships. Four of the vessels are lost though. Aeneas now worries. Perhaps the Trojans should settle in Sicily, however, Aeneas is visited by the ghost of his father Anchises who calls on Aeneas to visit him in the Underworld.

The decision is made to leave the women and children in Sicily and take only warriors to Italy. With the help of the gods the Trojans set sail for Italy. The Trojans are destined to arrive safely, all but the helmsman Palinurus who is taken by the gods and falls overboard to his death.

Sicily, Eyrx and Venus

In the final stages of the First Punic War (264-246BC), the city of Eyrx was one of the battlegrounds between the Romans and the Carthaginians. At the beginning of the First Punic War the Carthaginians held Eryx, but in 248BC the Romans captured the city. The Carthaginians managed to attack and retake most of the city by storm, but failed to capture a Roman garrison in the sanctuary, which held out until the end of the war. In the sanctuary of Eyrx was a temple dedicated to the Carthaginian Goddess Astarte. Historically also the inhabitants of Eryx were Elymians – who had their own traditions that they had journeyed to Sicily from Troy.

After the war ended the sanctuary was rededicated to the Roman Goddess Venus. During the Second Punic War, with the Carthaginian armies of Hannibal occupying much of Italy and war across Sicily, in 215BC the Romans built a new temple in Rome; the temple of Venus Erycina which mirrored the cult based in Eryx. The Romans then had made efforts to appropriate the cultural and historical traditions of the city of Eryx - the stout resistance of the Roman garrison at Eryx and the links to mythical Troy.

Task: Comparing Virgil and Homer

Read Book Five of the Aeneid and Book Eight of the Odyssey and also book Twenty Three of the Iliad.

What is similar between these texts and what is different?

Virgil and Homer

The funeral games to commemorate Anchises' death are an echo of those in the *Odyssey* in Book Eight as well as the funeral games of Patroclus in the *Iliad in Book* Twenty Three.

Homer has chariot races. Virgil has come up with a different race; the race at sea between warships. This is an attempt to be even more exciting than Homer, and as we might expect, the race is full of the tension and danger that Homer created in the *Iliad* Book Twenty Three. Yet again, the link is made between the Trojan warriors and Virgil's contemporary Romans, which emphasises Virgil's theme of the destiny of Rome and his writing of the glories of the Roman past.

Task: Women in the Aeneid

Write a response to the following question;

How far do agree with the view that the rebellion of the women in Book Five adds to the narrative?

Write three/four paragraphs that support and/or challenge this view

---

Women in Rome

Women were viewed by Roman men as inferior because they were thought to be weak physically and mentally inferior also. Therefore having established this premise the Roman men determined that women should be constantly looked after. Women were subject to the rule of their father or husband, or if neither of these were available then a brother or male relative or guardian. However under Augustus, laws were passed that women could become independent if they had managed to raise more than three children to adulthood.

The presentation of Women in Book Five

While the men enjoy the proper honouring of Anchises with noble games, the women have been left behind. They have not been idle however. Under the influence of the Goddess Iris they have been fomenting rebellion while left to their own devices.

A common stereotype to both the Greek and Roman mind (according to several writers) was that unsupervised women would misbehave and potential cause disaster.

This is well illustrated in Greek Tragedy. In Euripides' *Bacchae*, females, possessed by the madness of Dionysius are left alone on the mountainsides. These women, including the mother and aunts of King Pentheus deliberately leave the control of their men and city and are manipulated into destroying the king of Thebes Pentheus.

Uncontrolled women led men to fear that they were only one small step away from madness, uncontrollable passion, lust, rage, revenge and even murder.

Virgil is no different: without the men to calm them down, the grief stricken women have fallen under the influence of a malign goddess and become uncontrollable. The result is the fire almost destroys the Trojan ships and their quest, for without ships how may they reach Italy?

Just as fire once destroyed Troy, the women's rebellion in Book Five enables Aeneas to reflect on the nature of fortune, which gives him some peace of mind, and this in turn paves the way for Aeneas' dream of his dead father Anchises who tells him that he must visit the Underworld. This directs the plot forward and to the events of Book Six.

4.4 Book Six: Aeneas and the Underworld

This section will help you to;

• *Understand the events and structure of Book Six*

• *Continue to explore the character of Aeneas*

• *Explore and revisit other characters in Book Six*

• *Understand the mythical and historical references in Book Six*

• *Understand the role and function of the Sibyl in the Aeneid and in the Roman World*

Introduction

This section will help you to understand book six of the *Aeneid*. In Book Six Aeneas reaches Italy, visits the city of Cumae and enters the Underworld. Book Six is a very important book for students and one you should analyse deeply.

Take Note

It is also recommended that you read Homer's Odyssey Book Eleven in order to better understand the parallels between Homer and Virgil.

Task: Book Six Comprehension Questions

Try to answer without looking at the text

a) What does the Sibyl prophesise for Aeneas and the Trojans once they reach land?

b) What is the name of the dead comrade Aeneas must bury before entering the Underworld?

Book Six synopsis

The Trojans reach the Greek city of Cumae in Italy and land. As the Trojans make camp Aeneas goes up to Apollo's sanctuary on the acropolis in order to visit the Sibyl. The Sibyl, named Deiphobe, requests that Aeneas perform a sacrifice and a prayer to Apollo, which are duly carried out. The Sibyl predicts that a war will soon break out between the Trojans and the Latins; the reason for this war is revealed; an argument over a bride will cause this war.

Aeneas now requests that he be allowed to enter the Underworld. In order to do this the Sibyl instructs Aeneas to first of all retrieve a golden bough from a tree sacred to the Goddess Prosperina. Secondly he must also recover the body of the Trojan Misenus who was lost and bury him also.

The corpse of Misenus is recovered and Aeneas is guided by doves sent by his mother Venus to the sacred tree were he retrieves the golden bough. The burial of Misenus takes place on a hill and this mountain is now named Mount Misenus for posterity in honour of the dead Trojan.

Aeneas now begins his journey into the Underworld. He is accompanied by the Sibyl who acts as his guide. Aeneas performs a sacrifice before proceeding and Virgil now describes the sights Aeneas witnesses. Aeneas sees monsters and gods of the Underworld in the halls of the dead before reaching the river Acheron (also known in Greek myth as the river Styx). Here Aeneas speaks to his dead helmsman Palinurnus, who died at the end of Book Five. Aeneas persuades the God of this river, the ferryman Charon, to let him cross and he and the Sibyl enter the Underworld proper.

Now in the Underworld Aeneas sees monsters and dead heroes from the mythical past – including the multi-headed dog of the Underworld Cerberus, King Minos and also women from Greek myth (some of the stories of these women are recounted in Greek Tragedy). Aeneas also sees Dido and tries to speak to her; he feared, but did not know that she was dead. Dido however is now reunited with her husband Sychaeus in the Underworld. Next, Aeneas meets Greek and Trojan warriors who were killed in the war. Aeneas speaks to Deiphobus, a son of Priam who recounts to Aeneas the circumstances of his death and his betrayal by Helen. Aeneas also sees the punishment of evil doers and sinners.

Aeneas then reaches the spirit of his dead father Anchises. Anchises points out to Aeneas the future of the Trojan race and the spirits of those future Romans that will achieve greatness. Virgil presents his readers with a parade of these exalted Romans. Having seen the future destiny of the Trojans in Italy and the greatness of the city that his descendants will establish, Aeneas departs the Underworld.

The city of Cumae

Cumae was a city founded by Greek colonists from the island of Euboea around 740BC. Cumae was one of the first Greek colonies on the mainland of Italy and was established after the foundation of Rome. After a period of initial conflict between Rome and Cumae, Cumae remained a consistently loyal city to Rome during the Punic Wars and increasingly became 'Latinised'; adopting Latin as the cities' principal language around 180BC. Citizens of Cumae became eligible for full Roman citizenship by the mid-2nd Century BC.

Under Augustus Cumae was granted full colonial status (its citizens becoming Roman citizens) and Augustus also commissioned grandiose building projects in the city including the restoration of the harbour and the acropolis.

More famously however, Cumae was home to a religious sanctuary dedicated to Apollo and tradition maintained that a Sibyl was resident in the sanctuary producing religious prophecies.

Aeneas is guided by the Sibyl, an important figure in Roman religion. This shows us Aeneas' submission to the rule of the gods (as represented by the Sibyl) reminding us of the fate and the destiny of the Romans.

What was a Sibyl?

A Sibyl was a prophetic woman. In Greek and Roman myth Sibyl was a priestess of Apollo who refused the amorous attention of the god. Apollo then punished the Sibyl by granting her prophetic powers but also immortality without eternal youth.

The Sibyl in antiquity was an office or title, not an individual. Throughout the ancient world there were prophetesses who produced future readings of events in verse and often cryptic. The Romans identified at least ten catalogues of prophecies produced by some of these Sibyls in various locations;

- Persia

- Libya

- Delphi

- Italian Cimmerian

- Erythrae

- Samos

- Cumae

- Hellespont

- Phrygia

- Tibur

Rome and the sibylline prophecies

Rome maintained an interest in Sibyls and their prophecies from at least the 5th century BC. The first collection of sibylline prophecies arrived in Rome during the reign of the King Tarquinius Priscus. The prophecies were consulted in times of danger to the state by order of the Senate and thought to provide a solution to the present crisis.

Among the first collection of prophecies that were gathered in Rome came Cumae and were consulted only an order of the Senate. The collection increased steadily and was housed in the temple of Capitoline Jupiter (a temple destroyed by fire in 83BC).

A new collection was gathered and Augustus transferred this collection to the temple of the Palatine Apollo. The last known consultation of the sibylline prophecies was in 363AD.

Task: Aeneas and Dido in Book Six

Read Virgil's Aeneid Book Six Lines 450-477

Write responses to the following questions;

a) *How typical is the way Dido is portrayed in this passage of the way she is portrayed elsewhere in the Aeneid?*

b) *Using this passage as a starting point, discuss whether Book Six of the Aeneid is more optimistic than pessimistic.*

Mythical references in Book Six

There are quite a few references to Greek and Roman mythology in Book Six, below is a selection of comments to help you understand these references.

Acheron – the River of Hades, perhaps better known as the River Styx. This river was used to create unbreakable oaths that even the gods had to stick to if they swore by the Styx.

Briareus – A Hundred handed monster that in Greek myth fought Zeus and almost defeated him. The other Olympians helped Zeus and Briareus was overcome and thrown into the Underworld.

Cerberus – The monstrous hound of the Underworld. Cerberus had three heads (but is often depicted in Greek and Roman art as having only two. Cerberus was at times leashed and dragged out of the Underworld by a variety of heroes, including Heracles.

Deiphobus – A Trojan hero. Son of Priam and brother to Hector and Paris. Deiphobus was in myth one of the great warriors of Troy and after Paris was killed he married Helen. Deiphobus and Helen lived together until the sack of Troy when Deiphobus was killed and mutilated.

Hecate – Goddess of witchcraft and magic as well as crossroads. Hecate is one of the many gods of the Underworld.

Minos – A son of Zeus and mythical king of Crete. The Greek Historian Thucydides considered Minos to be a historical figure who first ruled the seas of Greece through the might of his navy. In myth Minos prayed to Poseidon to give him a great bull to offer up in sacrifice. Poseidon obliged, but the bull was so great that Minos refused to sacrifice the animal. Poseidon took offence at this and so made Minos' wife Pasiphae fall in love with the animal. The result was the Minotaur, which was placed in a labyrinth. When Minos' son Androgeos was killed by the Athenians, Minos demanded a sacrifice; seven young men and women each year to be fed to the Minotaur. This continued until the hero Theseus volunteered to go, and with the help of Minos' daughter Ariadne entered the Minotaur and killed it.

Minos was later killed in Sicily and after his death was appointed to serve as a judge if men in the Underworld.

Orcus – A Roman God of the Underworld.

Orpheus – Son of Apollo and a Muse, Orpheus was a renowned singer in myth and associated with many mythical stories. In one when Orpheus' wife Eurydice died, Orpheus journeyed into the Underworld to bring her back. He sang and performed for the God Hades, who was moved to release Eurydice. All Orpheus had to do was leave the Underworld, followed by his wife, and not look back.

Orpheus failed to do this and looking back, lost Eurydice for ever trapped in the Underworld.

Phoebus – another name and epithet for the God Apollo.

Pollux – Pollux (in Greek myth also called Polydeuces) was the brother of the mortal hero Castor and the son of Zeus. Together, the pair were called the Dioscoûri and were also brothers of Helen. When Castor died just before the start of the Trojan War, Pollux demanded to share the fate of Castor, the Gods decided to let the pair share immortality, spending one day in the Underworld and the next amongst the Gods.

Proserpina – The Queen of the Underworld. In Greek her name is Persephone, but in Virgil considered to be the 'Juno of the Underworld'.

Triton – A Sea God and attendant of Neptune.

The parade of 'future Romans'.

The list of the descendants of Aeneas starts in mythology, with Aeneas' son, but ends with the real-life and contemporary of Virgil, Marcellus and so reinforces the bridge between the mythical world of Aeneas and the contemporary world of Rome.

There is some dramatic irony and also *pathos* in Anchises' pleas to Caesar and Pompey not to wage a civil war; as a Roman reader would know, this was a useless plea since the civil war had already happened. Civil war was devastating for Rome, and as Romans viewed it, stood in the way of Rome achieving the status she had by the time of Augustus. Anchises also reminds us that Rome's proper role is as the world ruler and lawmaker and should not be enticed away from this by Greek culture and art.

In a world of war and chaos, the role Augustus wanted to promote for Rome was that of peacekeeper. This peacekeeping role (the famous *pax Romana* which Augustus helped bring about) was only achieved with Roman military intervention, bloodshed and demonstrations of Roman Imperium over subjected peoples.

> **Task: The Parade of future Romans**
>
> *Write a timed response to the following question;*
>
> *"How far do you agree with the view that Virgil uses 'history' (or 'future' to Aeneas) to underline Rome's imperial destiny?"*
>
> *This task requires you to analyse both the parade of future Romans in the Aeneid and the Augustan period in which Virail is writina.*

In Book Six Virgil presents Aeneas with a vision of the future. The city that will be in time established is Rome and Aeneas needs to see what kind of great men will come from this city in order to motivate him to confront and overcome the trials and tribulations that will come. This list of future great men begins with Aeneas' unborn son and continues with the kings of Alba Longa before reaching the foundation of Rome and great Romans, leading on down to Virgil's present.

The Catalogue of Roman imperial destiny

In Book One.254-297 Jupiter pronounced the future imperial destiny of the Trojans to Venus and now Virgil returns to this destiny and expands the details of this future imperial destiny in a list, a catalogue of great Romans to Aeneas. The Roman reader of course was aware of this destiny from a very early stage; now it is revealed to Aeneas, the main protagonist of Virgil's story.

Below is a little more information on this parade of future Romans as depicted in Book VI lines 756-892, where applicable dates are included.

Silvius: Son of Aeneas and Lavinia as yet not born.

The Alban Kings: Procas, Capys, Numitor and Silvius Aeneas. Virgil gives us a list of names of early kings from Alba Longa. These kings were according to Roman tradition rulers between the years 1053-753BC.

Romulus: The mythical founder of Rome. Along with his twin brother Remus, the pair is credited with the foundation of Rome. According to Roman myth, Romulus and his brother Remus were the sons of the God Mars and Rhea Silvia, the daughter of the Alban king Numitor and also a Vestal Virgin.

In Roman myth the brothers were exposed as infants to be left to die in the wild, they were saved however when a she-wolf suckled them. A shepherd later found them and raised them as his own. The twins grew into brave warriors and when Numitor was deposed at Alba Longa, they restored him. Desiring to found their own city, the twins established Rome and split it evenly between them prohibiting one to trespass onto the territory of the other. Remus however crossed this boundary and Romulus killed him and took over the whole of the city. After forty years of rule Romulus vanished and according to Roman tradition was transformed into the god Quirinus.

Caesar: 100-44BC. Gaius Julius Caesar of the Julian Patrician family claimed descent from Venus and Aeneas. Caesar first became Consul (the senior magistracy of the Roman Republic in 60/59BC and was allocated command of Gaul from 58BC. He conquered much of what is now France and Belgium and led military campaigns into Germany and Britain. The result was increasing wealth and fame that caused resentment in Rome. In 49BC Caesar, threatened with prosecution, determined to march on Rome with a single legion and started the Civil War which lasted from 49-46BC. Caesar became Dictator during this period of emergency on and off from 49-44 and was assassinated in 44BC by a Senatorial conspiracy led by Brutus and Cassius who feared that Caesar aspired to become King.

Augustus: 63BC-14AD

Numa: A Sabine King of Rome who ruled 715-673BC. Originally from Cures and credited with establishing many of the laws of Rome.

Tullus: Full name is Tullius Hostilius. A Latin King of Rome, who ruled in the years 673-642BC. Tullus was renowned as a warrior.

Ancus: Full name is Ancus Marcius. A Sabine King of Rome who ruled 642-617BC.

L.Tarquinius Priscus: One of the Etruscan kings of Rome. He ruled from 616-579BC.

L. Tarquinius Superbus: An Etruscan king of Rome. He ruled from 534-510BC. Superbus was the last king of Rome and was ousted in a coup led by the Patrician members of the Senate.

Brutus: Full name is L. Junius Brutus. A member of the Senate and a member of a Patrician family. Brutus led the conspiracy that ousted the last king of Rome and became one of the first two Consuls in the newly established Republic. Later Brutus would execute his sons for treason when they tried to help Tarquinius Superbus return from exile.

Task: The allusion to Brutus, killer of Caesar.

Read the following line and the preceding lines referring to Brutus;

'He is not favoured by fortune, however future ages may judge these actions –

love of his country will prevail with him and his limitless desire for glory.'

Virgil. Aeneid VI.823-824

These lines, in context with the reference to the original Brutus is a reference to the Brutus that assassinated Caesar.

Explore the following points;

- *What do you think is Virgil's view of Brutus?*
- *Is he supportive or critical in these lines?*
- *Why does he include these lines at all?*

Decii: This refers to two Romans. A Father and a son both with the name of P.Decius Mus. According to Roman tradition, these Romans both chose to kill themselves in sacrifice in order to achieve victories for Rome.

Drusi: A brief reference to the family of Augustus' wife Livia. Augustus' successor and adopted son, Tiberius was the son of Livia by her first husband.

Torquatus: Full name is T.Manlius Torquatus who lived in the 4th century BC. Torquatus was a general who fought against Gallic tribes in 361BC and in 340BC he led Roman armies against Latin cities that opposed Rome. Torquatus also executed his own son for the crime of breaking ranks in battle in order to seek personal glory in single combat against an enemy champion.

Camillus: Full name is M.Furius Camillus. Camillus is credited with recovering gold in 390BC given to the Gallic tribes that captured Rome. This seems to have been included as an oblique reference to Augustus. In 20BC Augustus succeeded in negotiating the return of Roman legionary standards that had been captured by the Parthian Empire in 53BC when a Roman army led by Crassus was destroyed.

Task: Caesar and Pompey

Read the lines referring to the 'The Spirits in Gleaming Armour' VI.826-834

These spirits are generally thought to indicate Caesar and Pompey.

What language does Virgil use in this part of book six?

What do you think Virgil is trying to say in these lines?

Mummius: Full name is Lucius Mummius. In 146BC Mummuius led a Roman army that sacked the Greek city of Corinth and clearly demonstrated to the other cities of Greece that power now lay with Rome.

Paullus: Full name is L.Aemilius Paullus. In 168BC Paullus led a Roman army against the kingdom of Macedonia achieving total victory at the battle of Pydna in that year. The Macedonian king Perseus was killed and Macedonia became a Roman province.

Cato: Full name M.Porcius Cato (Cato the Elder) lived from 234-149BC. Cato was an arch conservative Roman senator and considered to be the bulwark of Roman virtue and tradition.

Cossus: Full name A.Cornelius Cossus. In 246BC Cossus achieved the distinction of killing an enemy leader in single combat and received the award of the *Spolia Opima*.

Gracchi: Refers to two Roman politicians from the Gracchi family. T.Sempronius Gracchus (died in 133BC) and his brother G.Sempronius Gracchus (died in 121BC). Both Gracchi tried to bring about land and other reforms through the use of the office of Tribune in the face of opposition from more conservative members of the Roman Senate.

Scipios: An illustrious Roman Senatorial family. Virgil refers to two Scipios in particular; Africanus Maior, who conquered Spain during the Second Punic War, before invading Africa and defeating Hannibal at the battle of Zama in 202BC. Africanus Minor led the Roman army that captured and destroyed the city of Carthage in the Third Punic War in 146BC.

Fabricius: Full name G.Fabricius Luscinus was a leading Roman that refused to be bribed by Pyrrhus in the years 280-279BC.

Serranus: Full name is G.Atilius Regulus was a Roman General during the First Punic War. As Consul in 257BC he led an army that invaded Africa and defeated in battle, was captured. Regulus agreed to return to Rome with Carthaginian demands for peace; if he failed he agreed that his life would be forfeit. Failing to achieve peace, Regulus kept his promise and returned to Carthage to be executed. Serranus refers to the cereal crop he was planting when he was called to office as Consul.

Fabii: Refers to Q.Fabius Maximus nicknamed *'Cunctator'* (The delayer). During the Second Punic War, Cunctator achieved his nickname by avoiding battle against Hannibal (who had trounced several Roman armies). This strategy was widely criticised at first, but prevented Hannibal from achieving total victory and allowed Rome to recover to eventual victory.

Marcellus (I): Full name is M.Claudius Marcellus. A Roman General in the Second Punic War. Before the war, Marcellus was the last Roman to achieve the Spolia Opima in 232BC. He is credited with keeping Hannibal contained in a corner of Italy and also conquering the city of Syracuse, which had sided with the Carthaginians.

Marcellus(II): Full name is identical to the Marcellus above. The son of Octavia and (in 25BC) adopted son and heir of Augustus. Born in 42BC he died in 23BC. Marcellus was married to Augustus' daughter Julia and granted extraordinary political powers similar to Augustus' own in 24BC. Marcellus was probably intended to be Augustus' recognised heir.

Aeneas and Anchises and future destiny of Rome

In Book Six the ghost of Anchises gives Aeneas a tour of future Romans in the Underworld. He also gives Aeneas some advice;

"Others, I do not doubt it, will beat bronze into figures more softly. Others will draw living likenesses out of marble. Others will plead cases better or describe with their rod the course of stars across the sky and predict their risings.

Your task, Roman, and do not forget it, will be to govern the peoples of the world in your empire. These will be your arts – and to impose a settled pattern upon peace, to pardon the defeated and war down the proud".

Virgil. *Aeneid VI.848-853*

What Virgil is having Anchises say here is that other countries and people may be better at arts, science, crafts and even law, but what Rome will do better than anyone else is to impose order and imperium on the cities and peoples of the world. Rome's art form then is to rule.

4.5 Book Six: Aeneas and Rome

This section will help you to;

• *Explore similarities and differences between Homer and Virgil*

• *Continue to explore the character of Aeneas*

• *To consider Aeneas' role in Rome's imperial destiny*

• *To explore the moral values implicit in Book Six*

Introduction

This topic focuses on the *Aeneid* Book Six and the role of Aeneas in Rome's imperial destiny as well as on moral values. However, Virgil's particular aims in Book Six extend to include the aims of the *Aeneid* overall. For example, Virgil shows us the grand sweep of Roman history (in Aeneas' future but of course in a contemporary audience's past) which reminds us of Aeneas' role in Rome's imperial destiny. For Aeneas as a character, this vision of his descendants' greatness acts as a pick-me-up after his despondency of feeling that he is getting nowhere.

Aeneas' melancholy has already been revealed when he is confronted with the foundations of the city of Carthage, so now this personal vision of the future generations that will create Rome provides him with his own inspiration. Finally, Virgil does not miss the opportunity to exercise his poetic imagination on all the features of the Underworld, and to include some deeper or philosophical thinking on the nature of life.

Similarities between Book Six of the *Aeneid* and the *Odyssey*

Book Six marks an important stage in the *Aeneid*, marking as it does the half-way point in much the same way as did Book Twelve and Thirteen of the *Odyssey*,. In these books Homer marked the transition from the 'fantasy-world' of Odysseus' travels to the 'real-life' problem he faces in defeating the suitors on Ithaca. The similarities between Aeneas' visit to the Underworld and Odysseus' in Book Eleven of the *Odyssey* are clearly apparent. Virgil is consciously imitating Homer; if Odysseus finds it necessary to enter the Underworld in order to achieve his goal of returning home, so too must Aeneas enter the Underworld to see the future destiny of his efforts to settle in Italy.

Task: Anchises in the Underworld

Reread the passage Book 6 lines 679-703

From 'Father Anchises was deep in a green valley

To ... as light as the flight of sleep.'

Now answer the following question;

"Using this passage as a starting point, what do you think Virgil is trying to tell us about life and death?"

Anchises also shows Aeneas what the Underworld is like. It is very different from that of Book Eleven in the *Odyssey*, although similar in that it is also a place of rewards and punishments, each according to his deserts. In contrast, the Underworld of Virgil seems to be happier, with the dead well-catered for, rather than the blood-thirsty insubstantial shades of the *Odyssey*.

Virgil uses the character of Anchises to explain the meaning of life and death, including Virgil's philosophical ideas on reincarnation. This was a doctrine popular among the Roman elite, and was compatible with one of the philosophies popular at the time, Stoicism.

Roman attitudes to death

The Romans strictly separated the world of the dead from the world of the living. A family or household that experienced death was considered to be temporarily unclean or polluted and this pollution could potentially affect neighbours or visitors. In order to warn neighbours and to help assuage the pollution was marked out by decorating the place with cypress tree branches. After eight days a body was transferred to a cemetery and buried. Cremation was the normal method of disposing of the body with the ashes and bones buried subsequently.

The spirits of the dead were considered to be in a state of migration or a journey, from the community of the living and the journey to the community of the dead was thought to take about forty days. The community of the dead were called the *di mánes* and collectively the community of the dead were considered to be a collective divinity; as such they received ritual and cult practices as a result.

The unburied dead were called *lemurés* and thought to be wandering ghosts who would haunt the living. Pragmatically, the

Romans instituted a cult festival called the *Lemuria* in order to appease these wandering unfortunates.

Moral values in the *Aeneid*

Moral and philosophical values permeate the *Aeneid* and Virgil has much to say about both. The journey that Aeneas undergoes throughout the entire work has its moral dimension. Not only is Aeneas fated to found and establish the Trojans in Italy, but it is also his moral prerogative to do so, since Rome will come to enshrine civilisation in a world which (according to the view of the Romans) was full of chaos and barbarism.

Here are some further examples:

- The importance of burial, which shows respect for the dead and is one of the values which *pius* Aeneas holds as important is shown in Book Six. Palinurus begs for burial, and it is important for Aeneas to honour this request of his dead companion.

- Aeneas' meeting with Dido in Book Six is highly emotionally charged, since it is only here that the hero discovers that Dido is not only dead, but that she committed suicide. The tragedy that overcame Dido is arguably one of the greatest prices that Aeneas had to pay in order to fulfil his destiny and that of the Trojans. The sadness that Dido reminds us of makes us again revisit Aeneas' choices. This helps us to evaluate the moral values of the *Aeneid* and prevents Virgil's message being simplistic. If anything, Virgil is stressing that following what has been fated, or the will of the gods, is never all plain sailing.

Task: The end of Book Six

Does anything surprise or confuse you about the ending of Book Six?

A false dream? The end of Book Six

If you found the ending of Book 6 a little surprising, then you are not alone. Several commentators and readers of Virgil have also expressed some surprise at the way in which Aeneas departs the Underworld, since he leaves by the gate of ivory, which Virgil tells us represents the gate of false dreams.

If the whole the entirety of Book Six had been some kind of a 'false dream' that Virgil's audience is meant to disbelieve, this then could lead the audience to doubt the confidence placed in Rome as sovereign ruler of the world. Or perhaps Virgil has Aeneas leave the Underworld by the gateway of false dreams because in the Underworld, he is a 'false dream' since he is not a ghost or an image, but a living man that was tolerated to enter. There is no definitive answer here.

It could be considered that this episode along with Dido's death in Book Four and looking forward in the *Aeneid* to the war in Italy provide the audience with a strong and significant undercurrent of darkness that Virgil intended as a counterpoise the pro-Roman propaganda that it was Virgil's own stated aim to compose.

In Part Seven of this study guide we explore the role of philosophy in the *Aeneid*. We will return to the ending of Book Six again as we explore the role Epicurean philosophy has in the *Aeneid*.

Task: Examination style task: Book VI

Read Virgil's Aeneid Book VI, lines 450-477

Write responses to the following questions;

a) *How typical is the presentation of the character of Dido in this passage to other parts of the Aeneid?*

b) *'Overall Book VI is more of a positive rather than a negative book'. To what extent do you agree with this statement?*

PART FIVE: Books Seven to Nine of the *Aeneid*

PART FIVE

5.1 Book Seven – Beginning Virgil's "Greater Work"

5.2 Exploring Mythical allusions in Book Seven

5.3 Book Eight: The Shield of Aeneas

5.4 Analysing the Shield of Aeneas

5.5 Book Nine: Nisus and Eurylaus

5.1 Book Seven – Beginning Virgil's "Greater Work"

This section will help you to;

- *Understand the events and structure of Book Seven*

- *Understand the mythical and historical references in Book Seven*

- *Consider Virgil's use of Intertextuality in Book Seven*

- *Compare the similarities and differences in Book One and Book Seven*

- *Continue to explore similarities and differences between Homer and Virgil*

Task: Comprehending Book Seven

Read Book Seven of the Aeneid

Once you have, write brief responses to the following questions;

- *How has Virgil chosen to start this Book?*

- *What does Virgil mean by the 'greater work'? (VII.46)*

- *What do you think Virgil has focussed on in Book Seven?*

Introduction

This section will help you to understand the seventh book of the *Aeneid*. Here Virgil introduces his audience to the story of Aeneas and the Trojans that have now arrived in Italy and desire to set up their new home. The Trojans are now close to achieving their destiny of settling in Italy where in time, their descendants will found Rome and achieve the Imperial destiny that has been established and confirmed by Virgil's contemporary ruler Caesar Augustus.

Quick Questions: Book Seven

- *Why do you think that Aeneas is largely absent from Book Seven?*
- *In what ways does Book Seven resemble Book One?*

Book Seven Synopsis

The Trojans sail from Cumae and travel north, to that part of Italy known in the *Aeneid* as Latium, but is better known to us as the region where the city of Rome will later be constructed. As the Trojans sail they pass the island of Circe, as had Odysseus in the Odyssey. Unlike Odysseus however, the Trojans pass without incident. At the mouth of the river Tiber, the Trojans land.

After a second *proem* in which Virgil introduces the second 'greater' part of his epic, Virgil shifts the scene to the city of King Latinus, king of Latium and a descendent of the God Saturn. King Latinus has no heirs and therefore seeks a husband for his only daughter, Lavinia. Latinus' wife Amata wishes Lavinia to marry Turnus; a local hero and prince of the city of Ardea. Latinus however is not sure; omens sent by the gods indicate that Turnus and Lavinia will never marry.

The omens preventing Turnus and Lavinia from marrying are; a swarm of bees followed by Lavinia's hair set afire during a sacrifice. Latinus then seeks out the oracle of Faunus (his own father). This oracle instructs Latinus to marry Lavinia to a stranger. Do this, and the fame of the Latins and the strangers will reach the heavens.

Aeneas and the Trojans set up camp and eat a meagre meal of what remains of their food supplies. They spread what food they can on little wheat cakes (the wheat cakes were not normally consumed as part of the meal, as they were considered sacred to the Goddess Ceres). However, the Trojans are so hungry they eat the wheat cakes also, causing Ascanius to joke;

'Look! We are eating even our tables!' (VII.117)

This exclamation fulfils the prediction given in Book Three that the Trojans have now found their new home. The Trojans begin to build a city – in fact an armed camp which they will put to good use later. They send messengers to King Latinus informing his of their arrival and peaceful intentions. Once again the Trojan Ilioneus is called upon to lead the Trojan deputation and assure King Latinus of the Trojans' peaceful intentions. Latinus accepts the Trojans but insists

Tapas!

Aeneas and his men when they land eat small morsels of food on little wheat cakes. If you want to visualise these they seem to resemble Spanish Tapas. A Tapa is a piece of bread atop of which is cheese, fish, meat or fruit. Some can be very simple, others very ornate with a blend of tastes and colours.

that Aeneas himself come to meet with the king and also to marry his daughter.

The Goddess Juno however witnesses the arrival of the Trojans and is determined to cause trouble. She calls on the Fury Allecto to sow chaos and discord among the Latins and the Trojans. Allecto obliges. Allecto poisons Amata's mind and sends her running wild through the streets of the city and out into the countryside like a wild Maenad. Lavinia is hidden by her mother in the woods of Latium and the Latin women follow the lead of their queen.

Allecto then visits Turnus in disguise and tries to persuade him to fight for Lavinia, when he refuses and mocks the Fury; Allecto reveals her true form and drives Turnus mad for battle and bloodletting. Finally, Allecto visits Aeneas' son Ascanius whilst he is hunting. His hounds are driven mad and pursue a prize domesticated stag. Ascanius shoots the stag with an arrow which enrages the local farmers. A brawl between Latins and Trojans rapidly gets out of hand when the Trojans kill some of the Latins. Her work complete, Allecto leaves.

King Latinus witnesses his people prepare for war against the Trojans and he refuses to take part. However, Latinus is ignored by the majority of his people and the Latins and the Trojans prepare for war. What follows at the end of Book Seven is a catalogue of the Latin armies, their allies and their leaders and heroes.

The structure of Book Seven

- *The Second proem (lines 1-46)*

- *King Latinus (lines 47-109)*

- *The Trojan embassy (lines 110-282)*

- *Juno (lines 283-323)*

- *Allecto (lines 324-641)*

- *The Catalogue of the Latin armies and heroes (lines 641-end)*

The Second proem (lines 1-46)

Virgil innovates in Book Seven. He brings together the stories of Aeneas, the Latins and establishes a kind of new beginning for his epic. If we can crudely put it for the moment, Aeneas has completed his *Odyssey*; he now needs to survive his *Iliad*. To this end Virgil needs to create a new beginning, with new protagonists and a cause for strife between the Trojans and the Latins in whose land they are destined to build their city.

As a result Virgil creates a second *proem* that outlines the focus of this part of his work;

> *"Come now, Erato, and I shall tell of the kings of ancient Latium, of its history, of the state of the land when first the army of strangers beached their ships on the shores of Ausonia. I shall recall too, the cause of the first battle – come, goddess, come and instruct your prophet. I shall speak of fearsome fighting, I shall speak off wars and of kings driven into the ways of death by their pride of spirit... This is the greater work I now set in motion".*

In this second *proem*, Virgil clearly sets out his aims. The second part will be a story of the *Aeneid* will be one of battle and war. He appeals to one Muse to help him in this effort; the Muse Erato.

King Latinus (lines 47-109)

Virgil now shifts to King Latinus and his desire to find a worthy husband for his daughter. Omens seem to have eliminated the candidacy of Turnus; who is the favourite of his wife Queen Amata. The arrival of the Trojans gives Latinus an opportunity to obey the instructions of his father the divine Faunus whose oracle he consulted.

Of Lavinia's choice as to her future husband we are not told. It could be though that Lavinia would prefer the young and dashing Turnus, whom she knows, as opposed to the grizzled, older veteran of many a war whom she knows nothing and who is in any case only fated to live another three years.

Task: The Speeches of Ilioneus

Read the speeches of Ilioneus in Book I lines 520-579 and Book VII.211-249 again.

What is similar about the language of these speeches and what is different?

What is similar about the context of these speeches and what is different?

The Trojan embassy (lines 110-282)

Aeneas sends an embassy of picked men to King Latinus to assure him of their good intentions and to promise that they are peaceful. Ilioneus was the leading ambassador in Book One, now Virgil calls upon his services once more to set out the peaceful intentions of the Trojans.

Juno (lines 283-323)

As in Book One, Juno witnesses the Trojans arrival. Unlike in Book One they are no longer at sea, but safe on land. In Book One Juno sought help from Aeolus to cause a great storm. This time Juno enlists the help of a Fury; Allecto. Allecto's mission is to sow fear and confusion amongst the Trojans and the Latins and to drive them into conflict.

Allecto (lines 324-641)

The Fury Allecto wreaks havoc on the mortals. She does not target Aeneas or King Latinus directly however. She instead targets weaker, more vulnerable people and her primary weapon used to accomplish this is by instilling a sense of insanity amongst her victims. Both Queen Amata and Turnus are so afflicted. For Ascanius, it is his hounds that are targeted, and rash as he is with his love of hunting, he unwittingly fires the first arrow of the war by wounding a domesticated stag.

The Catalogue of the Latin armies and heroes (lines 641-end)

The final part of Book Seven is a catalogue of the Latin armies and heroes that are assembled to fight Aeneas and his Trojans. We should not be surprised to see such a catalogue. In the *Iliad*, Homer dedicates an entire book to describing the protagonists on both the Trojan and Greek sides; the heroes and leaders, as well as their homelands and backgrounds as well as (on the Greek side) the number of ships in which they set sail for Troy. For Virgil and his Roman audience then, such a catalogue is too expected from an epic.

Virgil catalogues thirteen groupings of Latins and their allies;

I.   Mezentius and his son Launus leading Etrurians from Agylla

II.   Aventinus, a son of Hercules leading the Sabines

III.   Catillus and Coras, brothers from Argos in Greece who lead the army of Tibur

IV.   Caeculus, a son of Vulcan from the city of Praeneste

V.   Messapus, a son of Neptune

VI.   Clausus, an ancestor of the famous Claudii family, leading Sabines

VII.   Halaesus, a Greek from the retinue of Agamemnon leading Italians

VIII. Oebalus, from the island of Capreae, leading Italians

IX.   Ufens, leading the Aequi

X.   Umbro, a priest from Marruvium

XI.   Viribius, the son of Hippolytus and Aricia

XII.   Turnus, the leader of the Latins in this war. From Ardea and commanding an army from across Italy

XIII. Camilla, a warrior women in the tradition of the Amazons leading the Cavalry of the Volsci

Many of these tribes and peoples were known to the Romans beyond Virgil. Italian peoples like the Sabines, Volsci and the Aequi would be defeated by the Romans as they achieved the domination of Italy in the years 700-400BC.

The decision to identify 13 groups of Latins and Italians may have been deliberate on the part of Virgil. When the Trojans were added to this number we arrive at 14; which was the number of *regio* (administrative regions) that the Emperor Augustus would later divide the city of Rome into for administrative purposes (this occurred probably in 7BC, after Virgil's death). The catalogue could also be used to help illustrate and describe from the outset the polyglot nature of the city of Rome with all the differing ethnic groupings that would eventually come together in the capital city of the Roman Empire and explain the mixture of beliefs and traditions that were bought together in that city.

Harpies

5.2 Exploring Mythical allusions in Book Seven

This section will help you to;

• *Continue to explore the character of Aeneas*

• *Explore the language used in Book Seven*

• *Explore links between the Latin past of Rome in the Aeneid*

• *Analyse the importance of references to Argos and Argive myths in Book Seven*

• *Consider Virgil's use of Intertextuality in Book Seven*

• *Continue to explore similarities and differences between Homer and Virgil*

Introduction

In this section we will explore and analyse Book Seven in greater detail. Here we will consider Intertextuality; the integration and referencing of other literary works in the present text. The importance and integration of mythical traditions into Virgil's work will be explored so that we can understand that, although Virgil is writing a new original work, we shall consider the extent to which he relies on other existing works and traditions to enrich his own story.

In this section we will also explore the references Virgil makes to the Latins and the important and vital ingredient of Latin culture in forming the melting pot that was Virgil's own contemporary Rome

Aeneas' *pietas* in Book Seven

Aeneas is largely absent in Book Seven. When Virgil does reveal him to the audience however he is invariably doing good deeds. At the very beginning of the Book Aeneas performs burial rites (VII.1-9), whilst a little later he prays and gives thanks for the Trojan's safe arrival in Italy (VII.137-149). Even though the focus of Book Seven is elsewhere, Virgil reminds his audience that Aeneas is a pious man, something that stands in stark contrast to the actions of almost all of the Latins in Book Seven, who are themselves victims of fate and the machinations of Juno and Allecto.

Exploring similes and metaphors in Book Seven

There are a few similes in Book Seven. Here we will reference two. In VII.460-468 Turnus' violence and lust for battle is likened to a fire causing a pot of water to boil over. In VII 700-706, Virgil likens the soldiers that follow Messapus to white swans; serene and graceful; at odds with what we might expect from a horde of soldiers lusting for battle.

Likewise, in a famous metaphor that has been commonly used throughout history; the state has been likened to a ship about to founder under the mad actions of the people, the king however has reached safety (VII.592-600).

> **Task: The Latins and Rome**
>
> *In Book Seven, try to identify as many references to Latin culture as you can.*

Homeric parallels in Book Seven

In addition to the catalogue of armies which closely resembles Book Two of the *Iliad*, Virgil also makes reference to other parts of Homer's poems in Book Seven. For start, Book Seven has in it a quarrel that results in part from a proposed marriage; that of Aeneas and Lavinia, at the expense of the jilted Turnus. Homer's epic cycle originates with a marriage dispute; the eloping of Helen with Paris. Likewise, in the *Odyssey*, Penelope is under pressure to choose a new husband, despite the imminent arrival of Odysseus.

The island of Circe, and the terrors if holds is also referenced early in Book Seven (lines 10-25) yet it is passed without incident by the Trojans. Why then does Virgil bother to mention it at all? The answer lay in that Circe's island was part of the epic tradition of Homer and thought to be close to the coast of Italy by the Romans – therefore it is referenced to add an additional layer of depth to Virgil's story.

Finally, Virgil appeals, like Homer does, to the Muses to help him describe the armies of the Latins (VII.641-648). The reference to Mount Helicon is apt as this mountain in Boeotia (Central Greece) was thought to be the home of the Muses.

Euripidean references in Book Seven

Virgil seems to have enjoyed Greek tragedy and his audience too would have enjoyed references to other myths that they would have encountered in other, older works from the mythical traditions of the past.

In Book Seven we can identify two intertextual references to Euripidean tragedies; the *Bacchae* and *Hippolytus*.

When Queen Amata is driven insane by the Fury Allecto, she acts like a worshipper of the God Dionysus; a *Maenad*. Amata runs through the streets of the city before escaping to the countryside, the Latin women following suit. This is a clear reference to Euripides' *Bacchae*; in which the God Dionysius sends the women of Thebes insane as punishment for doubting his own divinity and for slandering his mother Semele.

Euripides

Euripides was born in Athens around 484BC and first competed in the City Dionysia festival in 455BC and died around 407/6BC, not in Athens, but in the kingdom of Macedonia.

Euripides was a prolific writer, writing at least ninety plays, of which nineteen have survived and nine of these are datable.

According to some hostile and later commentators, relative lack of success at Athens prompted Euripides to leave his home city and travel to Macedonia at the invitation of the Macedonian King and it was in Macedon that he died.

Rome and the worship of Bacchus

The Greek mystery cult of the Bacchanalia was known in Rome and Italy from at least 400BC. Unlike in Greece, the worship of Bacchus could include both men and women and there were concerns about its orgiastic nature as well as its organisational levels which saw leaders of cells of worshippers having some power and authority over property and wealth that conflicted with established Roman family law.

In 186BC the historian Livy writes that the Roman Senate at last took steps to ban the worship of Bacchus and persecution of those who defied the Senate.

The second reference is to the play *Hippolytus*. During the catalogue of the Italian armies Virgil digresses on the origin of Virbius; a son of Hippolytus. According to the play by Euripides, Hippolytus is killed in an incident involving his chariot and a bull sent by the God Poseidon at the request of his father Theseus. Hippolytus however is restored to life in Virgil's version and dwelt subsequently in Italy.

The Hippolytus myth was very popular among both Greeks and Romans. Euripides himself wrote two plays on the story, and the Athenian Tragedian Sophocles also wrote a version of *Hippolytus* (now lost). Much later the story would be reproduced by Romans. Ovid would retell the story in his *Heroides* IV.

The Latins as early Romans

Despite the belligerent attitudes of the majority of the Latins towards Aeneas and his Trojans in Book Seven, Virgil is careful to deliberately identify customs and practices of the Latins that became keystones of Roman traditions in his own time.

One example is the identification of a great Senate House and temple known as the Laurentine Picus (VII.170-190); the ancestral home of King Latinus and from where he governed. A Senate is clearly identifiable indicating that the role and function of the Senate was inseparable from the foundation myths of Rome and an integral part of society.

The Gods Janus, Quirinus and Picus are also identified – these Gods of Latin origin continued to be an important part of the Roman religious pantheon.

Task: The Arch of Janus and the Gates of War

In Book Seven, read lines 601-640

Explore the language used by Virgil to describe one of the oldest institutions of Rome.

Finally, Virgil describes the gates of War. (VII.601-640) and their function in Roman preparations for war.

The Arch of Janus

Janus was the Roman god of door and gate; especially triumphal arches. A God with a face on both sides of his head, like a gate, he looks both ways.

His shrine of Janus Geminus was located in the Forum of Rome and almost always open, indicating that Rome was at war. When the shrine was closed, Rome was at peace.

Until the time of Augustus the shrine of Janus Geminus was closed only twice; first during the reign of King Numa, second in the year 235BC.

During the reign of Augustus the shrine of Janus Geminus was closed on no less than three occasions.

The role of the city of Argos in Book Seven

Virgil deliberately elects to link the Greek city of Argos into the narrative in Book Seven. We have already mentioned the image emblazoned on the shield of Turnus; an Argive myth. Turnus' ancestors originated in the city of Argos (VII.408-410)

We can also see that during the parade of the Latin armies at the end of Book Seven, no less than three of the leaders of the Latin armies; Catillus, Coras and Halaesus all come from Argos.

But Argos is also mentioned fairly early in Book Seven. Juno, the Queen of the Gods is travelling back from Argos when she spots that the Trojans have arrived in Italy (VII.287). Not only is Argos one of the beloved cities of Juno (another one being Carthage – visited by Aeneas in Books I-IV), but Argos was the centre of power of the Great Greek king Agamemnon who led the Greeks during the Trojan War. Argos was the scene of several bloody murders, committed by wives who betrayed and killed their husbands.

The latest victim of this apparent curse was Agamemnon himself who was killed by Clytemnestra and her lover Aegisthus on his return from Troy.

We will return to this crime and the myths associated with mariticide later when we explore the belt of Pallas in Book X.

Term: Mariticide

A Latin term used to describe the murder of a husband by his wife.

The shield of Turnus (VII.788-792)

In Homeric epic the armour and weapons are often described. Virgil too does this on occasion and in the catalogue of the Italian armies Virgil describes the arms and weapons of several of the heroes and the soldiers they lead. In Book Eight Virgil will fully describe the shield of Aeneas, but in Book Seven, it is Turnus' shield that is briefly described, foreshadowing the longer digression in Book Eight.

Turnus' shield is described as depicting a scene from Greek myth. Io having been abducted by Jupiter has been transformed into a cow. The Titan Argus is guarding her whilst her father Inachus pours a river from his upended urn. Why might Virgil have chosen to depict this particular mythical scene?

This image on the shield of Turnus indicates several interesting points that should be borne in mind as we continue through the *Aeneid*;

- Turnus is a loyal servant to the Goddess Juno (Hera)

- Turnus' ancestors originated in the city of Argos

- The Shield is a foreshadowing of another image described in Book X; on the belt of Pallas

Inachus

Inachus was an ancient hero and or river god of the city of Argos. He was the father of Io.

The Myth of Io

According to Greek mythology, Io was a priestess of Hera (Juno) at Argos who was desired by Zeus (Jupiter). Upon being seduced by the God, Hera punished Io by transforming her into a cow and instructing the monster Argus to guard her in the grounds of the temple of Hera at Argos (the site of the Argive Heraion can still be visited today). Argus was subsequently killed by the God Hermes (Mercury) but Hera punished Io to wander the earth, still transformed as a cow and tormented perpetually by a gadfly.

In time Io reached Egypt where Zeus restored Io to her original form. Here she also gave birth to Zeus' child a boy called Epaphus. Epaphus was the ancestor of Danaus, who would in Greek myth return to the city of Argos with his fifty daughters.

Task: Is Turnus to blame?

Write a response to the following question;

In Book Seven King Latinus declares;

"You are the guilty one, Turnus, and a grim punishment lies in store for you."

Considering what you have read in Book Seven, to what extent do you agree with the view of King Latinus that Turnus is to blame for causing the war between Trojans and Latins?

5.3 Book Eight: The Shield of Aeneas

This section will help you to;

- *Understand the events and structure of Book Eight*

- *Explore the characters of Aeneas and Evander*

- *Understand the importance of myth and history in establishing the narrative of the Aeneid*

- *Consider how Greeks and Latins are portrayed in Book Eight*

- *Understand terms and geographical places mentioned by Virgil in Books Seven and Eight*

Introduction

This section will help you to understand the eighth book of the *Aeneid*.

Book Eight of the *Aeneid* is very much about Rome. The reader is treated to a tour of Pallanteum/Rome conducted by Evander. Through this tour Virgil shows his audience the locations of the ancient famous sites of Pallanteum. These sites will come to be (in the present of his Roman audience) contemporary Roman sites and the customs and myths associated with them are linked back to the ancient past, thus providing Virgil's present day Rome with a pedigree and an authenticity that makes them all the more important.

Book Eight is also a book about the origins of Rome and Italy and the part that Aeneas, the Greeks and the Latins all had to play in establishing Rome. Virgil's narrative is that Italy is a land of migrants who together all contributed to the greatness and splendour that is Rome.

Book VIII Synopsis

As the Latins and their allies prepare for battle, they send a messenger to enlist the support of Diomedes, a famous Greek warrior who during the Trojan War fought and defeated several Gods including Aeneas' Mother Aphrodite (Venus) and even the God of War Ares (Mars).

Meanwhile, Aeneas is worried for the future of the Trojans and is aware that war is coming. Aeneas is advised the river God Tiber in a dream to travel to the city of Pallenteum and there seek help. Pallenteum is populated by Arcadian Greeks and their king Evander fights a continual war against the Latins. He will be a valuable ally in the fight to come.

Aeneas sets off – pausing only to sacrifice 30 piglets and their mother at the site of Ascanius' future city of Alba Longa. Aeneas arrives at Pallenteum and meets Evander and his son Pallas and immediately establishes a friendship and treaty of alliance with both. These friendships and treaties are based on their shared kinship and friendships that were established prior to the Trojan War.

Having feasted, Evander takes Aeneas on a tour of Pallenteum; the very site where Rome will be built later by Romulus and Remus. Several sites are identified on this walking tour and the legends attached to these places revealed.

The scene shifts to the Gods. Venus, fearful for the safety of Aeneas in the war to come appeals to her husband Vulcan and requests that he forge weapons and armour for Aeneas as he once did for Achilles (as told in Homer's *Iliad*). Vulcan agrees and the work begins at his forge underneath Mount Etna.

Evander and Aeneas discuss the upcoming war. The Arcadians are engaged in war with the Rutulians of Turnus. Evander advises Aeneas to travel on to Agylla to seek the help of the Etruscans. Their former king Mezentius fights on the side of Turnus and they may be keen to help Aeneas as well.

The leader of the Etruscans is Tarchon who has prepared a fleet as well as an army. Tarchon wants Evander to lead him in battle, but Evander has refused; he is too old. Instead Evander advises Aeneas to take command. Evander will also send Pallas with Aeneas to help him with a force of cavalry. A sign from the Gods encourages Aeneas to agree.

Aeneas and Pallas travel towards Agylla. On the way Venus appears before Aeneas and gives him the weapons and armour that Vulcan has made for him. Book VIII ends with a lengthy digression on the description of Aeneas' shield, which depicts events from the future that will establish the glorious present imperial status of Italy and Rome.

Task: Evander

How is Evander portrayed in Book Eight?

Explore the language used to portray this character.

How does Virgil want his audience to feel about him?

The structure of Book Eight

- *Aeneas travels to Pallenteum (lines 1-102)*

- *Evander and Aeneas (lines 103-182)*

- *The digression on Hercules (lines 183-279)*

- *The Tour of Rome (lines 280-369)*

- *Venus and Vulcan (lines 370-453)*

- *Evander counsels Aeneas (lines 454-625)*

- *The Shield of Aeneas (lines 626-end)*

Aeneas travels to Pallenteum (lines 1-102)

Book VIII commences with the Latin leaders; Turnus, Mezentius, Messapus and Ufens continuing to prepare and gather their forces. They also send an emissary to enlist the support of Diomede. This particular narrative thread indicates several possibilities;

That Virgil envisaged another potential link to the Trojan War and a possible confrontation between Aeneas and Diomede. This possible narrative thread was, as we shall see, never to take place and so is unlikely unless we consider that the *Aeneid* was never fully completed by Virgil and this might have been one of several possible revisions.

Secondly, and more likely is the suggestion that the Latins are careful in their preparations. They desire as much help as they can get (as does Aeneas). Diomede had taken the measure of Aeneas during the Trojan War and his help would be invaluable.

Finally, it is possible that Virgil is suggesting that, subconsciously at least, the Latin leaders are aware that they face a great threat in the form of Aeneas and his Trojans. They are not as confident as they may seem in the result of the upcoming confrontation.

Aeneas too, is experiencing worries and Virgil is clear in presenting Aeneas as a worried man. He however seeks comfort from the advice of the river god Tiber who talks to him in a dream. Tibur assures Aeneas that;

- He is destined to bring the city of Troy to the fields of Latium

- It is destined that the Gods of Troy will establish themselves here

- Ascanius will found a city called Alba where Aeneas finds thirty piglets and their mother in thirty years' time

Having been assured by the god that he is destined to succeed, Aeneas is instructed to travel up Tiber to the home of Evander – a natural ally.

Aeneas awakens and immediately gives thanks to Tiber. The piglets and sow are encountered as promised and sacrificed to Juno – as commanded by Tiber.

The contrast between the Latins and the Trojans is clear. Whereas Aeneas places his faith and hopes on the will of the Gods, the Latins have chosen to place their trust and faith in mortals – themselves and also a distant Greek hero who may or may not want to join them in their fight.

Task: Evander and Aeneas

Explore the language used by Virgil to these speeches

What is the content and tone of Aeneas speech?

What is Evander's response?

Evander and Aeneas (lines 103-182)

This part of Book Eight is mostly comprised of two speeches; one by Aeneas, and another by Evander.

Aeneas is clear. He wants and needs help. He appeals to Evander on the grounds of shared kinship and possesses a good knowledge of Evander's background. Often in epic a hero needs to introduce himself. But not here; Aeneas has a good understanding of who Evander is and also that they have a shared problem in the form of Turnus and his Rutulians. Finally he assures Evander that Aeneas' own men are good allies to have, they are strong and powerful in war. Evander's reply is equally brief and to the point. He remembers his previous friendship with King Priam and Anchises. He offers his alliance and invites Aeneas and his men to share in a feast.

The character of Evander

Although Virgil has presented foes for Aeneas in the shape of Turnus and his allies, not all of the non-Trojan characters are simplistically presented as inferior, foolish or weak in war. Virgil creates in Evander and Pallas a pair of very likeable characters; both are kind and friendly and generous.

This pair of Evander and Pallas both hold up a mirror to Aeneas and his son Ascanius, and show us another ideal and loving father-son relationship. Evander and Pallas are therefore worthy associates of Aeneas and his family because they are good people too and share his values. In fact, this relationship is vital for the plot: Aeneas finds genuine hospitality (*xenia*) and refuge at Pallanteum, the home of Evander and Pallas and the future site of Rome, which was sadly denied to him at the home of King Latinus through the machinations of the Goddess Juno.

As a marker of Evander's deep trust and regard for Aeneas, he entrusts his son to Aeneas' care, to which Aeneas agrees, showing us that both men are of like mind and temperament.

> **Task: Pallas**
>
> *How is Pallas portrayed in Book Eight?*
>
> *Explore the language used to portray this character.*
>
> *How does Virgil want his audience to feel about him?*

The character of Pallas

Pallas is a particularly memorable and appealing one. Like Ascanius, he is young, fresh and open much as we might imagine Aeneas' son, and is eager but like Ascanius, has not yet had a real taste of what warfare is like. He is therefore eager to make his name as a hero and so establish his reputation, and looks up to Aeneas as kind of father-figure. This strengthens the ties between the families of Aeneas and Evander since they share duties of *xenia* and since Evander can offer Aeneas a solution to war; the alliance with the Etruscans.

> **Task: Hercules**
>
> *Read Book 8 lines 190-279.*
>
> *What do you think is the effect of the 'Hercules' digression on the narrative of Book Eight?*

The digression on Hercules (lines 183-279)

The Romans adopted and integrated a great deal of their mythology and legend from the Greeks. Many Italians honoured Hercules, which can be seen as an indication of the growing influence of Greek culture in Italy.

Hercules (in Greek Heracles) was a Greek hero in myth that had widespread appeal – he was acknowledged by the Carthaginians (who knew Heracles as Melqart) and Egyptians as a hero and they adapted and added to the myth of Heracles themselves. The inhabitants of Italy were no exception to this appeal and they too adapted and integrated Heracles into their own pantheon of Gods – giving him the name Hercules.

The Historian Dionysius of Halicarnassus wrote about the deeds of Hercules in Italy in his works (I.40.1) and Dionysius was in turn probably influenced by now lost writings from earlier Greek writers in Italy and Sicily or from 5th century Greek writers such as Hellenicus of Lesbos or Hecataeus of Miletus.

The Romans particularly admired the legend of Hercules. In it, they saw a paradigm for the heroic mortal who (with a little help from the gods, of course) defeats many enemies and overcomes many seemingly impossible obstacles. There are obvious parallels to make between Aeneas and Hercules, both of whom take on the impossible and eventually overcome. Both, also, are destined to receive immortality as the reward for their labours.

According to mythical tradition, Hercules confronted and killed Cacus after this monstrous bandit stole several of the cattle Hercules was bringing from Spain to Greece as part of his labours. After killing Cacus, Hercules created an altar to Jupiter on the Palatine Hill and then dined with Evander and his father Faunus. Hercules was also credited with teaching two families – the Potitii and the Pinarii the sacrificial rites that would be performed in Rome at the site of the *'Ara Maxima'* (The Great Altar) which was located in one of early Rome's oldest locations; the *'Forum Boarium'* . These traditions can be dated in Rome to the mid-6th century BC – but could be even earlier.

The digression on Hercules then can be well understood as Virgil acknowledging the influence that this God-hero had on Rome in his own present day and through his identification of Hercules in the mythical tradition of the establishment of Rome, we can see that Virgil is integrating this tradition into his own attempts to acknowledge the contribution of the Trojan hero Aeneas into the foundation tradition of Rome.

The Tour of Rome (lines 280-369)

Any visit to Rome today it is not complete without a tour of the spectacular sights. Much like a modern tourist, Aeneas too is treated to a tour. Evander's tour of the sites of what will be Rome identifies several locations that were identifiable in Virgil's time and indeed are still identifiable today;

Evander identifies;

- The cave of Cacus on the Aventine Hill

- The Carmental Gate and the altar of Carmentis at the base of the Capitol Hill

- The Lupercal, a cave in the base of the Palatine Hill, only rediscovered in 2007

- The citadels of the Janiculum and the Saturnia atop the Palatine Hill

- Evanders' home which would be the site of the future Roman Forum

By describing these identifiable sites, Virgil is explaining to Aeneas and the audience the antiquity of Rome and also Aeneas' role in the future destiny of the Imperial city. It would have been exciting for the Roman audience to be able to stand where the hero Aeneas had stood in the past. Virgil then is helping to establish the credentials of Rome as a city whose origins are established by myth – like the cities of Athens, Troy and Thebes for example, but also to demonstrate that out of these same, shared mythical stories has emerged a city like Rome which is so much greater than all others; past and present.

This tour helps Aeneas to understand what it is that he and his men will be fighting for. A future vision of greatness and destiny.

Venus and Vulcan (lines 370-453)

In a reference to the story of Homer's *Iliad*, Virgil now has her husband, the God Vulcan, craft weapons and armour for Aeneas. In the *Iliad*, the nymph Thetis makes a similar request to Hephaestus (the Greek name for Vulcan) for Achilles after his own armour is taken from the body of his friend Patroclus.

Virgil describes the forge of Vulcan, the Cyclops who helps him in his labours and also maintain the war gear of the Gods and the act of the forging commencing.

Evander counsels Aeneas (lines 454-625)

There is another allusion to Homer in Book Eight. As Evander dresses and prepares for the day he does so in a very similar way to the young Telemachus in Book II of the *Odyssey*. In the early stages of Book II, Telemachus dresses, arms himself and then accompanied by two dogs walks down to consult with the Ithacans. In Book Eight, Evander does something very similar.

Evander tells Aeneas of the city of Agylla and the cruel king Mezentius who was exiled from that place. Mezentius is an ally of Turnus and the people of Agylla, led by their new king Tarchon have long sought allies in their war against Mezentius and Turnus. They are natural allies then for Aeneas.

As Evander bids Aeneas and Pallas farewell there is another parallel to Homer. Like Nestor in the *Odyssey* and *Iliad,* Evander is old, too old for fighting, but that does not prevent him from telling his audience that in his prime he too, like Nestor, was a fierce and skilled warrior. Evander tells of his battle with Erulus of Praeneste, who had three lives. Evander has to kill him and strip his body of armour no less than three times to put an end to him.

> *Task: Mezentius the cruel.*
>
> *Read Aeneid Book VIII.480-502*
>
> *Write a response to the following question;*
>
> *Consider the portrayal of Mezentius in Book VIII.*
>
> *What similarities and differences can we identify between Mezentius and Tarquin Superbus?*
>
> *Why might Virgil introduce such a character?*

Mezentius as a forerunner of Tarquin Superbus?

King Tarquin Superbus was notorious historical figure in Rome.

According to the historian Livy (I.49-II.21), Tarquin Superbus was the last king of Rome whose exile resulted in the establishment of the Roman Republic. As such Tarquin is an important part of the historical tradition of Rome.

Livy records that Tarquin was a brutal tyrant who usurped the throne. He established his position by embarking on a policy of exiling and or murdering those who he thought were a threat to him, or whose wealth and property he desired. Particular targets were Senators.

Tarquin refused to consult with the Senate and made his own decisions arbitrarily. He made a strategic alliance with the Latins of Latium, but insulted and offended them. One; a Latin named Turnus was executed by Tarquin.

Tarquin's son then stole the wife of one of his own comrades and raped her. This was Lucretia, who was famous in Roman tradition. Lucretia committed suicide after this violation, but not before she told her family of what had happened to her. Her family, led by a Senator named Brutus then overthrew Tarquin and drove him into exile.

Tarquin tried on several occasions to recapture Rome, but failed. A conspiracy of some Senators to try to bring Tarquin back also failed. Finally, Tarquin raised an army and tried to capture Rome by force, but he was defeated at the battle of Lake Regillus. Tarquin survived but remained an exile. He would die at the city of Cumae.

The Shield of Aeneas (lines 626-end)

The final part of Book Eight is a description of the Shield of Aeneas. Since we will explore this in greater detail in the next topic, we will say no more here.

A brief glossary of terms in Book Seven and Eight

Books Seven and Eight have exposed the modern reader to a range of new words and geographical places that we may or may not be familiar with. We will explore some of them here;

Etruscans: A people of Italy. The Etruscans dominated much of Italy prior to the rise of Rome, but they were centred in the region NW of Rome as far as the river Arnus. The Etruscans had their own language and culture distinct from the Latin peoples of Italy and they traded extensively with the Greeks and Phoenicians. The Etruscans established the earliest cities in Italy. The Etruscans had an important role to play in establishing early Rome as the Tarquin kings of Rome were probably Etruscan. By the 5th century the Etruscans were subsumed into the Roman political and social spheres

Latium: A region of Italy. The coastal plain region from the River Tiber in the North to the Apenines in the East, and to Campania towards the South. Latium is dominated by the dormant volcano called *Albanus Mons* – in antiquity *Albanus Mons* was the site of the important Latin sanctuary of *Jupiter Latiaris*.

Latins: The name used to describe the ethnic group of people who inhabited central Italy. The Latins shared a common name, language and religious practices. At the beginning of the 5th century BC, Livy tells us that the Latin city of Aricia and Rome were engaged in a war. This war ended with a peace established in 493BC.

King Latinus: King of the Latins. In Roman mythical tradition Latinus was transformed into *Jupiter Latiaris*; *'Jupiter of the Latins'*.

Pallenteum: The city of Evander which occupies the site that one day will be Rome.

Sabines: A people of Italy who dwelt to the NE of the Latins. In Early Rome traditions they were soon integrated into the population of Rome in the story 'The Rape of the Sabine Women'.

Samnites: A people of Italy who occupied the central Apenine region. The Samnites fought a series of wars against Rome in the 4th and 3rd centuries BC. The Samnites supported invaders such as Pyrrhus of Epirus and the Carthaginian Hannibal in the 3rd century BC. Thereafter, they were increasingly integrated into the Roman social and political sphere.

Volsci: A People of Italy. The Volsci were rivals of Rome and the Latins in the early 5th century BC. By the end of the 4th century however Rome had comprehensively defeated the Volsci.

Task: Quick Questions on Book Eight

Try to answer these without reference to the text.

a) What does the god of the River Tiber prophesy for Ascanius?

b) Who is Aeneas to make his ally?

c) Describe three features of the 'Golden Age' which Evander discusses with Aeneas?

5.4 Analysing the Shield of Aeneas

This section will help you to;

- *To read the Aeneid Book Eight*

- *To compare and contrast the shield of Achilles from the Iliad and the shield of Aeneas*

- *To consider the symbolism of the shield of Aeneas*

- *To examine the role of the gods and the power of fate*

- *Explore a differing account of the Battle of Actium in 31BC*

Introduction

This topic focuses on the *Aeneid* Book Eight and in particular analysis of the shield of Aeneas. The climax of Book eight is the description of the shield of Aeneas forged by Vulcan, which is then described in great detail.

There is an obvious parallel between Homer and Virgil in the description of Aeneas' shield in Book Eight and the description of the shield of Achilles in Book Eighteen of the *Iliad* lines 478-608.

> **Task: Comparing the shields of Achilles and Aeneas**
>
> *Read Book 18 lines 478-608 of Homer's Iliad*
>
> *What parallels can you draw between this passage and the shield of Achilles in the Iliad?*

Venus has persuaded Vulcan (the Greek: Hephaistos) to forge the shield of Aeneas that will protect him and help him to defeat his enemies. The description of Vulcan's forge is highly evocative, and the later description of the shield is a prime example of an ekphrasis.

Just as it is Hephaistos in the *Iliad* who forged Achilles' shield with a vast array of moving figures and scenes, Aeneas' shield is likewise impressive and not intended by Virgil to be 'realistic'. Remember that both shields are the work of a god, and as such possess qualities which go far beyond mere mortal craftsmanship.

> **Task: The Shield of Aeneas**
>
> *Make a bullet point list of all the scenes depicted on the shield of Aeneas by Virgil.*
>
> *Write a response to the following question;*
>
> *What do you think is the symbolism of the shield of Aeneas?*

The shield of Aeneas

> **Key term: Ekphrasis**
>
> *A description of a work of art which was designed to be a rhetorical exercise*

Unlike the shield of Achilles, which does not include any history, whether legendary or contemporary, the shield of Aeneas is decidedly historical as Virgil would have recognised it. In fact, Virgil is drawing heavily on the works of his fellow contemporary Roman author, Livy, who popularised the early history of Rome which included many of the stories told on the shield of Aeneas. (Don't forget that the shield shows Aeneas and his family's future but to a contemporary Roman, their past).

The shield is therefore far more heavily prophetic than that of Achilles in the *Iliad*. Virgil is clearly taking a famous Homeric technique and making it his own. Virgil's *ekphrasis* is closely tied to his own narrative aim: to show how firmly Aeneas and the Trojan myth is welded into Rome's imperial destiny. The shield, forged by Vulcan, shows us what is to come, that is, all the triumphs and glories of Rome (note the warlike nature of the scenes on the shield).

If it were in any doubt before about the inevitability of Rome and Aeneas' triumph before the audience witnesses this shield, we must surely be now utterly convinced that Aeneas will go on to unite the warring tribes of Italy, and his descendants would build a glorious empire with all its military conquests on the site of the old city of Pallanteum.

Most of the scenes on Aeneas' shield are drawn from Italian history (or mythical history). Around the outside of the circle are 6 scenes that are described over 41 lines;

- The founders of Rome; Romulus and Remus being suckled by a she-wolf.

- The rape of the Sabine Women, the subsequent war and subsequent peace.

- The punishment of Mettus Fufetius; dictator of Alba Longa who would desert the Roman king Tullus Hostilius during a battle.

- Scenes from the attack of the Etruscans on Rome in 508BC.

- The Gallic attack on Rome in 390BC.

- The punishment of Catiline in the Underworld for his attempted coup in 63BC.

The focus of the shield however is the depiction of Augustus' victory over Antonius and Cleopatra at the battle of Actium in 31BC and his subsequent triple triumph. This part of the description encompasses 54 lines.

Task: The battle of Actium

Read Book VIII.671-728

Write responses to the following questions;

a) *How are the opposing sides portrayed in this description of the battle of Actium?*
b) *How is Cleopatra presented?*
c) *How is Augustus (Caesar) presented?*
d) *Consider why Virgil might present this scene as he does?*

The Battle of Actium: 31BC

In the *Res Gestae* Augustus in his own words, outlines the popular support he had against Antonius and Cleopatra at the Battle of Actium;

"The whole of Italy voluntarily took oath of allegiance to me and demanded me as its leader in the war in which I was victorious at Actium. The provinces of the Spains, the Gauls, Africa, Sicily, and Sardinia took the same oath of allegiance. Those who served under my standards at that time included more than 700 senators, and among them eighty-three who had previously or have since been consuls up to the day on which these words were written, and about 170 have been priests."

Res Gestae 25

The Senate appointed Octavian (The future Augustus) as Consul and Antonius as an enemy of the state, simultaneously declaring war on Cleopatra. The oaths of allegiance taken by all of Italy and also the western provinces were something that was unprecedented. These oaths were sworn not to Rome, but to Octavian.

Reports were reaching Rome that Antonius was marching on Italy with his army and a fleet largely composed of Cleopatra's forces was supporting and supplying them. As well as some 300 Senators, Antonius had 30 legions and a fleet of 500 ships. Their intention was to militarily confront and defeat Octavian, who was coming to meet him.

The two sides met in Greece. Cleopatra's presence was both a blessing and a curse for Antonius. A blessing because she was paying for and feeding Antonius's soldiers as well as providing much of the fleet, but a curse because her very presence gave ammunition to the Octavian's claim that Antonius was a slave to her and that Rome was to be ruled by a foreign tyrant if they succeeded. Another problem for Antonius was that Cleopatra was unpopular with the Senators that had fled Rome. Desertions began.

Octavian left his friend Maecenas in charge at Rome and with his fellow consul Agrippa confronted Antonius. Agrippa commanded the Roman fleet and he succeeded in cutting off the supply route from Egypt and blockading Antonius's fleet at Actium. Antonius's rejected suggestions that he confront Octavian's army and instead attempted to break the naval blockade. Antonius's fleet failed to break out and was forced to retire, but Cleopatra's squadron broke clear and set sail for Egypt. Antonius followed in his ship and abandoned his army. The campaign was over and Antonius's army and the remainder of his fleet surrendered.

The Deaths of Antonius and Cleopatra

Octavian sailed after Antonius and reached Egypt in 30BC, where Antonius had been deserted by his few remaining soldiers, realising they were defeated both Antonius and Cleopatra committed suicide. Whilst Octavian was mostly merciful towards the rebel Senators and the children of Antonius and Cleopatra, but he considered Caesarion (the son of Cleopatra and Julius Caesar) and Antonius' eldest son (by his 1st wife Fulvia) as potential rivals. They were killed.

Egypt was seized, not as a province, but as the possession of Octavian. An Equestrian, Gaius Cornelius Gallus was appointed as Prefect responsible for the administration and control of Egypt. Octavian spent the remainder of 30BC in the East inspecting the provinces and client kingdoms. Antonius had reorganised them recently and by and large, Octavian felt little need to alter Antonius's arrangements.

Task: Cassius Dio's account of the battle of Actium

Read Cassius Dio's account of the battle of Actium Book 50.31-35 which was written approximately 200 years after the battle of Actium.

You can read this account online at;

http://penelope.uchicago.edu/Thayer/E/Roman/Texts/Cassius_Dio/50.html*

Write in your own words the major events of the battle in this account.

Consider;

   a) How are the main protagonists portrayed?
   b) How does the battle end?

   c) How reliable do you think this account is?

5.5 Book Nine: Nisus and Eurylaus

This section will help you to;

- *Understand the events and structure of Book Nine*

- *Explore the characters of Nisus, Eurylaus and Turnus*

- *Identify and explore Homeric parallels and stylistic techniques in Book Nine*

- *Consider the extent to which Book Nine is a 'Tragedy'.*

- *Explore the idea that Fate is consistently opposed to Turnus*

Introduction

This section will help you to understand the Ninth book of the *Aeneid*. Here Virgil focuses on the beginning of the war; an attack by Turnus on the camp of the Trojans. Virgil also focuses much of the attention of this book on two new characters; the Trojans Nisus and Eurylaus who are destined to die in the performance of a brave but futile act.

> **Task: The absence of Aeneas**
>
> *Aeneas is absent throughout Book Nine.*
>
> *Consider why Virgil chose to keep Aeneas out of the narrative at this stage.*

Book Synopsis

Juno now encourages Turnus to attack the Trojan encampment. The Trojans, despite the absence of Aeneas, are determined to defend themselves.

Finding the encampment well-fortified Turnus seeks an alternative way to hurt the Trojans. The battle begins with Turnus seeking to destroy the beached ships that the Trojans arrived in. However, Turnus is thwarted in this effort by the will of the Gods Jupiter and Cybele. The Trojan ships, cut from timbers from Mount Ida (A mountain sacred to Cybele), are transformed into sea nymphs who swim away unharmed. Turnus is undeterred however by this sign from the gods that perhaps all will not work out for him. He now turns to attack the Trojan camp.

The Trojans for their part man the walls and focus on defending themselves rather than emerging from camp to fight the Latins in open battle. Virgil directs attention to a pair of Trojans who are up to this point unknown to the audience; Nisus and Eurylaus.

Nisus is a veteran warrior and Eurylaus is a young but brave Trojan. The pair decides that Aeneas must be told that the Trojans are under attack. They decide to go themselves and warn him. The duo ensures that they do things properly; they do not leave all of a sudden, but instead they seek permission from the leaders of the Trojans in the camp and wait for the darkness of night. The permission is duly granted and should they succeed they will be well rewarded.

The pair sneaks out of camp at night and enter the lines of the besieging army. Here they set about killing many of their sleeping foes before escaping into the woods and Eurylaus takes a trophy before he escapes; a polished helmet. This Nisus and Eurylaus run into some woods but do not know the way and are separated. Eurylaus is captured and Nisus determines to try to rescue him knowing that it will probably end up with them both dead.

After a fierce struggle both Nisus and Eurylaus are killed, but they slay many of their enemies also.

With the dawn comes the attack of Turnus on the Trojan camp. The news of the deaths of Nisus and Eurylaus reaches the Trojan camp and Eurylaus' mother has to be comforted by the Trojan elders.

The attack on the camp begins. The army of Turnus attack in ways known and understood by the Roman audience of Virgil; they use artillery and approach the walls in a shield formation known as a *'Testudo'* (Tortoise). The Trojans defend themselves well until one of the towers in the Trojan wall is brought down in flames.

Turnus manages to enter the camp and goes on a rampage. He kills many Trojans, but Ascanius in turn kills a prominent Italian who is overly boastful and arrogant towards the Trojans. Having taking the life of a single warrior the God Apollo intervenes and takes Ascanius to a place of safety; he will play no further part in the battles to come. Turnus breaks alone into the Trojan camp and kills many more Trojans. Eventually the Trojans work together to force Turnus to retreat.

The structure of Book Nine

- *Turnus and the ships (lines 1-120)*

- *The speech of Turnus (lines 121-169)*

- *Nisus and Eurylaus (lines 170-501)*

- *The attack on the Trojan camp (lines 502-589)*

- *The death of Numanus (lines 590-670)*

- *The Aristeia of Turnus (lines 671-end)*

-

> ### Task: Turnus in Book Nine
>
> *How is Turnus portrayed in Book Nine? Is it all positive or negative or a mixture of both?*

Turnus and the ships (lines 1-120)

The most prominent character in Book Nine is Turnus. Turnus is present at the start of Bok Nine and Turnus concludes Book Nine with his retreat from the Trojan camp. Turnus comes across in this first part of Book Nine as a pious man. He obeys the commands of Juno (sent through Iris) and he prays for victory.

Turnus arrives before the Trojan camp and challenges any to come forward and fight him in a duel, but none accept. Turnus is also amazed that the Trojans remain within their camp; this is not the act of an epic army full of heroes!

Finally, Turnus spots the Trojan ships and then believes that if he destroys them it will either force the Trojans out to defend them, or will dishearten them. The Goddess Cybele however has other ideas; these are ships made from sacred timbers from Mount Ida. She gave permission for the trees to be felled and the ships to be constructed. She intervenes to save them from the fire of Turnus. But before Turnus can set fire to them; the ships sink, to remerge a moment later as Sea Nymphs.

> **Task: The speech of Turnus**
>
> *What is the content of Turnus' speech?*
>
> *What does he have to say about destiny?*
>
> *What does he have to say about the Trojans, the Greeks and his own army?*

The speech of Turnus (lines 121-169)

In this part of Book Nine, Turnus is portrayed by Virgil as a brave warrior and commander. He commands the army on the march from the centre, he travels ahead to scout out the Trojan camp and challenge them to battle, and he comes up with a plan to try to force the Trojans to fight.

Turnus however is thwarted. He fails to get the Trojans to come out of their camp and fight. He fails to get a Trojan champion to emerge to fight him and he fails to destroy the Trojan ships.

Turnus' speech is one designed to raise the morale of his own men. They have just witnessed a supernatural act and are obviously shaken. Turnus' response is to denigrate the Trojans and to praise his own side. Just to be sure though, he calls a halt to any attack on the camp and is content to besiege the place for the night.

> **Task: The Trojan speeches**
>
> *Virgil deliberately chooses to extend the debate between Nisus, Eurylaus and the Trojan leadership*
>
> *Consider the structure and content of each of the speeches;*
>
> - *The speech of Nisus*
> - *The speech of Aletes*
> - *The speech of Ascanius*
> - *The speech of Eurylaus*

Nisus and Eurylaus (lines 170-501)

Virgil now shifts attention to the Trojans. The Trojans are recognizably Roman in their military practice of building a strong encampment. Virgil even refers to them as a 'legion'. The Trojans Nisus and Eurylaus embark on a discussion; they decide to try to seek out Aeneas at Pallanteum.

Duty remains key however and the pair is responsible. Nisus and Eurylaus determine to seek the permission of the Trojan leaders, but they take care not to abandon their post before they wake Trojans to replace them on watch. They seek and obtain permission from the leaders too.

Nisus explains his plan in his speech and Aletes offers thanks and suggests rewards.

Ascanius offers ample rewards if the pair return with Aeneas, including rewards that are not yet his to give including;

- Twelve female slaves from the Latins
- Twelve male slaves from the Latin armies
- The horse and weapons and armour of Turnus himself

Ascanius also offers Euryalus his friendship.

Before he departs Eurylaus requests that the Trojans look after his mother; he himself does not want to see her before he goes into danger. Ascanius promises to look after Euryalus' mother as if she were his own.

The Trojan duo now leaves the camp armed and ready for battle. In a complete contrast to the Trojan camp, the army of Turnus is drunk and sleeping with few guards. Nisus and Eurylaus attack the sleeping men and kill many.

Eurylaus also strips the dead and takes trophies; medallions and belts from the dead they killed, but Eurylaus also takes up the helmet of Measspus, a man they did not reach or kill. This helmet is fatal to their adventure as the glittering metal betrays their presence.

Eurylaus is captured in part because he lost his way, but also because of the weight of the plunder he had taken from the camp. Nisus seeks to free his friend, but is forced into a hand to hand battle and is finally killed.

The episode has elements of a tragic play. The hero with a plan, the eager comrade whose lack of control results in the taking of trophies at a time when the priority had to be to get through to Aeneas and the subsequent death of the Trojans, betrayed by the trophies taken on the one hand and the love of the other for the one captured.

With dawn the army of Turnus prepares to attack. The heads of

Greek tragedy terms

Agon: A debate

Anagnorisis: recognition

Hamartia: A fatal flaw or act

Kommos: A lament

Peripeteia: A turning point

Rhesis: A set speech

Nisus and Eurylaus are stuck on spears and paraded before the Trojans. Eurylaus' mother learns of the fate of her son and Virgil gives through her a speech, much in shape and appearance to a tragic *kommos* (a lament) which damages the morale of the Trojans before their leaders intervene and remove her from the walls.

Task: The presentation of battle in Book Nine

How successfully do you think Virgil portrays the battle scenes in Book Nine?

What elements might you consider realistic?

What elements might you consider fanciful?

The attack on the Trojan camp (lines 502-589)

The Roman audience would recognize in Virgil's description of the attack by its realistic elements. Virgil describes the Volsci in with their shields in Tortoise formation, the efforts of the Trojans to fire arrows at the attackers and to push scaling ladders away from the wall with wooden poles. The Roman audience would also recognize the use of artillery by the Latin army and their own use of arrows to try to clear the Trojans from their walls. So too is the use of fire to try to burn one of the wooden towers by Turnus.

Virgil is also successful in capturing the emotions of the combatants. The fear and terror of the Trojans as the tower collapses, the Latin leaders urging their men on to greater efforts as well as the contrasting futile bravery of the Trojan Helenus when he finds that he is surrounded and facing certain death against the equally futile attempt by the Trojan Lycus to flee.

Task: Numanus Remulus

How does Numanus portray the Trojans, Greeks and Italians in his speech in Book Nine?

The death of Numanus (lines 590-670)

Ascanius has a greater presence in Book Nine than he does in any of the earlier works. With the absence of Aeneas, Ascanius attempts to stand up and take command of the Trojans and he does this with some success. He is young, but nonetheless establishes some credentials that point towards ability in war by killing Numanus Remulus.

Numanus is arrogant, rude and violent in his attitude towards the Trojans. He taunts them and even manages to belittle the bravery and skill of the Greeks during the Trojan War. Ascanius kills Numanus with an arrow and is then taken away by Apollo to safety, having established that he too can fight.

Key term: Aristeia

An 'Aristeia' is an episode in epic whereby a single warrior performs great deeds of bravery and skill in war; typified by the deaths of many enemies and sometimes concluded by their own death.

A famous example of an Aristeia is that of Patroclus in the Iliad – he defeats the Trojans and drives them from the Greek camp, but is eventually killed.

The *Aristeia* of Turnus (lines 671-end)

In a moment of bravado, two Trojan warriors, Pandarus and Bitias, decide to challenge the Latins. They throw open the gates they are supposed to be defending and determine to fight the army of Turnus hand to hand. They begin to kill many Rutulians with the help of other Trojans who join them.

Turnus hears word of this and storms to attack Pandarus and Bitias and their comrades. In a series of descriptive passages Turnus cuts through many Trojans and when Bitias is killed by a spear thrown from a Latin siege engine, Turnus manages to enter the camp. Pandarus shuts the gate, trapping some Trojans outside and Turnus in the camp. Turnus kills Pandarus and routs the Trojans. Turnus could now open the gate and let his army in. However he decides to attack by himself. He kills many more Trojans but is at last driven from the camp by a more organised group of Trojans who push him out by driving him into the River Tiber.

Homeric Parallels in Book Nine

Because Book Nine is a book filled with battle and conflict, we should not be too surprised to identify elements that remind us of episodes in Homer's *Iliad*. The marauding in the Latin camp by Nisus and Eurylaus bears some close resemblance to that of Diomedes and Odysseus in Book X.

Another parallel is that of Turnus storming the walls and trying to burn the ships with the act of Hector in the Iliad. He too enters the camp of his enemy and tries (and fails) to burn the enemy ships. He too is driven out by overwhelming numbers in Book XV of the *Iliad.*

Pandarus

Strictly speaking Virgil should not include Pandarus in his epic. According to the *Iliad* Pandarus is an archer who is killed by Diomedes fairly early on in the epic. Both of these Pandarus (both Homer and Virgil) are named as close companions of Aeneas so the choice by Virgil to include this Trojan is a little strange. It could be that Virgil is electing to alter the epic narrative by ignoring Pandarus' death in the *Iliad.* The reason for this may be that Virgil wanted a famous Trojan to be killed by Turnus, however many of the more famous Trojans do not survive the Trojan War.

Task: Similes in Book Nine

Identify as many similes as you can in Book Nine.

Who or what do they involve?

What is the subject matter of these similes?

Is it possible to identify a pattern?

Similes in Book Nine

A good proportion of the Similes in Book Nine involve Turnus or the deeds of Turnus.

Turnus is described as wolf like in lines 57-69 – a dangerous predator and in lines 560-568 Turnus is likened to both the eagle of Jupiter and the wolf of Mars. Finally, in lines 791-799 Turnus is likened to a lion confronted by a group of hunters. Turnus then is presented as a dangerous predator in Book Nine and this description is certainly apt considering his actions in Book Nine.

In contrast, Eurylaus is presented in lines 429-439 as like a scarlet flower or a poppy in his death at the hands of Volcens and his men. Finally, the death of Bitias is in lines 702-716 likened to the fall or collapse of a massive pile of stones.

PART SIX: Books Ten to Twelve of the *Aeneid*

PART SIX

6.1: Book Ten: The deaths of Pallas and Mezentius

6.2 Analyzing the Belt of Pallas

6.3 Book Eleven: Drances and Camilla

6.4 Book Twelve: The end of the Aeneid

6.5 Analysing Book Twelve

6.1 Book Ten: The deaths of Pallas and Mezentius

This section will help you to;

- *Understand the events and structure of Book Ten*

- *Continue to explore the characters of Aeneas and Turnus*

- *Explore the presentation of the characters of Mezentius and Lausus*

- *Explore the language used by Virgil to describe the battle scenes in Book Ten*

Introduction

This section will help you to understand the tenth book of the *Aeneid*. Book Ten is a book of war and battle, with much of the content of the book focusing on a particular hero; who they fight, who they kill and also who they are killed by. Book Ten also contains within it a brief but crucial act that results in ensuring the death of Turnus at the end of Book Twelve.

Task: Comprehending Book Ten

Read Book Ten of the Aeneid

Once you have, write brief responses to the following questions;

- *Which characters does Virgil focus on in Book Ten?*

- *Of these characters – who fights whom and who is killed in Book Ten?*

- *Who flees the battle unknowingly? What is their reaction when they realise?*

Book Ten Synopsis

Book Ten begins with the Gods. Jupiter inquires of the other gods why the Trojans are being attacked by Turnus and his army. Venus appeals to Jupiter for mercy – if not for Aeneas, at least she hopes she can save Ascanius by taking him to safety.

Juno however has a different view. She blames the Trojans for the present war and Venus for the Trojan War. Jupiter however declares that all the gods should keep out of the battle; it is for Fate to decide what happens.

Having visited the gods and determined that they will not intervene (although some of them do, as we shall see later) Virgil now directs his audience's attention to the war in Italy.

Aeneas is sailing to the rescue with his Etruscan allies. Virgil gives us a catalogue of the Etruscan forces, their ships, leaders and an idea of their numbers. Aeneas is greeted by the Sea Nymphs that were once his own ships and they tell him of the situation back at the Trojan camp.

In a series of descriptive combats Virgil describes how Aeneas fights, confirming for his audience that he has lost none of his fighting skills since the fall of Troy. Virgil goes onto describe the actions and death of Pallas at the hands of Turnus. The Latins too fight bravely as is shown by the actions of Lausus and his father Mezentius; both of whom subsequently die at the hands of Aeneas.

Turnus, encouraged by his sister Juturna, fights and kills Pallas, which sends Aeneas into a berserk rage. He now fights without mercy or pity, even barbarically. His furor is so much so that Jupiter and Juno are convinced that Aeneas is receiving divine assistance from Venus (although nowhere does Virgil state this to be the case).

Juno saves Turnus from an early confrontation (and death) with Aeneas by deception. He is forced to leave the battlefield. The Latins are not without leaders though, Mezentius takes charge and kills many Trojans and their allies before both he and his son are slain by Aeneas. In an inverse of expectation, Virgil designs his narrative so that it is Mezentius and Lausus that have the sympathy of the reader, Aeneas comes across as callous, taunting and even cruel.

The structure of Book Ten

- *The Council of the Gods (lines 1-119)*

- *The catalogue of the Trojans and the ships (lines 120-217)*

- *The arrival of Aeneas (lines 218-308)*

- *The Aristeia of Aeneas (lines 309-360)*

- *The Aristeia of Pallas (lines 361-422)*

- *The death of Pallas (lines 423-509)*

- *The Furor of Aeneas (lines 510-606)*

- *Juno deceives Turnus (lines 607-689)*

- *The deaths of Lausus and Mezentius (lines 690-end)*

Task: The speeches of the Gods

What evidence does Venus use to support her case?

What evidence does Juno use to support her case?

The Council of the Gods (lines 1-119)

The Council of the Gods in Book Ten comprises of several speeches, almost like those debates that are a key feature of Greek Tragedies. Jupiter plays the role of the impartial Judge. He opens the debate with a question? Why are the Trojans and Latins fighting? Jupiter is neutral in this debate and his concluding comment reinforces this; since Juno and Venus cannot agree (and neither has it seemed can the rest of the gods), Jupiter decides that the Gods will play no role in the war between the Trojans and the Latins. It is up to the Fates to decide.

Venus on the other hand is appealing for justice for the Trojans. If the Trojans cannot settle in Italy, then let them return to Troy, or if that is impossible let Venus save Ascanius if she cannot save her son.

Juno takes a very different view. Juno rejects the idea that Aeneas is fated to be in Italy – she says the prophetess Cassandra put him up to it. Juno also blames Venus for the woes of the Trojans – after all, she was the cause of the Trojan War when she helped Paris steal Helen.

The catalogue of the Trojans and the ships (lines 120-217)

In Book Seven Virgil catalogued the armies and heroes led by Turnus. Now in Book Ten, Virgil catalogues the forces of Aeneas. First of all he lists the prominent Trojans still besieged in their camp, but for the most part of this section Virgil describes the Etruscans that are sailing to the aid of the Trojans. The warriors are named and several of the thirty ships on which they sail are likewise named and described as are their home towns.

The towns and geographical locations named in this catalogue are mostly identifiable. The cities of Pisa and Mantua are in Northern Italy, as is the region known as Liguria.

The arrival of Aeneas (lines 218-308)

Aeneas still knows nothing of the attack on his people. This ignorance is rectified by the arrival of the Sea nymphs – the ships that were transformed in Book Nine. They tell Aeneas of the plight of the Trojans and he is determined to get there as swiftly as he can. Aeneas offers a prayer to Cybele in a manner that stands at odds with the presentation of Aeneas during the heat of the battle.

Turnus witnesses the arrival of the fleet and sees an opportunity to defeat the enemy forces while they are divided. He is presented as cool and calculating here. Tarchon, the king of the Etruscans is much less so. He is so excited by the prospect of war that he runs his ship aground on a reef and is prevented from taking part in the battle to come.

Task: The Aristeia of Aeneas (lines 309-360)

How does Aeneas fight in this part of Book Ten?

What language does Virgil use in this part of the fighting?

The *Aristeia* of Aeneas (lines 309-360)

Aeneas begins fighting in style and with a coolness and calmness that is abandoned later on. He is confident in his own abilities as is shown when he instructs Achates to pile up spears for him to throw. Aeneas is fierce, but he is controlled. He does not taunt his enemies but simply does what he needs to do. Contrast this with later in Book Ten.

The *Aristeia* of Pallas (lines 361-422)

Pallas too has arrived and has joined in the fighting. He sees that his own men are in difficulties and rallies them with words and deeds; re-inspiring his men. Pallas kills many Latin warriors and is likened in a simile to a shepherd who was constructed many fires in order to clear land for farming.

> **Key terms: Aristeia and Furor**
>
> *An 'Aristeia' is an episode in epic whereby a single warrior performs great deeds of bravery and skill in war; typified by the deaths of many enemies and sometimes concluded by their own death.*
>
> *A famous example of an Aristeia is that of Patroclus in the Iliad – he defeats the Trojans and drives them from the Greek camp, but is eventually killed.*
>
> *Furor is a Latin term from which the English words 'Fury' and 'Furious' originate.*
>
> *In the Aeneid Furor occurs when emotions or other violent urges are uncontrolled.*

The death of Pallas (lines 423-509)

Pallas however is matched by a young warrior on the other side, Lausus, the son of Mezentius. Both share common features, both are young, skillful in war and noble in appearance. Both will also die at the hands of a greater warrior in Book Ten; Pallas by Turnus and Lausus by Aeneas.

Turnus now arrives and challenges Pallas who is eager to fight him; either way he says he will achieve glory, either in killing Turnus, or being killed by such a great warrior.

Turnus is less charitable with his words. As he kills Pallas he taunts his corpse and his father Evander. He is giving Evander the son he deserves for giving hospitality to Aeneas.

In Book Nine the Trojan Eurylaus took trophies, a helmet that alerted the enemy to his presence and belts and medals that slowed his escape. Now Turnus too takes a trophy, the belt of Pallas that is embossed with *'an abominable crime'* (lines 490-509).

We will explore this belt and its meaning further in the next topic.

> ### Task: The Furor of Aeneas (lines 510-606)
>
> *How does Aeneas fight in this part of Book Ten?*
>
> *What language does Virgil use in this part of the fighting?*
>
> *What is different from before?*

The *Furor* of Aeneas (lines 510-606)

Aeneas renews his efforts in the fighting. He is no longer cool and skillful; he becomes a bloody slaughterer of his enemies. Aeneas is now fighting in a way that is no longer civilized. He is bent on revenge and retribution. This is no longer *aristeia*; it is *furor*.

- Aeneas takes some prisoners – only so he can sacrifice them later

- Aeneas kills Magus in cold blood when Magus appeals for mercy and offers a ransom

- Aeneas kills an attired priest (we are not told if the priest is a combatant or not)

- Aeneas taunts and kills Tarquitus – the brother of King Latinus whilst he begs for mercy and refuses to bury his corpse

- Two brave Latins; Lucagus and Liger are similarly taunted and dispatched when they confront him in their chariot

Aeneas' *furor* is useful and necessary as it enables him to turn the battle in his favour and breaks the siege of the Trojan camp.

However, it stands in stark contrast to the Aeneas we have been presented with in the earlier parts of the epic. In Book Two we have a foreshadowing of this rage when he tries to murder Helen during the fall of Troy. Now however this *furor* has been unleashed and the audience witnesses the consequences.

In part this *furor* is understandable; his Trojans are retreating and one of his main allies and youthful friends has just been killed. Aeneas is distraught not for himself, but for the grief that he has caused Evander when he learns his son will not be returning from the battle.

Juno deceives Turnus (lines 607-689)

Virgil shifts the scene to Jupiter and Juno, they believe that Venus must be helping Aeneas; but Virgil gives us no evidence of this. Juno rightfully fearing for Turnus if he should confront Aeneas now is granted permission to save him with the warning however that Turnus' fate is sealed.

Juno concocts a phantom in the form and shape of Aeneas and Turnus pursues this phantom, mistakenly believing that Aeneas is fleeing from him. Turnus pursues the phantom onto a ship which is then pushed out to sea by Juno. Turnus realizing he has been deceived despairs. He cannot help in the battle now and is afraid that his own side thinks that he has deserted them. He contemplates suicide, but is prevented from further action by Juno.

> **Task: The death of Mezentius**
>
> *Compare the deeds and actions of Mezentius and Aeneas in Book Ten.*
>
> *What evidence is there to suggest that Mezentius is the more sympathetic character of the pair in Book Ten?*

The deaths of Lausus and Mezentius (lines 690-end)

With the defection of Turnus, the Latins gain a new commander in the form of Mezentius. Virgil gives this warrior an *aristeia*; he kills many of Aeneas' men. Mezentius may have been portrayed by Virgil as a bloody usurper in Book Eight, but he also presents him here as a brave warrior as well.

Mezentius confronts Aeneas and the pair square off. Mezentius' spear is deflected and kills a comrade of Aeneas, Aeneas' return throw wounds Mezentius, but Aeneas is prevented from finishing the contest by the intervention of Lausus. Lausus tries to protect his wounded father and confronts Aeneas himself.

Aeneas kills Lausus, but on seeing the face of his enemy and finding him resembling Pallas in so many ways, Aeneas feels pity and his *furor* passes. He takes the body in his arms and grieves for the young warrior.

Mezentius too learns of the death of his son and is determined to fight Aeneas; wounded as he his. He calls for his horse, Rhaebus to carry him back into battle. Mezentius throws spears at Aeneas from his horse until Aeneas kills Rhaebus, he then finishes off Mezentius as he lies pinned under the horse.

Virgil clearly here is trying to invoke the audience's sympathy for the Latins that are dying at the hands of Aeneas; even Mezentius; the scorner of gods is sympathetically portrayed. In contrast, Aeneas, transforms from heroic warrior to berserker when exposed to the death and carnage he has witnessed and caused.

Task: The battle

Write a response to the following question;

To what extent do you agree with the view that Virgil tries to present both armies favourably in the battle in Book Ten?

6.2 Analyzing the Belt of Pallas

This section will help you to;

- *Understand and explore a key part of Book Ten*

- *Consider Pallas as a heroic victim*

- *Explore the myths and legends Virgil uses to add depth to the Aeneid*

- *Consider the links of the myth of the Danaids to Augustan Rome*

- *Attempt a set of examination style questions*

Introduction

In Book Nine the Trojan Eurylaus took trophies, a helmet that alerted the enemy to his presence and belts and medals that slowed his escape. Now in Book Ten, Turnus too takes a trophy, the belt of Pallas that is embossed with *'an abominable crime'* (lines 490-509). His topic focuses on this belt and its meaning.

Pallas: the heroic victim

The death of Pallas is one of the key events that really pushes the narrative forwards to its imminent climax in Book Twelve.

In Book Eight where we saw at first hand the relationship between Pallas and his father Evander, and the presentation of the endearing character of Pallas himself, we might have been expecting this pair to have an important role in the plot.

Pallas' role in the *Aeneid* is to be similar to the role played by Patroclus in the *Iliad*. He is to be a heroic victim. Like Patroclus, Pallas takes on far more than he is capable of when he confronts Turnus. Perhaps Pallas is foolish to even attempt to fight Turnus, but not only is this necessary to the direction of the plot of the *Aeneid*, it is also indicative of Pallas' bravery and manliness. To compound his victory over this young warrior, Turnus steals Pallas' belt as a trophy.

As mentioned in the previous topic. The news of Pallas' death is important to Aeneas; he was entrusted with the boy and with his safety by his honoured comrade Evander. It is not at all surprising that Pallas' death should incite Aeneas to extreme *furor*, and that Aeneas is overcome with a lust for blood.

There is then a clear and deliberate parallel between Aeneas and Achilles in the *Iliad*: both failed to protect their beloved companion. However, Aeneas or Achilles cannot be held to much to blame for this failure, since both Pallas and Patroclus made the decisions themselves to enter battle, despite knowing the limitations of their own prowess and most importantly, both were destined to die.

After hearing the news of the deaths of their close friends, both Aeneas and Achilles become consumed by a passionate desire for revenge. In both the *Iliad* and the *Aeneid*, it is this theme of revenge that really directs much of the subsequent plot.

The Myth of Danaus and the Danaids

According to Greek mythology, Danaus was a descendent of Zeus and Io (through his ancestor Epaphus) who lived in Egypt. According to Greek mythology Danaus was one of the forefathers of the Greeks. Danaus had fifty children, all of the daughters who married Egyptian husbands, but these husbands angered Danaus. Danaus fled to Argos with his daughters to escape these husbands, but they followed and caught up with their errant father in law.

Danaus now came up with an evil plan. He ordered his daughters (the Danaids) to murder their husbands. All but one of the fifty did so. The daughter who disobeyed was called Hypermestra and her husband Lynceus. In time Hypermestra and Lynceus would have children and from these children would become the line of the Argive kings.

The Danaids remarried (to Greek husbands) and lived out their lives, but for their crime of murder and for breaking the laws of hospitality they were punished in death by being continuously forced to pour water from leaking vessels.

The Danaids and Augustan Rome

In Rome Augustus embarked upon a series of great building and renovation project intended to make Rome a city worthy of the Imperial splendour of the Empire.

According to several Roman writers (Propertius II.3, Ovid. Ars I.73-4 and Tristia III.1.61-2) a series of statues were installed close to the new Temple of Apollo constructed by Augustus' orders on the Palatine hill. These statues depicted the Danaids. Why these statues were installed here has been debated. Several reasons for these statues have been argued including;

- A deliberate act of atonement for the bloodshed in the Civil Wars and the proscriptions following Caesar's assassination

- The triumph of civilisation over barbarism (the 'Greek' Danaids overcoming their Egyptian husbands)

- The Danaids are an allusion to Cleopatra who was thought to have murdered her husband's Ptolemy XIII and Ptolemy XIV (who were also incidentally her brothers). As a result she was guilty of mariticide amongst her other crimes against the Roman state.

Note!

One of the Mythical Danaids had the name Cleopatra – a common enough name in Ancient Greece, but also very convenient for use in Augustan propaganda!

6.3 Book Eleven: Drances and Camilla

This section will help you to;

- *Understand the events and structure of Book Eleven*

- *Explore the language and style of the speeches of Book Eleven*

- *Continue to analyse the descriptive language of battle in the Aeneid*

- *To consider the characters of Camilla and Lavinia*

Introduction

Book Eleven could be described as a book of two halves. In the first half the bulk of the narrative is comprised of speeches and dialogue between a variety of characters; Aeneas, Evander, Drances and Turnus. In keeping with Virgil's love of Tragedy, there is also a Messenger Speech bringing the response of Diomede.

The second part of Book Eleven is a description of a battle between the cavalry forces of the Latins and the vanguard of Aeneas' army. Neither Turnus nor Aeneas take part in this fight, but Virgil offers his audience the exciting spectacle of a fierce warrior woman fighting and dying heroically.

Book Eleven Synopsis

Aeneas and his victorious army build trophies and bury their dead after the battle before the Trojan camp. Pallas' death is lamented by Aeneas and Pallas' body is sent back to his father with a suitable honour guard.

Aeneas also receives a deputation from the Latins requesting permission to take up and bury their dead soldiers. Aeneas grants this and also uses the opportunity to repeat his desire for peace. Aeneas is replied to by Drances; a Latin who hates Turnus. A twelve day truce is granted.

Evander who receives the body of Pallas and he too grieves. Virgil now describes the burial rites of the Trojans and Latins; amongst the Latins the people are divided between those who hate Turnus and those who support him. The Latins are in discord with Drances heaping abuse on Turnus.

News arrives from the Greek hero Diomede. He has heard the request for assistance from the Latins and his response has arrived. Diomede's response is that the Trojan War is over, everyone lost much in that conflict and that it would be unwise for the Latins to reject Aeneas. Drances once again abuses Turnus in a speech and

Turnus replies; he will gather his allies and continue the fight against Aeneas.

The truce ends and Aeneas is determined to end the war. He marches on Latium and Turnus and his allies prepare to renew the battle. One warrior in particular is focused on in Book Eleven; the warrior woman Camilla. Camilla's background is told and how the goddess Diana loves her. Diana knows that Camilla is fated to die in the upcoming battle, but she instructs Opis, one of her divine companions, to observe the battle and kill in turn the man that slays Camilla.

A cavalry battle ensues and Camilla is prominent in the fight. She has an *aristeia*, slaying many of the Trojans and their allies, but she is stalked across the battlefield by Arruns. As Camilla is blinded to all other dangers when she targets the gaudily attired Chloreus, she does not see Arruns stalking her in turn. Arruns mortally wounds Camilla but is in turn shot down by Opis. The battle turns on the death of Camilla and the Latins begin to panic.

Book Eleven ends with the arrival on the battlefield of both Aeneas and Turnus, setting the scene for the long awaited confrontation.

The structure of Book Elven

- *Burying the dead (lines 1-201)*
- *The Latin Council (lines 202-530)*
- *Camilla (lines 531-598)*
- *Camilla fights and dies (lines 599-end)*

Task: Exploring the speeches in 'Burying the Dead' (XI. 1-201)

Read Book Eleven 1-201

Explore the language used by Virgil to describe the speeches and dialogue in this part of Book XI.

Burying the dead (lines 1-201)

Book Eleven begins with Aeneas burying the fallen warriors of his army and erecting a trophy to mark the victory. The trophy is the bloodied arms and armour of Mezentius; the *Spoilia Opima* of a fallen enemy commander.

The bulk of this part of Book Eleven is occupied by a series of speeches and dialogue;

- Aeneas makes a brief speech to encourage his allies to make a final effort to end the war, but first they must do what is right and bury their dead (lines 12-29).

- Aeneas' lament for Pallas (lines 40-59)

- Aeneas' address to the Latin envoys (lines 109-120)

- Drances' reply to Aeneas (lines121-131)

- Evander's lament for Pallas (lines 151-181)

This part of Book Eleven ends with a description of the funerals of the Trojans and their allies.

Spoila Opima

The spoila opima were the offerings dedicated to the gods by a Roman commander that had personally slain an enemy commander in single combat.

The presentation of Aeneas in Book Eleven

Aeneas is uncharacteristically conversational in Book Eleven. Despite Aeneas being the primary character of the epic, he often says little (or is not even present). This is not the case here, and in these speeches Virgil is providing his audience with more evidence of Aeneas' piety and generosity. This is important that he does this as Aeneas came across as rather bloodthirsty at the end of Book Ten. By presenting Aeneas in the central role of a leader *after* the battle – it shows that Aeneas' actions in battle stand at odds with his usual personality; as a leader of men that is genuinely caring of their wellbeing. Aeneas is also pious and generous to his defeated enemies; he bears their dead no malice. At the same time tough Aeneas is determined to achieve peace through any means;

including renewing the battle and achieving peace through the elimination of all opposition.

Task: Funerals in Book Eleven

Read Book Eleven 181-219

These lines describe the burials of the fallen; both Trojan and Latin.

Explore the language used by Virgil to describe the funeral scenes on each side.

In what ways are they similar and in what ways are they different?

The Latin Council (lines 202-530)

Like the first two hundred lines of Book XI, the next three hundred and thirty lines also is dominated by a series of speeches and dialogue;

- The 'Messenger Speech'; the response of Diomede to the Latins (lines 242-298)

- King Latinus' Speech (lines 302-335)

- Drances' Response (lines 340-377)

- Turnus' Speech (lines 379-487)

Task: Exploring the speeches in 'The Latin Council'

Read Book Eleven lines 202-530

Explore the language used by Virgil to describe the speeches and dialogue in this part of Book XI.

In what ways are the tone and language of these speeches different to those earlier in Book Eleven?

This part of Book Eleven ends with Camilla and Turnus planning the next battle against Aeneas. If the first part of Book Eleven is one of sadness at the losses suffered by Aeneas, it is also tinged with a tone of determination to end the war successfully. The Trojans and their allies are united and determined to win.

The second part of Book Eleven contrasts strongly with the first. Here the tone is one of sadness with the funerals of the warriors; but Virgil presents the Latins as divided and in varying degrees of despair. Their hope that Diomede will come to fight Aeneas is thwarted. Diomede expresses that it is Fate that has brought Aeneas to Italy. He will establish a city and the ghosts of the Trojan War will be laid to rest. Diomede has no desire to begin a new Trojan War in Italy.

King Latinus is mindful to negotiate with Aeneas and is tactful as regards Turnus *'I accuse no one' (XI.313)*. However, if Latinus cannot or will not point the finger of blame for his people's plight at anyone (including himself), this view is not shared by Drances. Drances hates Turnus and places the blame for the war squarely on the shoulders of Turnus.

Turnus in turn defends himself with spirit. He rounds on Drances, calls him 'scum' and a traitor. Turnus himself will defend his people from the Trojan threat. Turnus reminds Latinus and Drances that there are still many allies eager to fight the Trojans. If they fight so too will Turnus.

Camilla (lines 531-598)

Virgil uses a digression to describe the character of Camilla in some detail. Camilla's birth and origins are detailed, as are her skills in war.

The method Virgil uses if for the Goddess Diana to tell the story of Camilla to her companion Opis. Diana also tells Opis that Camilla will die in the upcoming fight. She instructs Opis to witness the battle and kill in turn the man who kills Camilla.

The character of Camilla

Camilla is a warrior maiden, a huntress in the model of the goddess Diana, the virgin huntress. Camilla has taken on the man's role of fighting. Camilla challenges the established Roman gender stereotypes of women, and dies a death that any Roman hero would be proud of.

Although it is Camilla's tragedy that even her patron goddess Diana cannot save her, since fate is against her. She is one on the role-call of those who must die in the establishment of Rome as supreme power, and the bitterness of her fate leads us towards the final climax and ending of Book Twelve.

Task: Lavinia and Camilla

Compare and contrast the characters of Lavinia and Camilla in Book Eleven.

Lavinia

Camilla occupies about half of Book Eleven, and since she is an interesting and exciting character, this seems a sensible plotting decision on the part of Virgil.

However, in comparison, Lavinia has been almost invisible in the narrative so far. This is rather strange when you consider how little description we have of Lavinia, in contrast, who surely has a greater role to play in Aeneas' and Rome's ultimate destiny.

Lavinia is Aeneas' future wife, and her marriage is one of the reasons for the conflict between Turnus and Aeneas, and yet she only has a few lines in Book Eleven. Instead of taking a key position in the narrative of the *Aeneid*, Lavinia is treated as if she were as the cause of the present evils. This is true to some extent, though this is rather unfair to Lavinia, since it is Fate that is causing the conflict between Turnus and Aeneas, not the actions or choices of Lavinia herself.

Lavinia herself has done nothing, since she is the model of a good Roman maiden: chaste, virtuous, modest, unassuming and beautiful. Perhaps Lavinia does not excite Virgil that much because she is such a well-established Roman stereotype, whereas Camilla is not.

Camilla fights and dies (lines 599-end)

The final half of Book Eleven is dedicated to another battle. The scene is before the walls of the city of King Latinus. As the Trojans and their allies approach Turnus takes a portion of the forces to lie in wait in ambush. This is a little weak on the part of Virgil, but it does remove Turnus from the remainder of the action in Book Eleven.

Aeneas too will be absent from the battle in Book Eleven. He accompanies the main body of his army. The fight that will be detailed is a cavalry skirmish in which the leading parts of the Trojan army are attacked by the cavalry forces of the Latins led by Camilla.

The cavalry battle is graphically described and may have been found of interest to the elite Roman aristocracy that was the target audience of Virgil as these men typically went to battle mounted on horses. Virgil uses a simile in lines 624-629 to liken the rapid movement of attack and withdrawal to the ebb and flow of the sea as each side charged and counter charge in turn.

Camilla is an unusual warrior – not only is she a woman (and accompanied by women bodyguards), but she is highly skilled in the use of many weapons. Unlike other fighters in the *Aeneid*, Camilla uses a variety of weapons such as a sword, axe, spear and bow. Virgil even has Camilla fire arrows from horseback using the famous 'Parthian Shot' in lines 650-659.

Virgil uses another simile to describe Camilla in battle; she is like *'the Sacred Falcon'* in lines 70-72

The Trojans and their allies have their leaders too. Having finally extricated himself from the shipwreck of his vessel in Book Ten, The Etruscan king Tarchon bloodily kills Venulus; as described through the use of another simile; Tarchon is described as a Tawny Eagle that grasps a snake in lines 750-757.

Camilla's death comes through a series of hunting parallels. Camilla is stalking the rather gaudily dressed Chloreus (line s770-779), who seems oblivious to the peril he is in. But in turn Camilla is unknowingly hunted by Arruns. Arruns sees an opportunity and throws a spear which fatally wounds Camilla.

Camilla is permitted a brief dying speech, calling on Turnus to come and join the fight. Arruns is offered no such speech; he is swiftly killed by Opis.

Task: Women in the Aeneid

Write an essay style response to the following question;

To what extent do you agree with the view that Virgil always presents mortal women characters in a sympathetic light?

6.4 Book Twelve: The end of the Aeneid

This section will help you to;

- *Understand the events and structure of Book Twelve*

- *Continue to analyse the descriptive language of battle in the Aeneid*

- *Explore the language and style of the speeches of Book Twelve*

- *Continue to explore Homeric parallels in the Aeneid*

Introduction

The final book of the *Aeneid*, The long awaited confrontation between Turnus and Aeneas is about to happen. Given the repeated references that it is Aeneas' fate to achieve victory, the audience knows that Turnus is doomed. It does remain however for the audience to learn how Turnus will meet his own fate and under what circumstances.

This section focuses further on the culmination of the *Aeneid* in Book Twelve and the comparisons that can be made between Homer and Virgil. We will also explore the ending of the *Aeneid* and consider if it is a satisfactory ending.

> *Task: The end of Book Twelve*
>
> *Read the Aeneid Book Twelve*
>
> *Consider especially how it ends.*
>
> *What strikes you about the ending?*

Book Twelve synopsis

The opposing forces of Turnus and Aeneas are camped outside the city of King Latinus. The forces of Turnus have been twice defeated now in battle; outside the Trojan camp and in the cavalry battle. Now Turnus has decided to act. He announces that he will challenge Aeneas to single combat.

Aeneas also prepares for battle and the next day sees the opposing armies assemble to witness the fight. The goddess Juno is no longer able to intervene directly but she still desires conflict and calls upon the nymph Juturna (Turnus' sister) to intervene and try to either save her brother or disrupt the truce.

Turnus and Aeneas approach the combat zone. Aeneas prays and swears that his men will respect the outcome in the event of his own death. The Latins however cannot help but compare Turnus against Aeneas and doubt the successful outcome they hope for. Juturna hears the mutterings of the Latins and acts; she deceives the Latins into witnessing a false omen and one of them, a Rutulian called Tolumnius acts first, throwing a spear at the Trojans. The truce is broken and battle erupts.

Aeneas tries to keep the peace but is wounded by an arrow. He is forced to leave the field and seek medical attention. Seeing this, Turnus rejoices and, helped by his sister goes on a rampage, killing many.

Aeneas lay wounded and in danger until Venus comes to heal him herself. Fully restored, Aeneas re-joins the fight and turns the tide. Juturna joins Turnus in his chariot and they continue to run amok, but are still unwilling to fight Aeneas. When he approaches, they flee.

The battle draws near to the city and Queen Amata in despair hangs herself, believing that Turnus is already dead. Turnus has an opportunity to flee, but his sense of honour prevents it. He agrees to return to the main battle and face Aeneas.

Aeneas and Turnus meet in battle; Turnus soon tries to flee again when his sword snaps and Aeneas pursues. Juturna intervenes once more to give Turnus a new sword. The scene then shifts to Jupiter and Juno. Jupiter forbids Juno to intervene anymore and urges her to accept Fate. Juno agrees reluctantly, but arrives at a novel way for peace; the Trojans can settle in Italy, but let them become absorbed into the peoples of Italy; let the Trojans become Latins (and in time Romans).

A Dirae is sent to ensure that Juturna also no longer tries to save Turnus. Transformed as a bird of ill omen the Dirae convinces Juturna to leave Turnus to his fate.

Turnus and Aeneas now meet in single combat. The duel renews and Turnus is soon overcome. He is wounded and begs for mercy. Aeneas is inclined to be merciful, but then notices the belt of Pallas. In a fit of rage (*furor*), Aeneas kills Turnus.

The structure of Book XII

Book XII can be most easily divided into the following sections;

- *Turnus demands a duel 1-257*

- *The Aristeias of Turnus and Aeneas 258-574*

- *The death of Amata 575-610*

- *Turnus and Juturna 611-699*

- *Aeneas pursues Turnus 700-790*

- *Jupiter and Juno 791-842*

- *The death of Turnus 843-end*

Turnus demands a duel 1-257

In the *Iliad*, Hector's actions seal his own fate when he kills Patroclus and the fight between Achilles and Hector bears some close resemblance to the fight between Aeneas and Turnus in the *Aeneid*.

In the tradition of a Greek Tragedy, the main protagonist commonly ends getting what they ask for, if not the outcome they expect. So for example, Oedipus discovers who killed King Laius in Sophocles' Oedipus *Rex*, but also discovers the awful truth that he murdered his own father and married his own mother. Agamemnon comes back from Troy in glory and to return to his wife Clytemnestra in Aeschylus' play *Agamemnon* only to end up brutally murdered shortly later at the hands of his wife and her lover.

So too in Book XII, Turnus demands a single combat with Aeneas. He demands that King Latinus make the arrangements; the winner will marry Lavinia and the loser will end up dead. Despite all the warnings of fate and the evidence that the Trojans have already defeated the Latins in two battles, Turnus still asks for what he will get; his own death.

> ### Task: Turnus demands a duel
>
> *Explore the dialogue in lines 1-257*
>
> *Who says what? What is the tone of their speeches and who or what is addressed?*

This part of Book XII is dominated by dialogue and exchanges between people;

Turnus speaks to Latinus (lines 11-18), Latinus replies (lines 19-45), Amata then speaks to Turnus (lines 59-65) followed by Turnus' response (lines 72-80). Again in the tradition of a tragedy, Turnus refuses to listen to what Lavinia and Amata have to say; King Latinus is saddened that the prospect of marriage of his daughter is the cause of all this conflict, but he agrees to participate as an adjudicator. Queen Amata also laments that her chosen champion Turnus is to fight and she declares that should he die, then she will also. Turnus consoles Amata, but remains adamant and prepares for battle.

Virgil then has Turnus address his spear in the form of a prayer. This apostrophé is a literary device used to increase the tension and drama of a situation. Perhaps the most famous example of an *apostrophé* is Shakespeare's Hamlet when Hamlet addresses a skull after he meets a gravedigger.

Virgil scene shifts to Aeneas likewise preparing for battle and then on again to the Gods. Here Juno addresses Juturna, a nymph and sister of Turnus. Juno calls on Juturna to help her brother for as long as Fate permits it. Both Juno and Juturna realise that Turnus is going to die and Virgil's audience can be in no doubt as to the eventual outcome: Turnus will die, it is only now to discover under what circumstances.

Both Aeneas and Latinus offer up prayers, not to their weapons, but directly to the gods. Note the contrast here between Turnus' prayer to his spear (which is futile), to Aeneas' prayer to the gods (which is answered). Latinus' prayer includes Aeneas – but there is no mention of Turnus. It is as if Turnus is already being excluded and that there can be only one winner. Even the Latin soldiers realise that Turnus stands no chance, when they compare Turnus against Aeneas.

In the *Iliad* Book V the truce that is arranged so that the duel between Menelaus and Paris is eventually thwarted when a Trojan is talked into firing an arrow by the machinations of a god; so too in the *Aeneid*, this truce is broken by Juturna, who persuades the priest Tolumnias to throw his spear.

The *Aristeias* of Turnus and Aeneas 258-574

As the fighting erupts once more the language used by Virgil shifts to description of battle and violence. There is some dialogue, but it is short and often taunting. Messapus taunts a solider he kills for example. Aeneas tries to keep the peace and his dialogue is conciliatory; however the response is an arrow that wounds him in the thigh and forces him to withdraw from the battle.

This clears the way for Turnus to have an *aristeia*; a series of fights in which he kills many of his enemies. This *aristeia* ends however when Aeneas is healed by his mother and returns to the fight.

Aeneas now has his turn to kill many Latins, but first and foremost he seeks out Turnus and to end the war. To achieve this he calls on the Trojans to storm the city of King Latinus.

The death of Amata 575-610

In an interlude from the carnage on the field of battle, Virgil shifts attention to Amata. Seeing the city under attack and no sight of Turnu, Amata fulfils her promise to Turnus and she commits suicide.

See Section 7.1 for more on Roman Values and a comparison of the suicides of Amata and Dido.

Turnus and Juturna 611-699

This episode of Book XII identifies well with aspects of tragedy. Whilst the city is under attack by the Trojans, Turnus is oblivious to events. He is on the edge of the battle chasing a few stragglers and making little or no contribution to the main part of the battle. Turnus begins to realise that he is fighting in the wrong place. Juturna, who is with Turnus in his chariot, tries to persuade Turnus to continue to fight as he is. He is still killing lots of Trojans, no matter what else is happening.

Turnus though is not so sure. He grieves for the dead on his own side.

A wounded messenger called Saces arrives – he brings terrible news. The city is under attack, Queen Amata has committed suicide and whilst a few brave Latins try to keep the defence intact, it is Turnus who is most needed, but he is avoiding his duty by wandering about and refusing to return to the heart of the fighting.

Turnus is distraught and realises that he can no longer avoid his fate. Virgil gives Turnus a beautiful -set of lines (677-680) to his sister;

'I am resolved to meet Aeneas in battle.

I am resolved to suffer what bitterness there is in death.

You will not see me put to shame again.

This is madness, but before I die, I beg of you, let me be mad.'

Turnus then calls on Aeneas to face him in single combat once more.

Aeneas pursues Turnus 700-790

Aeneas is just as eager as Turnus at this stage to fight a duel and the fight between the pair rapidly commences. Virgil uses an extended simile likening both combatants to a pair of bulls as they clash with each other.

However, Turnus is struck a new blow by fate; the sword he is using snaps against the armour of Aeneas and defenceless, Turnus seeks safety in flight. Here Virgil uses another simile; Aeneas is now a hunting dog pursing a stag.

Turnus for his part calls continuously for someone to fetch his sword, whilst Aeneas threatens those who might intervene. Aeneas is clearly not interested in chivalry. He wants to kill Turnus as he is; unarmed.

In another reversal, we see that the Trojans are guilty of some impiety; they have cut down a sacred olive tree sacred to Faunus line (770-771). The remains of this tree thwart Aeneas as he throws his spear and it is trapped in the tree stump. This delays Aeneas sufficiently for Turnus to be given his sword by Juturna. Venus too intervenes and gives Aeneas his spear back.

> **Task: Juno and the Trojans**
>
> *How is Juno reconciled at last to the Trojan cause?*
>
> *What does this tell us about the nature of the gods and their attitudes towards mortals?*

Jupiter and Juno 791-842

Virgil shifts the scene for the final time to the gods. Jupiter now commands Juno to accept Fate. Aeneas will become a god of Italy and Jupiter forbids Juno now to intervene further.

Juno accepts this command (note that up until this point in the *Aeneid*, Jupiter has not expressly commanded Juno to stop her harassment of the Trojans). She will accept Fate, but asks one thing of Jupiter; that the Trojans become Italians, and not the other way around.

Jupiter accepts this. He will ensure that the Trojans become Latins and those they will be united in blood, language and modes of worship.

In much the same way that Odysseus is required to placate Poseidon once he returns to Ithaca in the *Odyssey*; Juno must also be placated before any satisfactory conclusion can be reached.

This request being granted, Juno then switches her allegiance, reminding the audience of the fickle attitude to mortal affairs that the gods were thought to take. Events are doubly determined: peace between the two factions can now be possible. On the one hand because of Aeneas' promises, and also because Juno agrees to stop sowing discord on the other.

The death of Turnus 843-end

In Book Seven Juno sent the Fury Allecto to sow discord, now Jupiter commands one of the fearsome Dirae to recall Juturna. These savage and fearsome goddesses attend Jupiter directly and Juturna can be in no doubt who has sent the command for her to abandon Turnus. The Dirae needs no words, she is transformed into a black bird that screeches and dives continuously at Turnus' face.

Nonetheless, Juturma is distraught. She is abandoning her beloved brother on the commands of the God that on the one hand gave Juturna her divinity, but he only did so because she was, like many others, a victim and unwilling sexual conquest of Jupiter.

Turnus faces Aeneas once more, but he is afraid; afraid that the gods have condemned him to death. This fear impacts on Turnus to the extent that he fumbles the throw of a massive boulder. Virgil dwells on Turnus' fear (lines 912-913);

'...the strength we know we have, fails our body; we have no voice, no words to obey our will – so it was with Turnus'

Turnus is afraid, but Aeneas is certainly not. He throws his spear and wounds Turnus. Turnus tries to find pity in Aeneas, he talks about the grief he will cause his father; either dead or alive, he begs Aeneas, let him return to his father.

Aeneas is hesitant, but only for a moment. He spots the belt of Pallas that Turnus wears as a trophy and acts. Turnus is dispatched in a furious rage.

Virgil leaves it unanswered whether Aeneas will return the body to Turnus' father, or will he leave it unburied on the battlefield.

6.5 Analysing Book Twelve

This section will help you to;

- *Continue to analyse the descriptive language of battle in the Aeneid*

- *Explore the language and style of the speeches of Book Twelve*

- *Continue to explore Homeric parallels in the Aeneid*

- *Analyse the characters of Aeneas and Turnus*

- *Consider if we can call Book XII 'The tragedy of Turnus'*

- *Analyse the death of Turnus*

- *Consider how satisfactory you think the ending of the Aeneid is*

Introduction

In this section we will analyse aspects of Book Twelve in greater detail.

Task: Speeches of Book Twelve

What are the purposes of Aeneas' and King Latinus' speeches on the terms of the single combat?

Speeches in Book Twelve

There are several speeches in Book Twelve. We have already explored the early speeches.

Importantly, Aeneas promises in his speech before the duel that should he win, *he will not enslave the Italians to the Trojans*. Instead, he seeks a partnership of equals. We as the audience already know that Aeneas will win; the audience knows that Aeneas has witnessed in the Underworld (Book Six) of what is to be, and the omens and interventions of the gods have shown us the inevitability of what is to happen.

Aeneas' promises for the future are a reminder that although we know what is to happen, not all of the characters themselves are aware. Gradually, some (even his own allies) are becoming aware that Turnus cannot win, with the full realisation coming too late for Turnus.

The contemporary audience of Virgil knew also that Rome under Augustus was the culmination of all these earlier struggles and triumphs. They knew through reading Virgil that the Rome of their day, under the rule of Augustus, was the legacy of their forebears. Virgil encouraged the view in the *Aeneid* that the Romans of his day were the living embodiment of their ancestors' successes and achievements.

King Latinus' speech is likewise solemn; he swears an oath to Jupiter and the conditions are honoured with ritual sacrifices. It does not bode well that shortly, the conditions of the pact are broken. King Latinus' speech bears a close resemblance to that given by King Priam in the *Iliad* in Book V when Paris promises to fight Menelaus for Helen. As in the *Aeneid*, the truce made to witness the duel of Menelaus and Paris is betrayed by divine forces.

Task: Similes in Book Twelve

There are many similes in Book XII.

Identify at least five and explore their language and style.

Exploring similes in Book XII

There are many similes in Book XII. Many are used to describe Turnus and Aeneas as fighters, but some are used to describe goddesses' actions. Others are used to convey emotions in peripheral characters witnessing events or acting in the background.

Turnus is the focus of many similes;

- to a lion (lines 1-10)

- to a bull (lines 103-105)

- to the God Mars (lines 332-337)

- to a boulder (683-690)

Aeneas is similarly portrayed like Turnus as;

- an approaching storm (lines 451-457)

- a hunting dog (lines 749-758)

Together Virgil portrays Turnus and Aeneas as;

- Fires and rivers (lines 521-528)

- A pair of clashing bulls (713-722)

Juturna is likened as driving the chariot like a swallow (lines 472-478) and the Dirae is likened to an arrow (lines 855-860).

The Latin army is likened to a hive of bees defending their home in lines 588-592

These similes are interconnected to the overall narrative of Book XII on several occasions. The choice of likening Turnus to a boulder is revisited when Turnus picks up the boulder to throw at Aeneas for example. Juturna drives Turnus around the battlefield like a swallow, yet it is a small black bird that the Dirae transforms itself into when Juturna is commanded to abandon Turnus.

The similes deployed early in the book present Turnus as a fearsome warrior; at the end though he is afraid and scared, very unlike a lion, a bull or the God of war.

Task: The death of Turnus

Write a response to the following question;

To what extent do you agree with the view that Turnus does not deserve his death?

Comparing the climatic battles in Virgil and Homer

The single combat between Turnus and Aeneas (when it does finally happen) stands in contrast to the duels in the *Iliad* and also in stark contrast to the slaughter in the Hall of Ithaca at the end of the *Odyssey*.

In the *Iliad* there are several duels;

- The duel of Menelaus and Paris

- The duel of Hector and Ajax

- The fight of Achilles and Hector

In the duel of Menelaus and Paris; the duel rapidly becomes a farce as the outmatched Paris is hidden by Aphrodite (Venus) once it is clear that Menelaus is going to win. This duel ends with an arrow fired by the Trojans (by the archer Pandarus who is tricked into it by a God), which wounds Menelaus in the thigh and causes the fighting to start. This duel resembles in part the one at the beginning of Book Twelve of the *Aeneid*.

In the duel of Hector and Ajax, both warriors establish themselves, but both survive. The fighters exchange gifts. There is no parallel to this in the *Aeneid*.

In the fight between Achilles and Hector (we should not really call it a duel), Hector is pursued around the walls of Troy by a vengeful Achilles and only stops to fight and die when he is tricked into it. He believes his brother Deiphobus is coming to help him; when in fact 'Deiphobus' is nothing more than a phantom. Virgil has drawn upon this fight earlier in the *Aeneid*. In Book Ten Turnus pursues a phantom of Aeneas which draws him away from the battle. Likewise, in Book Twelve, Turnus is pursued by Aeneas after his sword snaps.

There are other similarities though, one side of the protagonists is fated to die, and in both cases, the unlucky one only realises this too late.

The Suitors in the *Odyssey* and Turnus are also similar in that they fail to recognise that it is their fate to die, until too late. Like Turnus though, some are resolved to meet danger and death face-to-face, rather than to hold back from the fight once they realise there is no avoiding the battle. Some however do not, but trapped in the hall, they cannot escape.

Task: The death of Turnus continued

How satisfied are you with the end of the Aeneid?

Did you expect this ending?

How is Turnus portrayed? How is Aeneas?

This can be a difficult question to answer, and of course many have disagreed over interpreting this death.

The presentation of character in Book XII: Aeneas and Turnus

Both Aeneas and Turnus undergo a transformation in Book XII. Turnus begins Book XII in rage, anger and fury (*furor*). He refuses to listen to the warning words of Latinus and Amata and becomes a victim of circumstances beyond his control. He should meet Aeneas in a duel early in Book XII, but this duel is delayed through the machinations of Juno and Juturna. During the resulting battle Turnus comes to realise that he is doomed and in doing so dooms himself when he succumbs to fear. Fear and madness together combine to make him challenge Aeneas to a duel for a second time, but when he suffers the misfortune of his sword breaking, he has no alternative but to flee; and when he flees he is ashamed to do so in front of all the assembled allies and enemies.

When it comes to the end of Book XII Turnus is barely able to fight. He tries to throw a rock but his own fear saps his strength. However, when it comes to his death, Turnus recovers his courage. He bravely requests of Aeneas to kill him or spare him and places his fate in the hands of Aeneas. Turnus' journey through Book XII then is a transformation from rage to fear to acceptance of fate.

Aeneas' journey in Book XII is the opposite of Turnus'. Turnus is already accepting of fate. He accepts that he is fated to establish the Trojans in Italy; that he is fated to marry Lavinia. This remains constant.

However, Aeneas begins Book XII as pious. He prays to the gods that he will be fair by the Italians *when* he wins. He shows good faith in accepting the challenge of Turnus. He perseveres in trying to maintain the truce even after violence erupts.

Aeneas however is wounded and this, combined with the sight of Turnus running amok through the ranks of the Trojans drives Aeneas to fury (*furor*) he determines to destroy the Latins in battle and even to sack the city of his future bride to be.

When Aeneas fights Turnus he shows him no mercy. He is determined to kill Turnus, even if he is unarmed (as he is when his sword snaps). Aeneas only seems to hesitate right at the end after he has wounded Turnus, but any thoughts he might have of mercy are rapidly overcome by rage when he sees the belt of Pallas. Once he spots this belt Turnus is doomed.

> **Task: Book XII 'The tragedy of Turnus'?**
>
> *Explore the language, tone and content of Book XII.*
>
> *To what extent can we consider Book XII to be the tragedy of Turnus?*
>
> *In what ways does the evidence support this statement?*
>
> *In what ways does the evidence challenge this statement?*

Turnus and Book XII as a tragedy

Turnus can be seen as undergoing the journey of a Tragic Hero in Book XII. He takes part in an *agon* in the early stages (with Latinus and Amata), his *hamartia* (fatal flaw) is false belief that he can win against Aeneas. A *peripeteia* (turning point) is realised through the messenger speech (another feature of Greek tragedy) of Saces as well as the kommos (lament speech) of Juturna. Finally Turnus undergoes an anagnorisis (recognition of fate) when he realises that he will die.

The death of Turnus

When Aeneas catches sight of Pallas' belt being worn by Turnus the decision that Aeneas makes to kill Turnus is a sudden one; a decision driven by emotion. You could say it is murder.

However, the decision may not be as sudden as it seems. In Book Eleven there are several suggestions that this decision is to be expected;

- Aeneas has been identified as feeling guilty and responsible for failing to carry out this duty towards protecting Pallas. (Book XI.40-50)

- Evander also states that it is the duty of Aeneas to avenge Pallas' death by killing Turnus (Book XI.178)

These two long-standing duties inform the audience that Aeneas' decision to kill Turnus is inevitable. It could also be added that Aeneas has always been an unwilling fighter and a somewhat unwilling leader of men ever since he departed his beloved Troy.

As we have seen, it is consistently destiny and his own sense of duty that has driven him on, as it always has done, and perhaps Aeneas is only carrying out the commands of Fate (that he should marry Lavinia and that Turnus should die) in the *Aeneid*.

The killing of Turnus, when Aeneas is on the point of mercy, achieves the dual purpose of fulfilling destiny as well as his own sense of duty.

Task: Speeches of Turnus in Book Twelve

Explore the language, tone and content of Turnus' speeches in Book XII.

In what ways do they stay the same, and in what ways do they change?

A Modern ending?

In Homer's epic poems the *Iliad* and *Odyssey*, the end of each of these poems is about reconciliation and a purging of violence and anger. Achilles relents his rage and gives Priam the body of Hector in the *Iliad*, whilst in the *Odyssey*, Odysseus makes peace with the Ithacans who naturally want revenge for the deaths of their sons and loved ones.

Virgil does something different, something more 'modern' at the end of his story. In many, many Hollywood films and in many fiction books today for example, the end of the film or book sees a climatic encounter between the hero and the villain and all too often, the villain ends up dead, or in prison or in another posture of defeat. The hero is then either satisfied that they have solved the problem through the elimination of their enemy. This is exactly what Virgil does in the *Aeneid*.

The end of the *Aeneid*

Whether or not the audience finds the death of Turnus satisfying, we should consider if this is a 'good' way for Virgil to end the *Aeneid*. Some have noted the rather abrupt and sudden finish, almost as if Virgil has broken off in mid-flow, rather than coming to a proper and rounded finish. Possibly this was not intended by Virgil. Virgil did die before he could complete the *Aeneid* so what we have is ultimately a draft version of the *Aeneid*.

However, Virgil has done a good job of preparing the 'true' ending for us. It could be that there were more books to follow.

The audience do know that Lavinia and Aeneas shall marry; that there will be concord and unity in Italy for the time being; that Rome will become great and that Aeneas' son Ascanius and his successors will bring the dream of Roman greatness closer to reality.

Virgil never needed to write any more books about all these things happening because the audience has already been reassured that they will happen.

Virgil has however completed the story of Aeneas. These other events also do not concern Aeneas directly, since he is fated to die only a few years later. The *Aeneid* is, as it has always been, about *pius* Aeneas, the Trojan hero who was to contribute to the foundation of what will be Rome.

PART SEVEN: Further analysis of the *Aeneid*

PART SEVEN

7.1 Roman Social and Religious Values and the Aeneid

7.2 Friendship in the Aeneid

7.3 Virgil; Philosophy and the Aeneid

7.4 The role of the Gods: Order vs Chaos?

7.5 Aeneas: flawed hero or Roman ideal?

7.6 Examination and extension tasks

7.7 Glossary

7.1 Roman Social and Religious Values and the Aeneid

This section will help you to;

- *Understand and explore some Roman social values*

- *Consider if Roman religion was in decline in the 1st Century BC*

- *The extent to which Augustus revived religion at Rome*

- *Understand what familia are and the role of familia in religion and morality*

- *Consider and explore examples of positive and negative values as relevant to the Aeneid*

Introduction

In this section we will explore a range of Roman social values including attitudes to religion under Augustus, attitudes towards friendship and also suicide. We will also explore these values in the context of Virgil's *Aeneid*.

Roman *familia*

Roman family society was quite stratified. The family unit (*familia*) was the principal social unit. In theory, the only person fully recognised under law was the *paterfamilias*; the male head of the family. Over his family, the paterfamilias had in theory, the legal right of life or death. This included those adopted into the family also. Full citizen rights were granted to male children when they reached about the age of 16-17. Women on the other hand, were excluded from holding office or power. They still had a great impact through their influence of the male members of the family however. Many non-poor Roman families possessed slaves, who lived with, served or worked with the family that possessed them. They could aspire to manumission and become free. At this point they blended in to the larger body of Roman citizenry.

Traditional Roman Values

Augustus encouraged traditional Roman values through his behaviour, through his demeanour and attitude towards the institutions of the state. Outwardly Augustus made efforts to respect the will and decision making of the Senate.

Alongside Augustus' social reforms and public behaviour in Rome, the surviving ancient sources tell us that Augustus wished to revive the traditional Roman values of the state which had fallen into a state of disarray. These 'values' included respect towards the traditional religions and gods of the state, the correct behaviour of the individual in public, and proper behaviour of children towards their parents.

Through a combination of supporting the renewed practice of religious ceremonies that had lapsed, as well as presenting both himself, his family and his associates, with demonstrations of piety.

After the death of Virgil in 19BC, Augustus proceeded with his policy of promoting a positive image for himself and his family. Those individuals that elected not to participate in Augustus' pious and moralistic behaviour were removed from view.

Augustus' daughter Julia for example, was exiled for her adulterous relationships. Agrippa Postumus too was exiled for his brutish behaviour. The future emperor Claudius was the brother of Germanicus. Deemed to be a simpleton and an embarrassment to the family, he was kept from the public view as much as possible in order to avoid potential embarrassment of Augustus and his associated family.

Augustus and Roman religion

Augustus was keen to present himself as a priest to the public. Indeed one of his first offices was as a priest of the college of Augurs. A few years after Virgil's death in 19BC Augustus inaugurated the *Ludi Saceculare* sacred games that were held once every century or so. These were held in 17BC.

These games celebrated Rome and honoured the traditional Roman gods, however at these games Augustus particularly elected to venerate the gods Diana and Apollo. Previously, gods of the Underworld held a special place at these ceremonies.

In 12BC with the death of Lepidus, the position of Pontifex Maximus became vacant. As the most senior priest of Rome, this was a prestigious position and Augustus ensured that it was he, and no other, that would now hold this position.

Augustus; *Lares and the Penates*

The *Lares* were the traditional spirits of the Roman household and also crossroads. As household gods they were also often associated with the *Penates*; the gods of the pantry. These household religions were favoured by more humble Roman families as they required little expense and as they were worshipped in the privacy of the home suited the small family, as they could be appealed to before dinner or before sleep.

Augustus cleverly linked the worship of the *Lares* to himself by including his 'genius' as a spirit of protection and benevolence along with the worship of the *Lares*. Augustus was not presenting himself as a God, but rather as a guardian, a protector over the home and the family that dwelt within it.

In the *Aeneid*, Virgil makes several references to the household gods of Aeneas and the Trojans. Aeneas rescues them from the fall of Troy in Book Two and makes several references to them in the early part of the *Aeneid.* Once he has succeeded in transporting them to Italy however Virgil does not reference them further.

Augustus and the beginnings of an Imperial cult in the provinces

Even by 42BC Octavian sometimes referred to himself as *'Divi filius'* or the 'Son of a God'. Whilst Augustus never claimed that he himself was to be worshipped as a God, he had no difficulty in making the claim that his adoptive father was a deity. This was a clever distinction, but the association was clear, He was not a God, but his adopted father had become one through his greatness.

The Hellenistic rulers of the East- the Ptolemies, the Seleucids and the Antigonids- had been worshipped as divine whilst still alive. Later, as Roman expansion to the East replaced these dynasties, the inhabitants applied these same honorifics to victorious republican Roman generals who had conquered. The city of Rome too, had become personified and worshipped as a Goddess 'Roma'. This happened much earlier than Augustus' Principate; the city of Smyrna for example had a temple to Rome as early as 195BC.

In 29BC, the cities of Nicopolis and Pergamum requested permission to build a temple to Roma *and* Augustus. Augustus granted these cities his permission so long as the temple was dedicated to both. Deliberate or not, the result then was that Augustus would be associated with Rome in the minds of the provincials.

These temples had committees responsible for their upkeep and to pay for the festivals and sacrifices. These ceremonies were useful in developing a sense of unity and acceptance of Roman rule. Because the worship of Rome and Augustus was being combined, the decades of successive practice of these festivities made the practice of Rome and Augustus inseparable.

In the provinces, Augustus also permitted himself to be associated with the worship of the divine. In the *Res Gestae* he claims that he ordered the removal of statues of himself from temples. However, Augustus did allow temples of Rome and Augustus to be constructed. The peoples of the Eastern provinces had a tradition of worshipping their leaders as if they were gods for the past few centuries. If the provincials wished to continue this practice,

Augustus did not attempt to dissuade them, even if he did not encourage them.

Augustus' family also encouraged provincials and Romans alike to combine Augustus and religion. In 12BC Drusus Elder erected and dedicated an altar to Rome and Augustus in the city of Lugdunum. Another altar similar in purpose has been identified at Cologne and dates to between 9BC and 4AD. In 13AD Tiberius dedicated an altar to *'Nomen Augusti'* at Rome itself. This altar worshipped not Augustus, but rather the Name of Augustus. This was a distinction between worshipping the man himself, but it was a fine distinction.

Augustus and the presentation of Egypt

Romans knew that the Egyptian civilisation was significantly older than their own. However there was some mistrust of gods that had the heads of animals and seemed markedly different from the more anthropomorphic gods of Rome.

During Augustus' personal conflict with Antonius and Cleopatra, the supporters of Antonius in Rome failed to defend their leader from Octavian's attacks that Antonius was attempting to distance himself from his traditional Roman roots. With the benefit of victory on their side, the poets Virgil and Horace present the struggle at Actium as a battle between East and West, between the Roman and the Egyptian Gods.

In the *Aeneid* Book Eight we see Virgil's presentation of Egypt as an uncivilised and barbaric state dominated by animalistic gods about to fall to the might of Rome and Augustus.

Later, Egyptian cults in Rome would be outlawed periodically as immoral and against the traditional Roman values, but these laws banning the Egyptian cults ignores the fact that these cults, especially the cult of Isis, had genuine appeal to many Romans. After Actium was won and Antonius and Cleopatra were dead, the date of Augustus' birthday became a public holiday that celebrated this event.

Augustus' family and the role of family in the *Aeneid*

Augustus was the nephew and adopted son of Julius Caesar and was eager to present to the Romans that he was Caesar's heir. This was crucially important when Caesar had a biological son, Caesarion; his son by Queen Cleopatra of Egypt. Caesarion was a political difficulty for Augustus, especially when this boy was under the control and authority of Augustus' great political rival, Antonius.

After Actium, Augustus sailed to Egypt and is rumoured to have had Caesarion murdered in his presence. Augustus would tolerate no possible rival to his position as the heir of Julius Caesar.

Augustus himself only had a single legitimate child; a daughter named Julia and it is tempting to see in this an interesting parallel between Augustus and King Latinus – whose sole daughter was the cause of the war between Turnus and Aeneas in the *Aeneid*.

Augustus was successful in almost his entire career, but he struggled constantly to find a suitable successor to follow him. In the end he was forced to recognise his step son Tiberius, who on paper was a worthy successor to Augustus, but in reality, was much less worthy.

Julia: Augustus' daughter

Julia was the daughter of Augustus and Scribonia, Julia was born in 39BC and died in 14AD shortly after her father. Julia was married three times; to Marcellus in 24BC, to Agrippa in 21BC and to Tiberius in 12BC. According to writers such as Tacitus, Suetonius and Vellieus Paterculus the marriage of Julia and Tiberius was not a happy one and Julia seems to have embarked upon a series of adulterous relationships after 12BC which were the scandal of Rome and to the acute distress of Augustus. As a result of these adulteries, Julia was exiled in 2BC (Tacitus. *Annals* I.52) and lived first on Pandateriai, an island off Sicily, and later at Rhegium. According to Tacitus and Suetonius, Julia was starved to death in 14AD through neglect, perhaps on the orders of her estranged husband and now Emperor Tiberius.

The importance of Julia

The succession centred on Augustus' daughter Julia. As Augustus' only biological child, Julia held single importance and it was through Julia that Augustus selected his designated heirs. Julia was married three times, each time to a potential or actual heir. Julia also had three male children who were likewise potential heirs. The children of Julia could likewise claim being connected to Augustus by blood.

Whilst the children of Julia had the advantage of being biologically connected to Augustus, and could be depended upon to maintain Augustus' legacy and potentially could inherit Augustus' position whilst relatively young, the husbands of Julia had on the other hand the experience of a political career and public renown in their own right.

Julia's male children and prospective heirs (all also Agrippa's children);

- *Gaius Caesar (died 4AD)*

- *Lucius Caesar (died 2AD)*

- *Agrippa Postumus (died 14AD)*

In the *Aeneid* we have seen that Lavinia is the shadowy yet somewhat reluctant bride of Aeneas. Could it be that Virgil is tactfully alluding to the dangers and difficulties of finding a suitable heir apparent through the use of a marriage alliance?

Claudius Marcellus: the heir apparent in the *Aeneid*?

Marcellus was Augustus' nephew. Claudius Marcellus was born in 42BC, the son of Octavia, sister of Augustus and Claudius Marcellus, a prominent Senator.

Marcellus served his uncle Augustus in Spain in 25BC and married Julia in 24BC. In 23BC Marcellus was appointed *Aedile* and organised magnificent games at Rome, but died shortly afterwards. Marcellus was buried in the Mausoleum of Augustus.

Virgil dedicates a section to Marcellus in Book Six of the *Aeneid*. He is the heir that Augustus never had. According to later Roman tradition, when Virgil recited Book Six in the presence of Augustus and his sister Octavia, Octavia was so overcome by grief that she fainted.

Suicide in Books IV and XII

Suicide was neither wholly approved of nor wholly condemned in Ancient Rome. It was seen as an appropriate response to shame or dishonour; however the method of suicide used by Amata is noteworthy. She hangs herself in despair; this was seen as a cowardly method for a member of the aristocracy.

Note that in Book Four Dido commits suicide by the far more respectable technique of stabbing herself (which was also seen as a more masculine method of suicide).

Task: Virgil and the Augustan regime

Write an essay style response to the following question;

To what extent do you consider praising Augustus to be the **only** *purpose of the Aeneid? Justify your response with reference to the Aeneid.*

7.2 Friendship in the Aeneid

This section will help you to;

* *Understand the concept of xenia and its use in the Aeneid*

* *Consider and explore examples of positive and negative xenia in the Aeneid*

Introduction

This section will help you to understand the role of friendship in the *Aeneid*. Although *Xenia* – or 'guest friendship' is a crucial part of Homer's *Odyssey* and lay at the crux of the whole of Homer's epic poem, friendship also has an important role to play in the *Aeneid*.

What is *Xenia*?

Xenia, or guest friendship, was an important cultural and social value that helped to establish and secure positive relationships across communities in the Ancient World. In an age when long distance communication was difficult and lengthy it was important for communities interested in trade and political alliance to be able build relationships.

The Greek word *xenia* has no direct translation into English. It is commonly rendered as 'hospitality' or 'guest-friendship', but its significance runs deeper than either definition given above. The practice of *xenia* was a code of conduct for dealing with strangers and visitors and was expected in the Greek world.

Before the rise of the Roman Empire city states across the Mediterranean relied on trusted members of one state to look after the affairs of others who lived in another city state.

In Athens for example one citizen would be responsible for looking after the interests of a city like Sparta for example and vice versa. This individual was chosen from a family that had previously established good working relationships with people from the selected city. Often these relationships would be developed over the course of generations.

The ritualised behaviour of *xenia* ensured that both the visitor and the host would be protected and honoured by the meeting. The good practice of *xenia* was an important part of the Ancient Greek moral code that Homer, and his audience, would take for granted. In the Classical Greek period (approximately 600-300BC) the sacrosanct nature of Heralds operating between often hostile cities was derived in a large part from the practice of *xenia*.

Broadly speaking, the practice of *xenia* ritualised the duties and obligations placed upon both a guest and a host. The guest, either whether expected or not was required to behave in a polite and respectful way to his host and where possible, to give a ceremonial gift of some expense, such as an item of weaponry, or a decorative item such as a plate, vase or platter.

In return it was the host's responsibility, as divinely ordained by Zeus, the patron deity of guests and thus of *xenia*, to offer shelter, food, drink and hospitality to any such strangers (or known guests) who might arrive on his doorstep.

It is this guest friendship that Virgil is referring to in the *Aeneid* on several occasions.

Typically, we see friendship in the *Aeneid* between equals; members of the aristocratic class who honour one another for being fellow aristocrats, but it is certainly a marker of civilisation, of civilized values and of humanity in the *Aeneid* and when *xenia* is breached, the result is hostility and war.

Task: Friendship in Virgil's *Aeneid*

Thinking about the *Aeneid* as a whole.

Complete the following table, recording examples of both positive and negative *xenia* in Book One.

Examples of *friendship* in the *Aeneid*	Negative experiences in the *Aeneid*

Task: Roman Friendship and Xenia

Write a response to the following question;

To what extent is xenia similar or different to Roman friendship?

Roman Friendship

When we discuss friendship from this point forward we are concerning ourselves with a discussion of formal friendships among the Roman elite; not the friendship of regular Romans Titus and Pullo as they drink wine in the streets of Rome. We shall briefly explore the following here;

- *Amicitia*

- *Cliens*

- *Hospitium*

Amicitia

Amicitia was the political term for friendship and could be between equals or unequal individuals.

There were no formal obligations towards each other in Amicitia but rather it was an informal association of mutual convenience. This did not mean it could not be a longstanding or even permanent arrangement.

Amicitia involved a ritualised exchange of gifts and services. So for example Caesar and Crassus were friends – Caesar gave Crassus political support in return for Crassus giving financial aid as part of their *Triumvirate*. Amongst the political elite in Rome, *amicitia* provided a political leader with a body of trusted advisors and or confidants. So Augustus may well have considered Agrippa and Maecenas as his *amicitia* and as Octavian his fellow Triumvirs of Antonius and Lepidus would consider him his *amicitia* for a time and they his.

The temporary nature of *amicitia* however is clear in these cases. Octavian/Augustus would violently clash with Antonius and oust Lepidus; Maecenas would fall from favour eventually and even the trusted Agrippa could arguably be more of a *cliens* than an *amicitia* to Augustus.

Cliens

A *Clien* was an individual who technically sought protection and favour from a superior. In return for beneficiaries and a degree of protection a clien would in turn support the career and actions of his patron; even to the point where they would visit them daily and even serve as an impromptu bodyguard and attendant when the patron is out and about on the streets of Rome.

A good example of this would be the relationship of Virgil to his patron Maecenas. Virgil receives through Maecenas wealth, access to the very court of Augustus and the ability to have his poetry better promoted.

Hospitium

Friendship or '*Hospitium*' could also between individual kings and the Roman Senate. In return for Roman military and political support, kings would send Rome corn and money. *Hospitium* was valuable for the Romans and non-Romans alike and had an instrumental role in 'Romanising' provincial elite and integrating into the upper echelons of Roman society.

> **Task: identifying different kinds of friendship in the Aeneid**
>
> *Think back over the whole of the Aeneid.*
>
> *Try to identify examples of amicitia, cliens and Hospitium from the text.*
>
> *Consider how successful these attempts at friendship were.*

The role of *friendship* in the *Aeneid*

Aeneas and the Trojans encounter on their travels in the first six books several states and individuals where they receive warm welcome. In part this welcome is guaranteed by previous relationships and knowledge of the people being visited.

We shall consider the following cases;

- Unexpected relatives
- Established ties of friendship
- Generational friendships
- New relationships that are less successful

Unexpected relatives

So for example, in Book Three Aeneas and the Trojans are surprised to see Helenus and Andromache at the city of Buthrotum. However, once they realise that Helenus is king of Buthrotum and Andromache is Queen, Aeneas knows he will receive safe harbour and a warm welcome.

Established ties of friendship

In Book Five the Trojans reach Sicily and visit Acestes. According to Virgil;

> *"Acestes had been born of a Trojan mother to the river god Crinisus and he had not forgotten his ancestry, but welcomed the returning Trojans and gladly received them with all the treasures of the countryside, comforting their weariness with his loving care."*

> Virgil. *Aeneid* V.39-40

Although the Trojan visit is unexpected, Aeneas knows Acestes will welcome him, as he has been there before and buried Anchises in Acestes' land as he alludes to at the end of Book Three.

Generational friendships

In Book Eight Aeneas travels to Pallenteum in order to secure a military alliance with King Evander. This turns out to be very straightforward as it turns out that Evander had previously met Aeneas' father Anchises as well as the old Trojan King Priam many years before. This relationship was marked by the traditions of gift-giving;

> *"When he (Anchises) was leaving he gave me a wonderful quiver filled with Lycian arrows, a soldier's cloak interwoven with gold thread and a pair of golden bridles which now belong to my son Pallas. So then, the right hand of friendship for which you ask has already been given in solemn pledge, and as soon as tomorrow's sun returns to the earth, I shall send you on your way and you will not be disappointed with the reinforcements and supplies I shall give you."*

> Virgil. *Aeneid* VIII.166-172

Xenia

'Guest friendship' is a bond of trust that imitates kinship and often ritualised;it creates obligations between individuals belonging to different social units.

New relationships that are less successful

In Book One the Trojans arrive at Carthage. They have no previous links to Carthage, the Phoenicians or Dido, but none the less they are made welcome. The reputation of Aeneas has preceded him; the Trojans are welcome to stay and even to settle in Carthage if they desire. This great and generous welcome by Dido is one that she will of course bitterly regret in due course. This does not stop Dido from giving the Trojans many rich and extravagant gifts.

Likewise in Book Seven, the Trojans are at first given a warm welcome by King Latinus. However, this welcome is soon ruined by the machinations of the Goddess Juno.

In Books One and Four we see both the best and worst of *xenia* – the practice of excellent *xenia* by Dido to the Trojans on the one hand, and the abuse of the laws of hospitality by Aeneas when he decides to slip away from Carthage rather than face Dido and tell her that he is leaving.

For Virgil, this in part explains the great hostility between the cities of Carthage and Rome and after many decades of war and hundreds of thousands of deaths in the three Punic Wars (264-246BC, 220-201BC and 149-146BC), peace only is achieved when Rome utterly destroys Carthage.

Extension Task: Reading about xenia in the Odyssey

For comparative purposes it may be useful to explore how Homer treats the concept of xenia in the Odyssey.

Read the following passages of Homer's Odyssey;

- *Book 3.30-80*

- *Book 3.470-488*

- *Book 4.20-75*

- *Book 4.650-672*

These are examples of the practice of xenia in the early part of the Odyssey.

7.3 Virgil; Philosophy and the Aeneid

This section will help you to;

- *Begin to understand and explore three prominent philosophical schools*

- *Begin to consider the impact of philosophy in the creation of the Aeneid*

- *Reconsider the plot and structure of Books IV and VI in light of these philosophical schools.*

Introduction

In this section we explore three philosophical schools of thought that were prominent in Rome amongst the Roman elite when Virgil wrote the *Aeneid*. These philosophical schools are;

- *Stoical philosophy*

- *Epicurean philosophy*

- *Peripatetic (or Aristotelian) philosophy*

It is important to state that this section goes beyond what an A level student of the *Aeneid* is expected to explore so please do not worry about incorporating this into your studies in any great detail. It is however useful to consider briefly to explore the *Aeneid* as a member of Virgil's Roman audience may have explored the poem in order to try to understand how and why it was constructed in its present form.

Also this section may help you explore in greater detail how and why Virgil chose to portray the central character of Aeneas and key parts of the plot (notably Books IV and VI) as he does.

Stoical philosophy and the *Aeneid*

Stoicism was a philosophical system formulated by Zeno of Citium (335-263BC) and subsequently refined by Chrysippus of Soli (280-207BC). Stoicism was very popular amongst sections of the Roman social and political elite for several centuries before being largely rejected by later Christian influenced teachings.

Stoicism consisted of three integrated parts; logic, physics and ethics. As a holistic philosophy stoicism can only really be understood when these parts are considered together. Generally speaking, Stoics had a materialistic and a fatalistic world view; the world consists of material objects that interact according to fate. For the Stoic, everything happens for a reason and in accordance with the will of fate which is to be considered divine. Even the gods are subject to fate.

In spite of this predetermination; Stoics believe that human actions and behaviour are as a result of a degree of free will and therefore human actions can be thought of as good or evil. Human beings therefore need to be morally responsible.

In the *Aeneid* of Virgil we see many examples of this interaction (or clash if you prefer) between fate and free will. In Book Four for example, Aeneas is conflicted. He may indeed love Dido, but he cannot escape his fate; to travel to Italy and establish a city there. In the end the conflict in Aeneas is resolved when he realises that it is destiny, and not his own desires, that must be obeyed.

Stoic teachings stressed the importance of rules and principles in moral reasoning. For the Stoic, virtue is good and external. Virtues come from fate and destiny and to be in harmony with the material world. Therefore to be virtuous is to be happy. Emotions on the other hand are internal and the product of the Self. Since emotions come from within ourselves, they can run counter to virtue and as a result should be considered to be bad. As a result these need to be controlled by our own will to ensure that they do not run counter to the will of fate. For the Stoic, emotions are inevitable, but they need to be controlled.

Task: Stoicism in the Aeneid

Reading through the Aeneid – try to identify as many examples as you can of evidence of Stoical beliefs and practices.

Consider in particular the characters of;

Aeneas, Dido, Juno and Turnus

Epicurean philosophy and the *Aeneid*

Epicurean philosophy takes its name from the philosopher Epicurus. Epicurus was born in Samos in 341BC and died in 270BC in Athens. Epicurus established a school in Athens in a location called '*κηπος*' or 'Garden'.

The Epicurean philosophers were what we might crudely describe as monastic hedonists with a scientific slant.

They dwelt together in closed communities and lived simply. Somewhat unusually for the ancient world, the Epicureans permitted women and slaves to be part of their communities. It is thought likely that Virgil himself dwelt for at least a time in one of these communities at Neapolis in Italy (near Modern Naples).

In the 1st century BC many Romans were influenced by the Epicurean poet Lucretius (whose work survives).

Epicurus argued that creation of the physical world was an accident and not due to any divine action; that humans had no divine spark and that any soul or mind they did possess was the result of the alignment of tiny particles that comprised all matter; 'atoms'. For Epicureans there was no afterlife and therefore nothing to fear from the gods; if they did exist they were aloof from human affairs.

For an Epicurean to have a happy life was all important. Pleasure was the prime object of life. But for a human being pain was also inevitable. Therefore the ideal state to be in was known as '*ataraxia*'; a state of calmness or tranquility.

Epicureans attracted some criticism for their beliefs and way of life. They were accused of living immorally (perhaps because of the closed nature of the community and tradition of permitting women and slaves to join them). They were also considered (somewhat inaccurately) to be atheists.

Epicureans also struggled to explain how their belief in pleasure or tranquility for the self was able to be combined with their practice of seeking community and the wellbeing of other people; surely if everyone was seeking pleasure, this would cause suffering elsewhere?

Task: Epicureanism in the Aeneid

How might an Epicurean consider the entirety of Book VI for example?

How might an Epicurean consider the relationship between Aeneas and Dido in Book IV?

Peripatetic (or Aristotelian) philosophy

If Stoical philosophy was the weight at one end of a set of scales and Epicureanism was at the other end, then the Peripatetic school of philosophy would be in the middle.

The philosopher Aristotle was by far the most famous philosopher of the Peripatetic school. These philosophers were originally based at the Lyceum, a sanctuary dedicated to the God Apollo that lay just outside the city of Athens. Aristotle in turn was heavily influenced by Socrates and Plato.

Aristotle

Aristotle lived from 384BC-322BC. He was the legendary philosopher, writer and tutor of Alexander the Great.

Aristotle was heavily influenced by Plato's writings and learned from Plato directly until Plato's death in 348/7BC.

Aristotle established the Lyceum school in 335BC and his writing influenced many subsequent philosophers, scientists and politicians including at Rome the politician and lawyer Cicero. In the 1st Century BC the Peripatetic school, as it began to be called, was revitalised under the leadership of Andronicus of Rhodes.

The *Aeneid* as a Peripatetic text?

Aristotle wrote on many different topics, but here we are most concerned with his works on ethics and moral philosophy. Aristotle argued that humans should aspire to '*Eudaimonia*' (literally 'human flourishing'); what we can probably better understand as good virtues and positive character traits that are to be exemplified. These include courage, justice and generosity.

Aristotle however acknowledged that sometimes these virtues could not be always adhered to. Humans, being imperfect, will sometimes fail to exhibit these virtues and instead fall short. Human beings become angry, fearful, jealous and envious. These negatives were nonetheless part of the human experience.

In his *Poetics*, Aristotle argues that good people often fall short of '*Eudaimonia*' through the occurrence of events beyond their control. A fierce storm, for example, can cause us to become afraid or we can become jealous of another person's good fortune or wealth. This means that even good people can sometimes act in a bad way.

Task: The Aeneid as a Peripatetic text?

Reading through the Aeneid – try to identify as many examples as you can of evidence of peripatetic beliefs and practices.

Consider in particular the characters and actions of;

Aeneas and Turnus

For Aeneas, whenever in the *Aeneid* he considers his own emotions – he can be conflicted between acting selflessly or selfishly. In Book Two for example, Aeneas is overcome by his emotion when he tries to murder Helen. It takes the direct intervention of his mother to force Aeneas to think beyond his own selfish desire and turn his thoughts to virtue – in this case, saving as many Trojans as he can and leading them to safely.

Task: Reading the Aeneid as a philosophical text

Reading through the Aeneid as a philosophical text is a challenging thing to attempt.

Consider the following parts of the Aeneid and try to explain them in light of the three philosophical doctrines explored in this section;

- *The attempt to murder Helen in Book II*
- *The abandonment of Dido by Aeneas in Book IV*
- *The journey into the Underworld in Book VI*
- *The death of Turnus in Book XII*

The treatment of Dido in Book IV as viewed by philosophers

In topics 4.1 and 4.2 we explored Book IV as a kind of Greek Tragedy. Here we will consider how Aeneas' treatment of Dido and the motives for her abandonment might have been considered by practitioners of the three philosophical schools mentioned above.

For Stoics and Aristotelian philosophers this episode presents no great difficulties – Aeneas must suppress his desires and obey the commands of fate. It is for the greater good that Aeneas abandons Dido and in obedience to powers beyond his own selfish desires. He is fated to settle the Trojans in Italy and this is what he now proceeds to do. For Stoics and Aristotelian philosophers alike then, Aeneas' conflict is understandable, but as a basically 'good' man, he obeys and puts the greater good before his own selfish needs.

For Epicureans though it is a little more complicated, though in the end Aeneas' actions can be explained. First of all, given that the Epicureans believe that the gods do not take a role in the affairs of men, the arrival of Mercury with Jupiter's command can be explained that it is Aeneas' own consciousness that makes him act.

Secondly, Aeneas is content and tranquil in Carthage, we see him happily building the walls of Carthage and wearing nice luxurious clothes. How then can he improve on this situation? This can be explained that Aeneas himself decides that all is not actually well with him in Carthage and with Dido after all.

Perhaps Aeneas has had a moment of clarity; if he leaves Dido and Carthage behind, he can achieve greater things elsewhere. He can build *his own* city, for *his own* people, with *himself* in charge. He might even find (as has been promised another, more suitable bride. This of course comes across as extremely selfish and is tough on Dido – but perhaps Aeneas can console himself (as he does in VI.457-463) that Dido might be better off without him anyway.

A false dream? The end of Book VI revisited

If you found the ending of Book VI a little surprising, then you are not alone. As mentioned earlier in this study guide we raise the somewhat surprising way in which Aeneas departs the Underworld, since he leaves by the gate of ivory, which Virgil tells us represents the gate of false dreams.

As mentioned in this section and elsewhere, Virgil may well have been an Epicurean. If this was the case then Virgil would not have believed in the possibility of an afterlife – therefore if we read the *Aeneid* as an Epicurean text then this event of Aeneas journeying into the Underworld could never happen.

The strange departure through the ivory gate of 'false dream' therefore suggests that this entire episode was actually nothing more than a dream experienced by Aeneas.

But as we mentioned earlier in topic 4.5 there is no definitive answer on this point of the text.

7.4 The role of the Gods: Order vs Chaos?

This section will help you to;

- *Understand and explore the roles of the Gods*

- *Compare the actions of Juno and Jupiter in the Aeneid*

- *Compare the role of Venus with Athena in the Odyssey*

- *Explore the prayers of Iarbus and Mezentius*

- *Reconsider the plot and structure of some parts of the Aeneid in this light*

Introduction

In this section of the study guide we explore the role of the gods across the *Aeneid*. In particular we will explore the roles of Jupiter and Juno, traditionally seen as representing the forces of order (Jupiter) and chaos (Juno). We will also consider the argument that Jupiter is a God that is purely focused on his own power *(Imperium)*.

Roman Religion

So varied and diverse is Roman religion that it is very difficult to define exactly what Roman religion was like across all the various gods, local and foreign cults, modes of sacrifice and religious practices. Certainly it is beyond the remit of this study guide and impossible to cover all aspects adequately here. We shall satisfy ourselves with a few points to help you understand Roman religion as it impacts upon our study of Virgil's *Aeneid*.

After the turmoil of the civil wars there was a conscious effort by Augustus to restructure and reorganise religion in the city of Rome. Augustus actively promoted the cult of Apollo, for example (his patron God) and dedicated new temples to Mars and Apollo in Rome. He also suppressed the worship of the Egyptian Goddess Isis – given his rivalry with Antonius and Cleopatra this was no real surprise - and Augustus also encouraged the promotion of an' Imperial Cult' based on himself and his family, with works of art such as the Ara Pacis altar.

Augustus also promoted the worship of the *Lares* and *Penates* – gods of the household and pantry that each household should honour. These god-spirits are identified in the *Aeneid* on several occasions with the gods of Troy that accompany Aeneas on his journey.

> **Task: Examination style task: Book VII**
>
> Read Virgil's *Aeneid* Book VII, lines 436-475
>
> Write responses to the following questions;
>
> a) How successful is Virgil in making this part of the *Aeneid* vivid and exciting?
> b) Victim or criminal? Using this passage as a starting point, which word best describes Turnus throughout the *Aeneid*?

Order and Chaos

The gods are ultimately beings apart for the mortal world. They live a blessed life on Mount Olympus, free from human concerns such as hunger, disease and death.

The gods' interventions in the *Aeneid* are generally similar in nature and form. The Gods help those that they wish to help and hinder those that they wish to hinder. The gods are partisan and callous towards those they are not concerned with. They even come across as cruel.

One commonly held view of the actions of Jupiter and Juno in the *Aeneid* is that they are diametrically opposed. Jupiter represents order whereas Juno represents chaos.

Jupiter and Rome

Jupiter is the father of the Gods – known as Zeus in Greek; Jupiter was a very important god for the Romans. Originally a weather god associated with the skies and storms, that Jupiter was held as the supreme God of the Romans is signified by his name and his priests always being named first in any religious list. Jupiter had the traditional epithet of *'optimus maximus'* – or *'best and greatest'*.

Jupiter had a temple dedicated to him on the Capitoline hill – which he also shared with Juno and Minerva, and together the trio served as Rome's patron deities. Jupiter as father of the Gods also represented power and the authority of the family and state. He was the god that oversaw treaties and oaths. As such Jupiter represented order.

Jupiter and the *Aeneid*

The presentation of Jupiter above then resembles closely the role Jupiter plays in the *Aeneid*. Jupiter stands as a neutral power in the narrative of the *Aeneid*. He neither helps nor persecutes the Trojans in their quest to reach Italy and he only intervenes in an active role in a few books of the poem.

- Book One – Jupiter consoles Venus with a prophecy of future Roman greatness (I.266-298)
- Book Two and Three – Jupiter is absent
- Book Four – Jupiter commands Aeneas (through Mercury) to leave Carthage (IV20-238)
- Book Five, Six, Seven, Eight and Nine– Jupiter is absent
- Book Ten – Jupiter hosts a council of the gods and commands the Gods not to intervene (X.1-117) but later permits Juno to save Turnus (X.606-633).
- Book Eleven – Jupiter is absent
- Book Twelve – Jupiter intervenes. He commands Juno to stop interfering and sends a Dira to recall Juturna (XII.791-869)

Jupiter then only intervenes in the narrative of the *Aeneid* on two occasions – in Book Four and in Book Twelve. He himself never deals with mortals directly and maintains a hands off attitude to affairs until the very end when he commands Juno and Juturna to no longer help save Turnus from his fate.

Task: The prayer of Iarbus

Read Virgil's Aeneid Book IV lines 199-218

What is shocking or surprising about this prayer to Jupiter?

The prayer of Iarbus

One prayer to Jupiter is of particular interest and needs to be explored further. It is the prayer of Iarbus in Book IV lines 199-218.

Iarbus is a son of the god – one of his many children that come about his habit of seducing or raping mortal women. Virgil presents Iarbus as a loyal worshiper of Jupiter. But his prayer is provocative and shocking as it contains the accusation that Jupiter is not a god;

> *"We bring gifts to temples we think are yours and keep warm with our worship the reputation of a useless god".*

Virgil. Aeneid IV.217-218

Surprisingly Jupiter does not punish this outright insolence. Instead he makes pains to prove Iarbus wrong. This is the only direct prayer in the *Aeneid* that Jupiter actually acts upon. It is almost as if Jupiter is eager to prove to Iarbus that he is no a 'useless god'. In short, Jupiter is eager to demonstrate that he has power '*Imperium*'.

Task: The prayer of Mezentius

Read Virgil's Aeneid Book X.845-856

What is shocking or surprising about this prayer to Jupiter?

Mezentius

Another figure worthy of consideration in relation to Jupiter is Mezentius. Mezentius is described by Virgil as a *'scorner of the gods'* (VIII.649). This unique epithet suggests that Mezentius is either an atheist or agnostic; he cares nothing for the gods.

Yet in Book Ten Mezentius is propelled by Jupiter into the fighting (X.689) It is Jupiter that intervenes to prevent Lausus and Pallas meeting in battle; both will be killed by greater warriors (Aeneas and Turnus respectively). Yet when Mezentius learns of the death of Lausus, he prays to the heavens (Jupiter) before confronting Aeneas and dying bravely.

Juno and Rome

Juno was another of the chief deities of Rome and an old Italian goddess. In Greece Juno was known as Hera. Juno represented the role of women in society and also as Jupiter's Queen *'Regina'*. Juno was also a goddess that had roles as a goddess of childbirth and marriage. Every year on the 1st of March Roman men would give gifts to their wives when Rome would celebrate the festival of *Matronalia*.

Task: Examination style task: Book X

Read Virgil's Aeneid Book X, lines 611-634

Write responses to the following questions;

a) How typical in the Aeneid is this portrayal of the goddess Juno?
b) Using this passage as a starting point, consider whether Fate or the Gods is more important to the narrative of Virgil's Aeneid?

Juno and the *Aeneid*

The traditional form of Juno presented briefly above then contrasts sharply with the Juno of the *Aeneid*.

Juno serves an extremely important role in the plot of the *Aeneid* since it was her enmity which drives much of the events. She has been depicted by Virgil as nursing a deep seated grudge against both Aeneas and the race of Trojans, and without the enmity of the Goddess being placated, troubles keep piling up for Aeneas and the Trojans.

However for Juno her anger is somewhat understandable, as she knows that she is struggling against the will of Fate. It is the knowledge that despite being the Queen of the gods as the wife/sister of Jupiter. Her actions therefore are ultimately futile.

Juno freely acknowledges this on several occasions. Juno knows that she cannot stop Carthage, her favourite city, from being destroyed eventually by the Romans and she cannot thwart Aeneas' fate to reach Italy, to settle his people there and to marry Lavinia.

However, what *is* in Juno's power is to throw as many spanners into the works as possible and this is what she does. Juno is responsible for or harasses the Trojans in almost every book;

- Book One – causes a storm that nearly shipwrecks them
- Book Two – is on the side of the Greeks as they destroy Troy
- Book Three – Ignores the sacrifices Aeneas makes to Juno on arriving in Italy
- Book Four – Juno tries to foil the prophecy of settling in Italy by encouraging Venus to help her make the Trojans and Carthaginians one people
- Book Five – Juno sends Iris to cause mischief amongst the Trojan women
- Book Seven – Juno sends Allecto to cause the Latins to fight the Trojans
- Book Nine – Encourages Turnus to attack the Trojan camp
- Book Ten – Blames the Trojans in a council of the Gods
- Book Eleven – Rescues Turnus from battle
- Book Twelve – Encourages Juturna to help her brother Turnus but is reconciled with Jupiter

Juno then is motivated by her desire to sow discord and chaos wherever she can.

There would have been peace between Aeneas and Latinus in Book Seven without Juno. For a Roman audience, the threat of war between two otherwise peaceable tribes destined to become one through intermarriage would have struck a bitter note, with memories of civil war still fresh in mind. Put this way then the war between Octavian and Antonius can be explained as being caused through the actions of another Goddess – this time a human one called Cleopatra (Cleopatra presented herself to her subjects and in her public image as a living god – an incarnation of Isis).

Without Juno, Aeneas would never have even travelled to Carthage. The irony here of course is that it is Juno's actions then that cause the great enmity between Rome and Carthage, that ultimately results in the destruction of her own favourite city.

Juno in Book Twelve – appeased or fooled?

Now that the end is near, Juno knows that she can oppose Fate no longer. But Juno must also be placated before a true conciliation can be reached. Juno has been so vehemently opposed to the Trojan cause, and now Jupiter commands her to desist from opposing Aeneas.

Juno sees a way to achieve a measure of victory. In return for her future benevolence to the union of the tribes of Trojans and Italians, all she asks for is that the name of Troy should disappear forever. This is a wish that is easily granted by Jupiter.

It seems a little petty to a modern audience that all Juno really wanted was to see the end of the name of Troy. But even in this she is actually thwarted. The poet Virgil of course is recounting the story of Aeneas; the Trojan. He is not Italian and in recounting the story of the Trojan Aeneas to the Romans, the name of Troy lives on in memory and in fact. The Romans themselves considered themselves to be descended in part from Troy. If they remembered, then Juno never truly gets her wish.

Juno then is duped at the end of the *Aeneid*. She easily switches her allegiance, reminding the audience of the fickle and inconsistent nature of the gods, who have been duped by mortals before – the gods accepted the sacrifice of the waste parts of an animal for example; when tricked by the sight of the fat that actually concealed the bones.

The 'Savage King'

Jupiter intervenes in events finally and conclusively in Book Twelve when he sends one of the Dirae to force Juturna to abandon Turnus (XII.843-855). The use of a fearsome force to carry out his commands is ironic as it is exactly the same technique that Juno used in Book One and in Book Seven. Virgil at this point calls Jupiter a *'saeuus rex'* or *'savage king'* (line 849).

At this point of the *Aeneid* Juno is no longer a force of chaos, it is now all order and power that is being demonstrated. Jupiter issues the commands for Juno to desist. Jupiter commands Juturna to abandon her brother and Jupiter demonstrates his power and authority by sealing the fate of Turnus and ending the war being fought.

Comparing Venus and Athena in epic poetry

There is a parallel between Venus/ Aphrodite in the *Aeneid* and the *Iliad* and Athena in the *Odyssey*. Both goddesses hold the hero of the epics as their favourites, but for different reasons. In the *Odyssey*, Athena sees in Odysseus much of her own character and therefore much she can admire, whereas Venus/ Aphrodite is Aeneas' mother, and not only has a maternal bond to this offshoot of the Trojan royal family, but also Paris, the son of King Priam, who selected her as the most beautiful goddess in the contest of the golden apple. In the *Iliad* then Venus/Aphrodite takes care of both Aeneas and Paris, saving them from otherwise certain death.

Both Venus and Athene seem fond of disguise when appearing to mortals. Both goddesses disguise themselves though whereas Athene and Odysseus have some warmth in their relationship, there does seem to be less evidence of affection at first between Venus and her son in the *Aeneid*. In Books One and Two of the *Aeneid*, Venus and Aeneas interact, but do so in ways that seem commanding or even callous. As the *Aeneid* progresses however the bond between Aeneas and Venus grows – she makes more of an effort to help him; bringing him weapons and armour in Book Nine and healing him at a key moment in Book Twelve.

> ### Task: Aeneas and the Gods
>
> *Write an essay style response to the following question;*
>
> *To what extent are the gods more of a hindrance than a help to Aeneas?*

7.5 Aeneas: flawed hero or Roman ideal?

This section will help you to;

- *Understand and explore the character of Aeneas*

- *Compare Aeneas to Odysseus and Achilles*

- *Explore the idea of Aeneas as being an imperfect hero*

- *Consider the extent to which the character Aeneas is a reflection of Augustus*

- *Reconsider the plot and structure of parts of the Aeneas in this light*

Introduction

In this section we will return again to the character of Aeneas and consider the extent to which Virgil intended Aeneas to be a reflection of Augustus. Using a range of episodes drawn from across the *Aeneid* we shall consider whether Aeneas is a flawed hero or the image of an ideal Roman or a combination of the two. We shall also explore some episodes that might suggest that Virgil is critical of the Augustan regime which he is supposedly promoting.

We shall explore Book Six in particular so it may be worth going over that book and sections 4.4 and 4.5 again.

Aeneas – the defence of a hero

Aeneas is often portrayed in the *Aeneid* as brave, strong, good looking, pious, generous and a great leader of men. In Book One Aeneas demonstrates his leadership skills in encouraging the Trojans after the great storm before heading out to hunt food and scout the local area. In Book Two for example, Aeneas bravely leads the Trojans in the desperate but futile battle to save the city of Troy. In Book Five Aeneas exhibits his generous spirit and leadership skills as he leads the Trojans in a series of games designed to promote unity and celebrate their own 'Trojan-ness', having survived many ordeals at sea in the years since leaving Troy. In Book Six Aeneas braves the terrors of the Underworld in order to obtain key information. In Book Eight Aeneas personally seeks military and political alliances. In Book Nine Aeneas' absence is felt by the Trojans as they desperately try to hold onto their camp. It is Aeneas' rampage in Book Ten that breaks the army of Turnus in battle and saves the Trojan camp.

Odysseus and Achilles – as imperfect heroes of Homer

Aeneas then is undoubtedly a great hero, as great a hero as Odysseus in Homer's *Odyssey* or one of the leaders of the Greeks at Troy in Homer's *Iliad*. Yet neither Odysseus nor Achilles are perfect heroes. Odysseus is a broken man when he is first encountered in the Odyssey – a man imprisoned by a goddess with no hope on his own of escape. Odysseus fails to keep his men in line – if he had been a better commander, perhaps his men would have obeyed his commands on occasion and survived to reach Ithaca. The end of the Odyssey shows Odysseus as more than a little vengeance obsessed. He fights his own townsfolk and tries to kill them even as they run away. It takes the command of Athena to bring him to heel.

Achilles is the greatest fighter the world has ever seen. No-one can match him in battle and no one can escape from him when he chases them down. But he too has flaws. He is impetuous in council and tries to challenge the established order by arguing with Agamemnon. Achilles refuses to fight and in doing so causes many Greek warriors to be killed or wounded as a result. The Greek army is on the verge of being destroyed and rather than save the day himself, he sends out Patroclus to fight in his stead (pretending to be him) and as a result Patroclus is killed. When Achilles returns to the fight he is an inhumane force of nature that terrifies friend and foe alike and his treatment of the brave Trojan Hector is despicable, respecting neither the rules of the living nor the dead. Achilles however does manage to find his own way back to reason and sanity; he treats King Priam with respect and eventually relents of his anger by cleaning and returning the despoiled body of Hector.

Task: To err is to be human

The fifth century AD Roman commentator Tiberius Claudius Donatus once described Aeneas as 'devoid of every fault'.

To what extent do you agree with this view?

The shortcomings of Aeneas

Aeneas then will be a hero more in keeping with those in Homer's poems if he has a few failings, and he does indeed have a few.

Aeneas gets enraged on several occasions. He exhibits *furor*. In Book Two, carried away in the heat of battle at Troy, Aeneas tries to murder the defenceless woman that is Helen; it takes his Mother Venus to intervene directly in order to save Helen. In Book Ten *furor* once again takes a hold of Aeneas as he slaughters his way through the Latin army – and he comes across as taunting and cruel as he kills without pity. In the final act of the *Aeneid*, Aeneas is once again consumed with anger as he slaughters the defenceless Turnus. Now all of these actions are justifiable to an extent – Helen was the cause of the ten year conflict that results in the destruction of Aeneas' home and loved ones, in Book Ten Aeneas has learned that his young friend Pallas has been killed by Turnus, and in Book Twelve the leader of the enemy army and the main cause of his troubles and sufferings has now been defeated and deserves punishment for his actions.

Aeneas is not just an angry man though. He is insensitive to others. When the helmsman Palinurnus is taken by the actions of the gods and drowned in (Book V.828-870), Aeneas rather unfairly blames him for dereliction of duty. Again, when Aeneas encounters the ghost of Dido in the Underworld (Book Six.457-563);

> *"I could not have believed that my leaving would cause you such sorrow"*.

Here then Aeneas is either gullible or lying. In Book Four, He knew that Dido was besotted with him, yet he abandoned her without even trying to explain why he had to go. Her speech in Book Four made it plain that her love for Aeneas and his abandonment had dishonoured and disgraced her (Book IV.300-330).

Aeneas is also not always pious or dutiful in the *Aeneid*. He conveniently forgets that he has a duty to fulfil when he chooses to stay in Carthage with Dido and he tries on several occasions in Book Three to settle the Trojans in places other than Italy – despite being told this is where he should go in Book Two by Creusa. One of these cities he founds named after himself, Aeneadae, in an egotistical act. His next settlement of Pergamea on Crete was the result of misinterpreting the oracle of Apollo on Delos.

Again these actions can be justified. Aeneas is perhaps trying to console the ghost of Dido and alleviate some of the guilt he feels for abandoning her. When he encounters the ghost of Palinurus in the Underworld, Aeneas learns of the true fate of his helmsman and makes amends. When he settles the Trojans in Crete and raises Pergamea it is because of an error in interpretation.

Aeneas is also overemotional; he cries a lot, and this stands in contrast with manly Roman virtues.

What is clear then is that Aeneas is not perfect. He makes mistakes like all of us do; including the archetypical epic heroes Odysseus and Achilles.

Aeneas as the Stoic or Epicurean Ideal?

In section 7.4 we explored some of the philosophical schools that may have influenced Virgil when he wrote the *Aeneid*. It has been argued that Aeneas is the ideal stoic character. But is this true?

Stoicism argues that it is a virtue to be as indifferent to pleasure and pain as possible and that it is also a virtue to act according to the designs of Fate as closely as possible. Aeneas' coldness of character on occasion can be seen to be evidence of Aeneas being virtuous.

However, if the *Aeneid* is an Epicurean text then Aeneas' coldness is a vice to be overcome. Likewise, Aeneas' overemotional acts – his expressions of grief and fear would be stoical vices, but Epicurean virtues as through these expressions he purges himself of pain and suffering in order to feel better; pleasure.

Conversely Aeneas' *furor* (rage in battle) is for a stoic a vice. Yet for an Epicurean it could be argued that Aeneas' *furor* is in some ways pleasurable. He fights with fury because he wants and chooses to; in this way Aeneas' *furor* can be considered to be a virtue.

Aeneas and Anchises and the death of Turnus

In Sections 4.4 and 4.5 when we explored Book Six the ghost of Anchises gives Aeneas a tour of future Romans in the Underworld. He also gives Aeneas some advice;

Your task, Roman, and do not forget it, will be to govern the peoples of the world in your empire. These will be your arts – and to impose a settled pattern upon peace, to pardon the defeated and war down the proud".

Virgil. *Aeneid VI.851-853*

What Virgil is having Anchises say here is that other countries and people may be better at arts, science, crafts and even law, but what Rome will do better than anyone else is to impose order and imperium on the cities and peoples of the world. Rome's art form then is to rule.

But Anchises also gives Aeneas here some instructions. Aeneas has a duty to impose peace. He is also to pardon the defeated and war down the proud.

In Book XII Turnus by the end of the book is defeated and humbled. According to Anchises' instructions, Aeneas should pardon him. He fails to do this. In failing to spare Turnus, Aeneas fails to live up to his epithet of *pietas*. Rather, at the end of the *Aeneid*, Aeneas has succumbed to his *furor*.

Aeneas as a parallel to Augustus

Virgil is generally considered to have written the *Aeneid* in order to honour Augustus and promote his regime. Other contemporary writers and poets such as Ovid, Livy and Horace all equated Augustus with mythical heroes, and it is reasonable to suppose that Virgil wanted to equate the deeds, actions and character of Aeneas with Augustus also.

There are indeed some clear parallels between Aeneas and Augustus; Aeneas founded a city, Augustus founded many cities and also is credited with re-founding Rome. Both Aeneas and Augustus claimed to be sons of Gods; Venus for Aeneas and Julius Caesar for Augustus (and by extension Venus also). Aeneas was brave and victorious in war, and Augustus was credited with being the same (the whispered comments that Octavian stayed in his tent during the battle of Mutina in 43BC was wisely not mentioned or alluded to by Virgil).

There are clear episodes in the *Aeneid* when Augustus and the Augustan regime are obviously being promoted;

The shield of Aeneas in Book VIII (VIII.625-end) is clearly pro-Augustan propaganda, as is the first speech of Jupiter in Book One (I.255-297), when the God announces that a Caesar will rule the earth.

If then, Aeneas is meant to be Augustus, we must consider the question - why does Virgil create in Aeneas a hero with such obvious character flaws? Is he more critical of Augustus than it seems?

There are strong grounds for this argument. Virgil is keen to present many of the opponents of Aeneas in a positive light. Turnus for example is a young brave warrior whose opposition to Aeneas is justifiable on the grounds that it is his beloved wife to be Lavinia is unfairly snatched away from him and given to a much older stranger.

Are Rome and the Roman Empire flawed?

The *Aeneid* presents the periods of civil war from the death of Caesar in 44BC to the victory of Augustus at Actium in 31BC in a neutral way.

In Book VI lines 829-831 and also in lines 820-825 Virgil is careful to neither assign blame or praise to some of the major protagonists in the civil war period. Julius Caesar and Pompey are characterised by the great battles they will have, whereas the comment on the elder Brutus has hints of the actions of the Brutus that assassinated Caesar in 44BC.

Rome's great enemy the city of Carthage is consistently presented sympathetically. At the beginning of the *Aeneid* (Book One lines 12-20) a great city is described, one which should have a bright future, but it is doomed. This city is Carthage and It will be destroyed by the descendants of Troy and Aeneas; the Romans. Over the course of three great wars the power of Carthage will be stripped and appropriated by Rome, before the city is annihilated.

It is the actions of the Gods and the Trojans themselves that cause the Carthaginians to become hostile to them. The Carthaginians give the Trojans safe harbour without demands in return in Book One. Rather than be treated as pirates or as shipwrecked refugees that can be taken advantage of, the Trojans are invited to join the Carthaginians in their new city. Their repayment is to see their Queen disgraced and dead and the Trojans do not even leave without giving thanks for the Carthaginian hospitality.

Virgil then is gently saying that perhaps the Carthaginians were justified in their hostility to Rome.

However, Augustus re-founded other cities than just Rome. Augustus also re-established Carthage as a Roman colony in order to better control Roman Africa and to find homes and farms for some of the tens of thousands of Roman soldiers he pensioned off after the Civil Wars. This re-establishment of Carthage by Augustus restored the city and eventually brought great wealth to the inhabitants of Carthage. The city survives to this day; Tunis, the capital of Tunisia.

Task: Augustus in Book VI

Read Book VI lines 791-800 – in which Virgil describes Augustus.

How is Augustus presented in this passage?

In what ways could this passage be viewed as a critical of Augustus and in what ways is this passage praise?

Criticism of Augustus in the *Aeneid*

We have already presented a case that if Augustus is supposed to be represented by or a parallel of the character of Aeneas that Virgil is presenting a hero; a great man, but one with flaws nonetheless.

However in Book Six Virgil turns to describe the spirit that will be Augustus directly;

> "Here is the man whose coming you so often hear prophesied, here he is, Augustus Caesar, son of a god, the man who will bring back the golden years to the fields of Latium once ruled over by Saturn, and extend Rome's empire beyond the Indians and the Garamantes to a land beyond the stars, beyond the yearly path of the sun, where Atlas holds on his shoulder the sky all studded with burning stars and turns on its' axis. The kingdoms round the Caspian Sea and Lake Maeotis are even now quaking at the prophecies of his coming. The seven mouths of the Nile are in turmoil and alarm."

Virgil. *Aeneid* VI.791-800

On the one hand this presentation of Augustus is extremely praising. Augustus is predestined, a son of a god. All his enemies will fear him. On the other, the picture portrayed is one of war and conflict and turmoil. There is no mention of peace and prosperity here; just one of conquest and of a man that leads an all-powerful empire. This passage praises Augustus' Imperium. But his morality is entirely absent.

Conclusions

It is fair to say then that on balance the *Aeneid* is not a one-sided piece of pro-Augustan propaganda. There are far too many suggestions contained within that more than hint that Virgil was not an outright supporter of Augustus and all of his actions.

Augustus was the victor in the Civil wars because he eliminated all possible opposition.

The proscriptions that saw innocents and guilty alike killed for their political beliefs, or deprived of wealth and land, or both. More killed because they may one day oppose Augustus, or to satisfy the egos of others like the murder of Cicero to please Antonius. Virgil's family themselves may have suffered as a result of the proscriptions.

The great rivalry between Augustus and Antonius became a battle to the death. Even by 40BC it was clear that sooner or later one would have to die in order to safeguard the other. Augustus murders the boy Caesarion; killed because he was the biological heir of Julius Caesar and Cleopatra and therefore too politically dangerous to be left alive.

Virgil was a witness to these events and it should come as no surprise that he himself had a view on these matters. What is more of a surprise is that he would dare to voice his opinion on some of these matters in a poem that was commissioned to support the Augustan regime and celebrate the reign of Augustus.

Augustus too might have agreed with Virgil. He had to fight for a long time, and use some extremely questionable tactics in order to achieve his victory.

7.6 Examination and extension tasks

Task: Examination style task: Book II

Read Virgil's Aeneid Book II. Lines 200-219

Write a response to the following questions;

   a) Explain how Virgil stresses the strength and power of the serpents in this passage. Write out **three** examples and explain their effect.
   b) 'The audience relives the horrors of the fall of Troy but feels no pity for the Trojans.'
   To what extent do you agree with this statement?

Task: Examination style task: Book IV

Read Virgil's Aeneid Book IV lines 653-683

Write a response to the following questions;

Using this passage as a starting point. Who do you think is most to blame for Dido's downfall?

Task: Examination style task: Furor

Write a response to the following question;

To what extent do you think a Roman audience would have criticised Aeneas for the furor (rage) that he shows in Books II, X and XII?

Extension Task: Book Seven: A warning for Aeneas?

Write a response to the following question;

In Book Seven it is proposed by King Latinus that Aeneas marry his daughter Lavinia.

Why might Aeneas be cautious in pursuing this marriage, in light of the references to the mythical traditions of Argos and the Trojan War in the Aeneid?

Consider:

- His destiny as explained in Book Two by the ghost of Creusa
- His relationship with Dido
- What we know of Lavinia's opinion on the matter of marriage to Aeneas
- The 'recent' history of Virgil's own time; particularly that of Antony and Cleopatra

Task: Examination style task: Essay responses

Write a response to the following questions within 45 minutes;

a) 'Virgil shows not just the glory and the pity of war but also the necessity of war.' To what extent do you agree with this statement?

b) 'Pietas to the gods, family and country is the most important element of the story of the 'Aeneid'.' To what extent do you agree with this view?

c) How do you agree with the view that the relationship between Mezentius and Lausus different from other relationships between fathers and sons in the 'Aeneid'?

Task: Examination style task Book X

OCR produced the following specimen paper for teaching with the new specification of this course unit;

Read Aeneid Book 10 lines 511-537

Questions

A) *Evaluate how successfully Virgil makes this piece of writing powerful? Use references to the passage to support your answer.*

B) *'Aeneas behaves in an unheroic way throughout the second half of the Aeneid'. To what extent do you agree with this statement? You may use this passage as a starting point.*

7.7 Glossary

Acheron: *the River of Hades, perhaps better known as the River Styx.*

Acta: *literally means 'things done'.*

Actium: *a decisive naval battle fought between Octavian (the future Augustus and Antonius and Cleopatra in 31BC.*

Affectio maritali: *a lasting marriage union*

Agon: *An agon is as a set debate in Greek tragedy. In an agon a character presents his or her case, in a formal manner, and another character refutes the points made. It has the feel of the 'law-court' about it.*

Allusion: *a direct or indirect reference to other literary texts. In Virgil we can most easily identify allusions to the works of Homer.*

Amicitia: *the political term for friendship and could be between equals or unequal individuals.*

Anagnorisis: *Recognition is a change from ignorance to the awareness of a bond of love or hate.*

Analepsis: *a form of 'flashback'; a digression by the poet when they refer to events that have occurred previously. Analepsis can be either brief or extended.*

Andromache: *Andromache was the mythical wife of Hector*

Apollonius Rhodius: *An epic poet*

Apostrophe: *An address by a character to an inanimate object, or alternatively an address to a non-living form.*

Apotheosis: *A literary device by which a character is transformed or elevated to a god-like status.*

Aristeia: *An episode in epic whereby a single warrior performs great deeds of bravery and skill in war; typified by the deaths of many enemies and sometimes concluded by their own death.*

Assonance: *Where the same sound is repeated —so meet, feet, greet.*

Briareus: *A Hundred handed monster that in Greek myth fought Zeus and almost defeated him. The other Olympians helped Zeus and Briareus was overcome and thrown into the Underworld.*

Catharsis: *Catharsis gives us our word 'cathartic' which we use to refer to something with a great cleansing or purging power.*

Carthage: *A large and prosperous city state situated in North Africa (the modern Tunis) and peopled by inhabitants of Semitic origin from the coasts of the Levant. Carthage was principally a trading city, her ships dominated the Western Mediterranean for centuries and her navies allowed Carthage to establish trading centres in Sicily, Corsica, Sardinia and the Iberian Peninsula (Modern Spain).*

Cerberus: *The monstrous hound of the Underworld.*

Cliens: *an individual who technically sought protection and favour from a superior.*

Cumae: *a city founded by Greek colonists from the island of Euboea around 740BC. Cumae was one of the first Greek colonies on the mainland of Italy and was established after the foundation of Rome.*

Conubrium: *A form of Roman marriage*

Cursus Honorum: *The career path of a Senator*

Cyclops: *Mythical creatures mentioned in the Odyssey*

Deiphobus: *A Trojan hero. Son of Priam and brother to Hector and Paris.*

Delos: *a small island in the Cyclades island group in the central Aegean Sea*

Deus ex Machina: *A literary device used by poets, playwrights and authors to bring about a resolution of a conflict or situation through the deployment of the actions of a god, character or action that may seem otherwise unrelated to the story.*

Ekphrasis: *A description of a work of art which was designed to be a rhetorical exercise*

Enjambment: *The sense of a line of poetry runs over from one line to the next, rather than stopping at the end of every line with a sentence end. This has the effect of creating a more 'flowing' verse structure.*

Epithet – *An epithet is a name bestowed upon a character which identifies a defining characteristic. For example in Virgil's Aeneid Aeneas is commonly referred to as 'pious' or 'dutiful' Aeneas.*

Etruscans: *A people of Italy. The Etruscans dominated much of Italy prior to the rise of Rome, but they were centred in the region NW of Rome as far as the river Arnus. The Etruscans had their own language and culture distinct from the Latin peoples of Italy and they traded extensively with the Greeks and Phoenicians. The Etruscans established the earliest cities in Italy. The Etruscans had an important role to play in establishing early Rome as the Tarquin kings of Rome were probably Etruscan. By the 5th century the Etruscans were subsumed into the Roman political and social spheres*

Familia: *family*

Fate: *The universal destiny of all. Even the gods are subject to Fate.*

Fides: Faithfulness. The Roman dictator Aulus Atilius Calatinus built a temple to Fides during the First Punic War in 249BC.

Furor: A Latin term from which the English words 'Fury' and 'Furious' originate. In the Aeneid Furor occurs when emotions or other violent urges are uncontrolled. It can also mean Rage.

Ganymede: In myth Ganymede was the son of a Trojan king called Tros. Ganymede was so beautiful that he was desired by Zeus (Jupiter). Zeus abducted Ganymede and made him his immortal cupbearer on Mount Olympus and also his lover. As a result Ganymede was greatly resented by Hera (Juno).

Hamartia: meaning 'to miss the mark' or 'to fall short'. In the context of Greek Tragedy, hamartia refers to a failing of the central character which brings about the catastrophe.

Harpies: Mythical creatures. They were encountered by the Argonauts on the island of Salmydessus off Thrace. They had been sent here to plague a blind seer named Phineus. The Argonauts agreed to drive away the Harpies in return for guidance. After the Harpies were driven away, they took refuge on the Strophades islands (where they were encountered by Aeneas).

Hecate: Goddess of witchcraft and magic as well as crossroads. Hecate is one of the many gods of the Underworld.

Helenus: A Trojan Prince, brother of Hector and mentioned in the Iliad. Helenus was in myth a priest of Apollo.

Hospitium: Friendship

Imperium: 'Supreme Power' Imperium was a term used to describe a Roman politician or military commander's authority and ability to carry out their commands and edicts.

Intertextuality: Often a writer or poet will make reference to the works of another writer or poet. For example it is often stated that Virgil makes direct or indirect references to the works of Homer.

Io: According to Greek mythology, Io was a priestess of Hera (Juno) at Argos who was desired by Zeus (Jupiter). Upon being seduced by the God, Hera punished Io by transforming her into a cow and instructing the monster Argus to guard her in the grounds of the temple of Hera at Argos (the site of the Argive Heraion can still be visited today). Argus was subsequently killed by the God Hermes (Mercury) but Hera punished Io to wander the earth, still transformed as a cow and tormented perpetually by a gadfly.

Kleos: Good reputation

Kommos: A lament or grief stricken speech commonly found in a Greek tragedy.

Lares: The Lares were the traditional spirits of the Roman household and also crossroads

Latium: A region of Italy.

Latins: The name used to describe the ethnic group of people who inhabited central Italy.

Manus: A form of Roman marriage including property exchange.

Mariticide: A Latin term used to describe the murder of a husband by his wife.

Matrona: matron, or married older woman

Media Res: this means that the story begins part way through.

Mens: 'Composure', 'Resolution' or 'clear headedness'. This quality is ascribed to Aeneas in Virgil. The Roman dictator Fabius Cunctator (more on him in Book Six) built a temple to Mens during the Second Punic War.

Metaphor: A common literary device that is present in everyday usage by us all. A metaphor is a merging of two different elements or ideas. For example to say 'My head is spinning' is a metaphor.

Metonym: A Metonym is the use of a part in order to represent the whole; the use of one item to stand for another for which it has been associated. An example of a Metonym is to refer to the police as 'the long arm of the law'.

Minos: A son of Zeus and mythical king of Crete.

Muses: Goddesses of the Arts

Octavia: Augustus' sister. She was married several times. First of all to Claudius Marcellus who died in 40BC. Despite this, Octavia was soon married to Antony in order to seal the treaty of Brundisium.

Octavian: The name of the future Augustus.

Orcus: A Roman God of the Underworld.

Orpheus: Son of Apollo and a Muse, Orpheus was a renowned singer in myth and associated with many mythical stories.

Pallenteum: The city of Evander which occupies the site that one day will be Rome.

Paris: Son of Priam and Trojan Prince that caused the Trojan War by eloping with Helen.

Paterfamilias: The male head of the family.

Penates: The gods of the pantry.

Peripeteia: Peripeteia refers to a (usually sudden) reversal or change of fortune of the central character.

Personification: Personification is when an inhuman object is given human characteristics.

Phoebus: A name and epithet for the God Apollo.

Pietas: Is the recognition of and the discharge of an individual's duty to gods, country and family.

Polydorus: A Trojan Prince, brother of Hector and mentioned in Greek Tragedy.

Proem: From the Greek word 'proemium', which simply means 'the introduction'.

Prolepsis: A 'fast-forward'; a digression by the poet or writer when they refer to events that have occurred previously. Like analepsis, prolepsis can be either brief or extended.

Proserpina: The Queen of the Underworld

Qunitus Ennius: Roman writer and playwright

Rhesis: A common feature of Greek tragedy, a Rhesis is the name given to a set speech by a character which is characterised by logical argument or ordered reasoning, yet may also include emotional appeal.

Sabines: A people of Italy who dwelt to the NE of the Latins. In Early Rome traditions they were soon integrated into the population of Rome in the story 'The Rape of the Sabine Women'.

Samnites: A people of Italy who occupied the central Apenine region.

Sibyl: A Sibyl was a prophetic woman. In Greek and Roman myth Sibyl was a priestess of Apollo who refused the amorous attention of the God. Apollo then punished the Sibyl by granting her prophetic powers but also immortality without eternal youth.

Sicily: A large island just off the 'toe' of Italy and part of the modern country of Italy.

Silvius: Son of Aeneas and Lavinia as yet not born.

Simile: A simile is a common literary technique that is a comparison of one item with another with which it intentionally similar. Generally speaking if something is like something else then this is a simile. So for example in Homer's Odyssey Menelaus likens Odysseus to a lion and the suitors to startled deer. Another example is to compare the love of a character to a beautiful flower such as a rose. As we shall see Virgil litters the Aeneid with similes like confetti at a wedding.

Spoila Opima: *The offerings dedicated to the gods by a Roman commander that had personally slain an enemy commander in single combat.*

Symbol : *A device used by writers and poets to substitute one thing for another. These symbols replace a word with an item associated with this word. So for example a Dove is commonly used as a symbol for peace. Red is a colour we commonly associate with danger and a snake is sometimes used as a symbol for temptation.*

Timé: *The pursuit of honour and esteem.*

Triton: *A Sea God and attendant of Neptune*

Tyche: *Fortune*

Volsci: *A People of Italy. The Volsci were rivals of Rome and the Latins in the early 5th century BC. By the end of the 4th century however Rome had comprehensively defeated the Volsci.*

Xenia: *Greek guest friendship*

CPSIA information can be obtained
at www.ICGtesting.com
Printed in the USA
BVHW040954021121
620548BV00014B/365

9 781731 238399

7.8 Bibliography and Further Reading

Cairns, F. (1989). *Virgil 's Augustan Epic.* Cambridge.

Camps, W. A. (1969) *An Introduction to Virgil's Aeneid*, Oxford University Press

Clausen, W. (1987). *Virgil's* Aeneid *and the Tradition of Hellenistic Poetry.* Berkeley.

Deryck Williams, R. (2013) *Aeneas and the Roman Hero (Inside the Ancient World)* Bloomsbury

Galinsky, K. (1969). *Aeneas, Sicily and Rome.* Princeton.

Galinsky, K. (1996). *Augustan Culture.* Princeton.

Galinsky, K (2003). *"Greek and Roman Drama and the Aeneid,"* in Gill, C. J., et al.. eds. *Myth, History and Performance in Republican Rome* Exeter 275-294.

Gransden, K. W. (2004) *Virgil: The Aeneid (Landmarks of World Literature),* Cambridge University Press

Griffin, J. (2013) *Virgil (Ancients in Action),* Bloomsbury

Martindale, C. (ed) (1997) *The Cambridge Companion to Virgil,* Cambridge University Press

Nicholson, A. (2015) *The Mighty Dead: Why Homer Matters,* William Collins

Williams, R. D. (1990). "The Purpose of the *Aeneid,*" in Harrison, S. J., ed., *Oxford Readings in Vergil's* Aeneid (Oxford) 21–36.